Online Product Activation at DrLam.com

1. Visit http://www.DrLam.com. New users click "Register Here" at top right and complete information required. Current users please sign in.
2. Click the blue "Redeem Bonus(es)*" button. Click the link under "Did you purchase a supplement package or did your purchase come with a PIN (example: 1234-56-7890)?", enter your PIN and click "I Agree, Submit". Your gift(s) will be in your Private Library.

Scratch off to reveal your PIN number

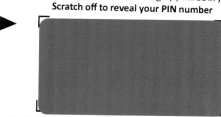

* Bonus promotional gift(s) provided with your purchase of this product is redeemable online only at DrLam.com based on your nontransferable and personal use at your private library limited to a single user per valid PIN number. Corporate or library use and access, as well as any direct or indirect sharing is strictly prohibited and will invalidate your access and/or PIN number. Access may not be shared, resold, or otherwise circulated. Access to the Bonus item(s) available in your Private Library may terminate 1 year after redemption. Online content may change without prior notice to you. Access is subject to your acceptance of detailed terms and conditions upon registration/redemption. Limit 1 PIN per customer. Offer good while supplies last. Access to the online material requires an actove account with DrLam.com, and is subject to the applicable terms. Other conditions may apply on additional gifts and coupons.

Adrenal Fatigue Syndrome Cookbook

Recipes to Reclaim Your Energy

Dorine Lam, MS, MRN, RDN
Dr. Michael Lam | Dr. Justin Lam | Dr. Carrie Lam

Adrenal Fatigue Syndrome Cookbook

Recipes to Reclaim Your Energy

Dorine Lam, MS, MPH, RDN
Dr. Michael Lam
Dr. Justin Lam | Dr. Carrie Lam

Adrenal Fatigue Syndrome Cookbook
Dorine Lam, MS, MPH, RDN
Dr. Michael Lam
Dr. Justin Lam
Dr. Carrie Lam

© 2016
Dr. Michael Lam, MD

Adrenal Institute Press, Loma Linda, CA 92354
All rights reserved.

No part of this book may be reproduced, copied, stored, or transmitted in any form
or by any means – graphic, electronic, or mechanical, including photocopying, recording,
or information storage and retrieval systems without the prior written permission
of the authors or Adrenal Institute Press, except where permitted by law.

Cover + Interior design: Rebecca Finkel, F + P Graphic Design
Editing: Melanie Stafford
Publisher: Adrenal Institute Press
Book Consultant: Judith Briles, The Book Shepherd

ISBN (Hard Cover): 978-1-937930-27-1
Library of Congress Control Number: 2015960696

ISBN (Soft Cover): 978-1-937930-28-8
Library of Congress Control Number: 2015960696

ISBN (e-Book): 978-1-937930-29-5
Library of Congress Control Number: 2015960696

Categories for cataloging and shelving:
1. Cookbook   2. Nutrition   3. Health   4. Adrenal Fatigue

10   9   8   7   6   5   4   3   2   1

Printed in Korea through Four Colour Print Group

We want to express our gratitude to the following people for helping us during the entire process of putting this book together:

Leh Ota, MPH, RD, my good friend and fellow Registered Dietitian for recipe ideas and research.

Cassandra Young for photography.

Christiane Wong for content management.

Other publications by
Michael Lam, MD, MPH

Books

*Adrenal Fatigue Syndrome:
Reclaim Your Vitality with Clinically Proven Natural Programs*

*Central Nervous System Disruptions and
Adrenal Fatigue Syndrome*

*Advanced Symptoms of Adrenal Fatigue Syndrome:
A Metabolic Perspective*

5 Proven Secrets to Longevity

How to Stay Young and Live Longer

Beating Cancer with Natural Medicine

*Estrogen Dominance:
The 21st Century Hormonal Imbalance*

CDs

Adrenal Breathing™ Exercise

Mind-Body and Adrenal Fatigue

Adrenal Fatigue in a Complex World

Adrenal Health and Anti-aging

DVDs

Adrenal Yoga™ Exercise Vols. 1–4

About DrLam.com

DrLam.com is a free public educational website offering cutting edge information on natural medicine. Founded in 2001 by Michael Lam, MD, nutritional medicine expert and board certified anti-aging medicine specialist, the site features the world's most comprehensive scientific, evidenced-based information on Adrenal Fatigue Syndrome.

Dr. Lam's mission is to educate and empower others to take control of their health. You can ask questions about your health concerns online. Because of his willingness to answer specific questions, Dr. Lam has helped legions of individuals learn how to use safe, effective, and clinically proven natural protocols for self- healing. This educational service is provided free.

Other resources on the website include:

- Quick 3 minute Adrenal Fatigue Test to assess your adrenal function.
- Sign up for free email Adrenal Fatigue Newsletter to stay up on the latest AFS research. Get the latest information presented in easy-to-understand language.
- Hundreds of cutting-edge original special reports and videos by Dr. Lam on everything related to Adrenal Fatigue Syndrome.
- An extensive and archive-rich library of answers to questions previously asked by others that are certain to help you in your recovery from Adrenal Fatigue Syndrome.
- Over 30 condition-based health centers with specific clinically proven natural protocols ranging from heart health to cancer.

Dr. Lam offers a worldwide, telephone-based, one-on-one, nutritional coaching service. Personalizing the natural principles discussed in this book, his coaching service has successfully helped countless Adrenal Fatigue Syndrome sufferers recover and reclaim their vitality.

For more information, visit *www.DrLam.com*

Contents

Preface ix

CHAPTER 1 Hypoglycemia 1

CHAPTER 2 Insomnia 31

CHAPTER 3 Low Blood Pressure 55

CHAPTER 4 Food Sensitivities 87

CHAPTER 5 GI Disturbances 95

CHAPTER 6 Toxin Overload 133

CHAPTER 7 Catabolic State 161

CHAPTER 8 Snacks 195

About the Authors 207

Glycemic Appednix 210

Histamine Appendix 212

Category Index 215

Food Index 221

Preface

This is a cookbook designed for those battling Adrenal Fatigue Syndrome (AFS). It is an attempt to rebuild the body's nutritional baseline through a fundamental facet of life: food. As a team of nutritional professionals helping people recover from AFS, many of whom are bedridden and in a catabolic state with severe fatigue, we have observed the wonderful, direct effects of nutrition, if done right, on a sensitive and weak body. This book encompasses our years of experience in developing recipes and dietary principles specifically for AFS recovery. The more you know about the science behind nutrition, the better you are able to self-navigate. In addition to recipes, we detail the science of macronutrients and explain the reasons behind different preparations of food and their clinical results on the neuroendocrine system to help you in your recovery process.

The nourishment concepts and strategies of this book incorporate wholesome food principles from ancient times, when food was cherished as a healing tool, exemplified by many biblical stories. These principles work then and now because the human body has not changed. The environment has, however. We therefore emphasize the importance of eating whole foods, especially vegetables and easily digestible proteins, and discourage consumption of pork and scavenger-type seafood because of their negative effects on the digestive system.

The recipes in this cookbook focus more on vegetables, beans, nuts, fish, and poultry because they are easily broken down into nutrients and are better handled by a weakened digestive system commonly seen in those with AFS, where the gastrointestinal assimilation is compromised. Many people with AFS are also sensitive to dairy products, so there are only a few recipes that contain natural cheese or goat cheese. For those who have gluten or wheat intolerance, rice noodles or gluten-free pasta can be substituted for spaghetti. We have seen clinical proof of success when these dietary principles are followed. The body possesses amazing rebound capability if we only give it the tools to nurture it systematically with these recipes.

As the body strengthens and is able to tolerate heavier nutrients, you can start adding meat strips, ground meat, and stronger cheeses. We strongly recommend organic or free-range meats (free of antibiotics and hormones).

It is important to remember that every body is unique, and you are the chef in charge of your own system. Listen to your body, and create dishes that feel nourishing to you.

Another tip to remember is that the body has a circadian rhythm that follows the seasons in your location. It is important to buy local foods and eat seasonally. When the body gets hot in the summer, eating "cool" vegetables such as zucchini and cucumber can help reduce the internal heat. In the winter months, the body needs to keep warm, so more hearty foods such as gourds and roots are better. This way, you not only save money by buying foods in season but you also follow your body's needs according to what the land has provided over thousands of years.

The recipes in this book are identified by easy, medium, and challenging preparation levels. Those with severe AFS can start with the easy preparation level and scale up from there if they feel stronger and healthier over time. We hope that people with AFS use this cookbook as a guide to strengthen their nutritional base and regain wholesome balance to their health.

—Dorine Lam, MS, MPH, RDN
Michael Lam, MD, MPH
Justin Lam, ABAAHP, FMNM
Carrie Lam, MD

CHAPTER 1

Hypoglycemia

What Is Hypoglycemia? 3
Proteins and Fats 5
Frequency of Meals 5
Just Say NO to Sugar and Flour 6
Listen to Your Body 7

meal one
Black-eyed Pea and Kale Soup 8
Bok Choy Cherry Salad 9
Tuna Salad Wraps 10

meal two
Cream Cheese Chicken Casserole 12
Sugar Snap Peas with Wasabi Dressing 14

meal three
Orange and Mint Peas 15
Sautéed King Oyster Mushrooms 16
Mahi Mahi with Cucumber- 17
 Pineapple Salsa

meal four
Grilled Eggplant Fans 18
Teriyaki Chicken with Summer Squash 19

meal five
Braised Red Cabbage and Apple 20
Kale Salad with Avocado 22
Lemon Chicken Breasts 23

meal six
Leeks with Lemon and Garlic 24
Quinoa, Celery and Almond Salad 27

meal seven
Lemon Basil Pasta 28
Tomato Eggs 29
Marinated Carrots with Mint and Garlic.... 30

What Is Hypoglycemia?

Reactive hypoglycemia is one of the more common signs of Adrenal Fatigue Syndrome (AFS), especially for those in Stage 3 (adrenal exhaustion). People with AFS need to eat frequently, usually every two to three hours, to avoid symptoms of hypoglycemia including brain fog, anxiety, fatigue, racing thoughts, and lethargy, just to name a few. Additional symptoms of hypoglycemia could be cold sweats, dizziness, nausea, hunger, waking up at night and not being able to go back to sleep, and waking up in the morning feeling jittery. However, laboratory testing will reveal normal blood sugar levels. Therefore, the velocity of the drop in blood sugar within the normal range is likely responsible for these symptoms, not the absolute level of blood sugar.

> **The velocity of the drop in blood sugar within the normal range is likely responsible for these symptoms, not the absolute level of blood sugar.**

Three hormones play a vital role in regulating blood sugar in our bodies: insulin, cortisol, and growth hormone. Cortisol is the most important for people with AFS because an inadequate level makes the body's conversion of glycogen, fats, and proteins into glucose extremely difficult, resulting in hypoglycemia. Typically, when a person has both AFS and reactive hypoglycemia, a combination of low cortisol levels and high insulin levels contributes to the difficulty of managing a stable blood glucose level.

There are different schools of thought about what constitutes hypoglycemia and when medical attention is required to treat it. For those with AFS, it is even more difficult to diagnose because its manifestations are more often than not subclinical; that is, when blood tests are conducted, the blood plasma levels, fasting serum blood sugar, and glucose tolerance tests are all within the acceptable range. An experienced clinician who creates a detailed history has by far the best chance of ascertaining the presence of reactive hypoglycemia.

People with AFS have a greater need than people without blood sugar issues for a continuous supply of energy throughout the day. In situations where this demand is not being sufficiently met through adequate food consumption, the body will use the existing sources of protein and fat it has stored. Those in Stage 3 and beyond should eat every two to three hours to maintain an optimal blood sugar and insulin balance and avoid hypoglycemia. These do not have to be large meals—just a small snack to avoid the dip in blood sugar levels. Be proactive. Always carry a snack, and eat on a regular basis throughout the day. Do not wait for symptoms to surface because that is already too late. Most people with AFS can tell when symptoms will arise; they sense the drop in blood sugar ahead of time. Learn to listen to your body, and eat a snack about 30 minutes before the symptoms arise.

Reactive hypoglycemia is in itself a symptom, not a disease. After you correct the underlying root problem, the low blood sugar will automatically resolve. Eating frequently to avoid reactive hypoglycemia is a short-term solution. Resolving the underlying adrenal weakness remains your key priority. That usually requires nutritional supplementation along with lifestyle and dietary changes over time. As recovery proceeds, so too will the reactive hypoglycemia

improve. For those in Stage 2 of AFS, it is possible to go for a stretch of four to six hours without eating. As your AFS and hypoglycemia improve to Stage 1, skipping a meal should be a minor inconvenience and not cause any major setbacks.

When signs of acute hypoglycemia are present, such as hunger or nausea (for a more comprehensive listing of the signs and symptoms, see Chapter 7, "Stage 3A, Early System Dysfunction," of Dr. Lam's *Adrenal Fatigue Syndrome* [2012]), an immediate and temporary fix is consuming 10–20 grams of carbohydrates, such as a segment of an orange or apple or a quarter cup of grape juice. It is not advisable to reach for sugar-laden sweets or beverages containing high fructose corn syrup. These quick fixes can cause more damage in the long run, and the symptoms will resurface in an hour or so. Listed here are some strategies to implement when considering what to eat at your mealtimes.

Proteins and Fats

When planning your daily menu, it is most important to consume proteins and healthy fats with each meal because this combination helps to slowly release the sugar into your body, thereby extending the time between meals before hypoglycemia sets in. Snacks such as nuts, containing both healthy fats and proteins, are an excellent nutritional choice and also convenient to carry at all times. Other foods to consider are meats, fish, poultry, and beans for protein, along with coconut oil, olive oil, whole milk yogurt, and avocados for healthy fats.

Frequency of Meals

Small frequent meals with snacks in between can be helpful. The following pages will contain sample meal plans that give you a starting point in creating your own meals after you understand which food combinations work well to keep your blood sugar levels from fluctuating. After you feel comfortable with the meal plan, you can peruse all the recipes in this book and create your own meal plan based on your food preferences.

Always, always carry portable snacks such as nuts, fruits, or soaked granola cookies (recipe in this chapter) in your bag or in your car to avoid hypoglycemic episodes and the temptation of purchasing sugar-laden junk food. We have experimented with numerous snack recipes and have come up with easy-to-prepare healthy recipes in this book. Do not be tempted to buy that bar of chocolate at the checkout counter; it will do you more harm than good. Try out these recipes instead.

Just Say NO to Sugar and Flour

If you go into your kitchen and look at nearly any food label, you'll find sugar or some other sweetener. For most people, this is okay in small amounts used occasionally, but others, especially those who are insulin resistant or on low-carb diets, should be very careful with these ingredients.

Sugar is considered a high-impact carbohydrate because it causes such a rapid rise in blood sugar levels. It enters the bloodstream quickly and can be a major cause of adrenal stress. When we consume sugar, we are giving our adrenal glands constant stimulation instead of much needed rest to rebuild and effectively conduct their purpose, such as cleansing the body of heavy metals. Other high-impact carbohydrates, such as refined white flour, essentially have the same effect.

Avoid refined white sugar and bleached white flour products. This would include typical store bought, processed desserts and packaged snacks. Included in this book are wonderfully healthy dessert alternatives for those who crave an occasional sweet. Use these instead!

One of the best ways to improve your health is to reduce the amount of additives in your diet, and one of the easiest ways to do this is to swap the sugar, high fructose corn syrup (HFCS), and other unhealthy sweeteners with natural sweeteners that are better for your health. Some of the best include:

1. **Stevia,** a sweet herb that can be purchased in a variety of forms and used in tea, coffee, or sweets. Stevia is low calorie, will not cause blood sugar to spike, and has a host of other health benefits. If you have a green thumb, you can even grow it yourself and simply use the leaves.

2. **Maple syrup.** When most people think of maple syrup, they think of pancakes or waffles or maybe bread, but the heart healthy, immune-boosting sweet stuff can be used to sweeten many foods.

3. **Honey.** Raw honey is an easily available natural sweetener with many health benefits. It does not cause blood sugar spikes, is high in antioxidants, promotes healthy digestion, and can even speed wound healing.

4. **Blackstrap molasses.** High in iron, potassium, and calcium, blackstrap molasses is a sweet nutrition powerhouse. However, blackstrap molasses is derived from sugar cane and does still contain sugar, so those with diabetes should use this sweetener cautiously.

5. **Agave nectar.** Similar to honey, agave nectar is a sweet syrup extracted from the agave plant. Agave nectar can help ease inflammation,

strengthen the immune system, and improve the absorption of some nutrients. Agave nectar should be used in moderation because most varieties contain between 70 percent and 90 percent fructose, more than HFCS.

6. **Date sugar.** Not actually sugar, date sugar is extracted from dehydrated dates. Date sugar is high in several minerals, including magnesium, zinc, selenium, iron, and calcium. Date sugar might boost cognitive function, improve the immune system, stabilize blood pressure, and relieve muscle soreness and migraines.

Listen to Your Body

Remember that these are not hard-and-fast rules. It is always important to listen to your own body. If you are having a particularly stressful morning, you might need to consume more snacks between your meals to curb that low-blood sugar dip. Because people with AFS have bodies that have endured more than their fair share of stress, anything you put into your mouth can either heal or harm you further. The recipes in this book are meant for you to use as part of your journey of naturally healing your adrenal glands and eliminating all the other symptoms associated with AFS. Make these recipes part of your everyday meals, and you should notice an improvement in your overall health and well-being.

Bon appetit!

MEAL 1: Black-eyed Pea and Kale Soup

SERVES: 10 | LEVEL: Easy

CALORIES: 129; Fat: 3.6 g; Protein: 4.2 g; Carbohydrates: 21.4 g

Like many beans and legumes, **black-eyed peas** are high in both protein and complex carbohydrates. Complex carbohydrates are broken down into simple sugars by the body before they can be used for energy. This process slows absorption, so you get a steady release of energy and avoid the dizziness and anxiety that can come from low blood sugar and can quickly follow consumption of sugary foods.

Black-eyed peas also contain fiber consisting of linked sugars that the body is not able to break down. The fiber binds with excess cholesterol and sugar in the digestive tract and helps to remove them from your body, preventing them from being stored as fat.

1 lb. dried black-eyed peas, washed
1 large yellow onion, diced
1 tsp. garlic, minced
1 cup celery, sliced
½ tsp. crushed chili pepper
1 tsp. cumin seeds
1 tbsp. butter
1 tbsp. olive oil
Salt and pepper to taste
28 oz. can diced tomatoes
½ cup quinoa
½ lb. kale, cut into 2 inch slices
Mushroom extract to taste

GARNISH (optional)
Sour cream
Green onion, chopped

1. Fill a pot with water, covering the black-eyed peas by 2 inches. Cover the pot and bring to a boil for 2 minutes. Turn off the heat, and let it stand for at least 1 hour. Discard the water.
2. Stir-fry the onion, garlic, celery, chili pepper, cumin, salt, and pepper in the butter and olive oil.
3. Combine all ingredients but kale in a pressure cooker. Add 6 cups of water, and bring to boil. Cook for 20 minutes.
4. After the pressure cooker has cooled down, add the kale and cook for another 40 minutes or until all ingredients are tender. Add mushroom extract to taste.
5. When ready to serve, garnish with sour cream and green onions if you wish.

NOTES

1. This is a thick soup. You can add more water to create the consistency you like, and add more seasoning if you want to spice it up.
2. For estrogen dominance, substitute spinach or Swiss chard for the kale. It is okay to use kale or other cruciferous vegetables two to three times a week.
3. For AFS, use fresh tomatoes instead of canned. Also add more olive oil after you have dished out your bowl of soup, so you don't get hungry.

CHAPTER 1: **Hypoglycemia**   9

Bok Choy Cherry Salad

MEAL 1

CALORIES: 152; Fat: 12 g; Protein: 2 g; Carbohydrates: 12 g

SERVES: 6 | LEVEL: Easy

SALAD
2 cups bok choy, chopped
½ cup dried sweet cherries
½ cup walnuts, presoaked
½ tsp. ginger, chopped

DRESSING
2 tbsp. olive oil
1 tsp. sesame oil
1 tbsp. hoisin sauce
1 tbsp. vegetarian oyster sauce

1. Mix the bok choy, cherries, walnuts, and ginger in a bowl.
2. Mix the olive oil, sesame oil, hoisin sauce, and vegetarian oyster sauce in a separate bowl, then add it to the salad and toss. Serve in chilled bowls.

NOTES:
1. For estrogen dominance and hypothyroid, substitute mixed green lettuce for the bok choy. You should eat cruciferous vegetables only twice a week.
2. For weight loss, do not be afraid of the oil, which helps maintain satiety and prevent you from getting hungry until the next meal.
3. For AFS, when your body is very sensitive to different kinds of readymade dressing, just use oil, sesame oil, soy sauce, and maple syrup.

Cherries have a low glycemic index when compared with many other fruits, making them a great choice for stabilizing blood sugar. In addition, cherries get their bright red color from a variety of antioxidants that can help control your blood sugar levels by managing your insulin output.

Cherries are also quite high in melatonin. You might be familiar with melatonin as a sleep aid, but that is not its only benefit. Melatonin readily crosses the blood-brain barrier and soothes the neurons, calming irritability and relieving headaches.

Cherries have substantial anti-inflammatory properties, making them a great post-exercise snack. In one study, a group of marathon runners drank either tart cherry juice or a placebo for seven days prior to a race. The cherry juice group reported significantly less muscle pain after the race than the placebo group.

MEAL 1 — Tuna Salad Wraps

SERVES: 6 | LEVEL: Medium

CALORIES: 209; Fat: 5.3 g; Protein: 20 g; Carbohydrates: 21 g
NOTE: Nutritional values do not include wraps, salad greens, or crackers.

Tuna is a tasty saltwater fish most commonly found in warm seawater. Although tuna can be a good source of omega-3s, there are issues to be aware of before consuming it. Researchers in the Department of Marine Science at Coastal Carolina University in Conway, South Carolina, found that no tuna (not only canned albacore but also canned light tuna and wild ahi tuna) was able to meet the omega-3 recommendation (500 milligrams daily of EPA plus DHA) without exceeding the daily limit for mercury (6.8 micrograms). Pregnant women in particular have been warned to limit their intake of certain types of fish, including tuna, because of the risk of mercury. However, the study did find that other fish—such as salmon, trout, shrimp, and tilapia—provided the desired amount of omega-3s without going over the mercury limit. Therefore tuna should not be consumed more than three times per month.

When tuna is prepared for canning, the fish is steamed for several hours. This process yields a liquid referred to as cooking juice, typically discarded by manufacturers as a waste product. However,

- 2 6-oz. cans chunk light tuna, drained
- 2 medium-sized tomatoes, coarsely chopped
- 1 medium-sized apple or 1 stalk of celery, coarsely chopped
- 2 scallions, trimmed and sliced
- 2 stalks parsley, coarsely chopped
- 2 tbsp. extra-virgin olive oil
- 2 tbsp. lemon juice
- ¼ tsp. salt
- 1 15-oz. can small white beans, such as cannellini or great northern, drained and rinsed
- Freshly ground pepper to taste

1. Combine all ingredients except the beans. Mix well.
2. Last, toss in the beans and gently mix.
3. Refrigerate until ready to serve.
4. Serve in a gluten-free or lettuce wrap, on a bed of salad greens, or on crackers.

recent studies have discovered that this cooking juice contains protein fragments known as peptides that contain powerful antioxidant properties. The same peptides are produced when you steam, sear, or broil fresh tuna at home, so be sure to consume the cooking juices with your tuna for the greatest nutritional impact.

Tuna also contains beneficial compounds such as B vitamins, selenium, and potassium. Selenium is an antioxidant that assists the body's immune system. Recent research shows that tuna contains a form of selenium known as selenoneine that appears to bind with mercury and might reduce the amount absorbed by the body. Contrary to popular belief, people who eat tuna might actually have less mercury risk and added antioxidant protection with the presence of selenium.

MEAL 2: Cream Cheese Chicken Casserole

SERVES: 8 | LEVEL: Medium | CALORIES: 405; Fat: 19 g; Protein: 28 g; Carbohydrates: 29 g

Chicken broth/stock helps your system digest more efficiently, and it has been used in GAPS (see page 104) and other gut-healing diets. The yellow fat of chicken broth/stock made from free-range chicken holds immune-boosting powers. It contains minerals from the bones that are easy to assimilate into the body and helps improve bone density. The gelatin from the cartilage aids in joint health. Consuming gelatin also counteracts the breaking down of muscles to provide energy and material to repair them when under stress.

PART A
1 tbsp. grape seed oil
1 cup onion, chopped
1 tbsp. fresh garlic, minced
2 tbsp. cornstarch
1½ cups chicken stock
4 oz. cream cheese
¼ tsp. kosher salt
¼ tsp. black pepper, freshly ground

PART B
2 tbsp. butter
1 8-oz. can/jar/fresh button mushrooms, sliced
2 tsp. grape seed oil

PART C
1 cup leek, chopped
½ cup celery, chopped
½ cup carrot, chopped
¼ cup cooking wine

PART D
3 cups brown rice, wild rice, and quinoa cooked and blended together (prepare ahead)
4 cups boneless, skinless, free-range chicken breast, cooked and chopped
⅓ cup fresh flat-leaf parsley, chopped
1 tsp. salt
½ tsp. black pepper

TOPPING
1¼ cups quinoa, toasted
2 tbsp. butter, melted

CHAPTER 1: **Hypoglycemia**   13

1. Preheat oven to 350°F.

2. PART A: Heat the grape seed oil in a saucepan over medium temperature. Add the onion; cook 6 minutes. Add the garlic and cornstarch; cook 2 minutes. Gradually add the chicken stock, stirring constantly; bring it to a boil. Remove from heat; stir in the cream cheese, salt, and pepper.

3. PART B: Heat the butter and grape seed oil in another saucepan over a medium temperature. Add the mushrooms.

4. PART C: Add leek, celery, and carrot to the saucepan from Part B: cook for 5 minutes, stirring occasionally. Stir in cooking wine and bring to a boil. Cook until liquid evaporates.

5. PART D: Combine the results of Parts A, B, and C with the ingredients for Part D and toss.

6. Spoon the mixture into an 11-by-7-inch baking dish.

7. Bake at 350°F for 25 minutes.

8. In a skillet, toast the quinoa over a medium heat. Stir constantly until golden brown. Add the butter to the quinoa. Mix well; turn off heat. Sprinkle topping evenly over the casserole when it comes out of the oven.

> **NOTE:** For weight loss, use nonfat yogurt or low-fat cottage cheese instead of cream cheese.

Sugar Snap Peas with Wasabi Dressing

MEAL 2

SERVES: 4 | LEVEL: Easy

CALORIES: 95; Fat: 5 g; Protein: 3 g; Carbohydrates: 10 g

Sugar snap peas are a sweet variety of peas that can be eaten raw or parboiled. A hybrid pea created by crossing green peas with snow peas, sugar snap peas are bred to have the fibers all going in the same direction so they can be easily eaten in the pod. Fresh sugar snap peas are high in fiber, vitamins, and antioxidants. However, a study found that storing sugar snap peas at room temperature caused overall antioxidant content to decrease. Because of this, you should buy fresh peas and eat them quickly.

Sugar snap peas have around half the calories of green peas and provide significantly more vitamins, minerals, and other nutrients. Just 100 grams of sugar snap peas in the pod contain a full daily recommended intake of vitamin C as well as more folate and vitamin K than green peas. Because they are eaten in the pod, they also contain a great deal of dietary fiber to help keep you feeling full.

3 cups sugar snap peas

DRESSING

1 tbsp. extra-virgin olive oil

1 tbsp. soy sauce

1 tsp. sesame oil

1 tsp. wasabi (from a tube)

1 tsp. vegetarian oyster sauce

1 tsp. agave nectar or honey

Pepper to taste

1. Bring a stockpot filled with water to a boil. Put the sugar snap peas in the boiling water, stir, and drain immediately. (Do not bring them to another boil.)

2. In a separate container, whisk together all the ingredients for the dressing. Put the dressing in a small dip container and place it in the center of a plate. Arrange the sugar snap peas around the dressing.

CHAPTER 1: **Hypoglycemia**   15

Orange and Mint Peas

MEAL 3

CALORIES: 106; Fat: 5 g; Protein: 4 g; Carbohydrates: 13 g

SERVES: 8 | LEVEL: Easy

PART A
½ medium-sized red onion, quartered and thinly sliced
3 tbsp. butter

PART B
4 cups frozen green peas
¼ cup freshly squeezed orange juice
Salt and pepper to taste

PART C
2 slices orange peel (only the orange outer part, not the white inner), thinly sliced
3 tbsp. fresh mint, finely chopped

1. **PART A:** In a medium-sized skillet, sauté the onion in the butter over medium-high heat.

2. **PART B:** Add the green peas, orange juice, salt, and pepper. Stir and cook for around 5 minutes; the peas should be heated through.

3. **PART C:** Remove the skillet from the burner, and stir in the orange peel and mint.

Oranges are a rich source of vitamin C, a powerful antioxidant that helps boost the immune system and protects cells against damage from free radicals. Free radicals can cause premature aging and damage eye health. A single medium-sized orange provides nearly three-fourths of the vitamin C you need every day.

In addition to protecting against damage from free radicals, vitamin C is also vital to the synthesis of collagen, an important building block of skin. Collagen helps keep skin healthy and wrinkle free.

The orange color is a result of the amount of vitamin A in the form of beta-carotene and other carotenoid compounds oranges contain. These compounds are essential to eye health and can protect against macular degeneration, a progressive eye disease that causes blindness.

The fructose in oranges can help satisfy your sweet tooth without causing a spike, and subsequent crash, in sugar levels, so you stay energized longer. The fiber in oranges helps to stimulate the digestive juices and relieve constipation.

MEAL 3 — Sautéed King Oyster Mushrooms

SERVES: 4 | LEVEL: Easy

CALORIES: 75, Fat: 3.6 g; Protein: 5 g; Carbohydrates: 9 g

4 king oyster mushrooms
1 tbsp. butter
1 tsp. spike seasoning

1. Cut king oyster mushrooms into 1-inch chunks.
2. Heat a shallow frying pan over a medium temperature.
3. Add the mushrooms, butter, and spike seasoning.
4. Cover the pan and slow-cook for 15 minutes, stirring several times.

Oyster mushrooms are the largest members of the *Pleurotus* family. The oyster mushroom has a thick stem and small brown cap. Mushrooms are high in a variety of nutrients and have been shown to boost the immune system, lower cholesterol, and fight tumors.

Mushrooms contain ergothioneine, a powerful antioxidant not found anywhere else that protects cells and builds immunity. A three-ounce serving of oyster mushrooms contains 13 milligrams of ergothioneine whether cooked or not. In fact, oyster mushrooms should always be cooked to an internal temperature of at least 140 degrees. This is the temperature needed to destroy ostreolysin, a protein that ruptures red blood cells and can be toxic.

King oyster mushrooms are an excellent source of iron and a good source of zinc; potassium; calcium; phosphorus; vitamins C, D, B1, B2; folic acid, and niacin.

Mahi Mahi with Cucumber-Pineapple Salsa

MEAL 3

CALORIES: 174, Fat: 2 g, Protein: 22 g, Carbohydrates: 17 g

SERVES: 2 | LEVEL: Medium

2 mahi mahi fillets (4 oz. each)
½ medium lime
½ tsp. olive oil
Salt and pepper

SALSA

1 cup fresh or frozen pineapple, chopped
¾ cup cucumber, finely chopped
1 stalk green onion, finely chopped
¼ cup cilantro, finely chopped
½ cup lime juice
¼ tsp. paprika
¼ tsp. crushed red chilies
1 tsp. agave nectar
2 tbsp. frozen pineapple juice or fresh pineapple juice when chopped

1. Marinate the mahi mahi filets in lime juice, olive oil, salt, and pepper for 30–60 minutes.
2. Combine all salsa ingredients, and add salt and pepper to taste.
3. Heat a grill to medium high, and cook the fish for 3–4 minutes on each side.
4. Serve with the salsa.

MEAL 4: Grilled Eggplant Fans

SERVES: 4 | LEVEL: Medium

CALORIES: 255; Fat: 14.6 g; Protein: 5 g; Carbohydrates: 30 g

3 Asian eggplants
2 medium-sized tomatoes
1 large red bell pepper
1 red onion
Salt to taste

SAUCE
4 tbsp. red wine vinegar
4 tbsp. extra-virgin olive oil
2 tsp. minced garlic
¼ tsp. ground pepper

1. Preheat oven to 350°F.
2. Thinly slice the eggplants lengthwise, from the end to 2 inches from the head (DO NOT cut all the way to the head). Split the parts into 4–5 slices to create a fan shape. Flatten the eggplant head by smashing it.
3. Liberally rub salt onto each eggplant slice. Let them stand for 15 minutes while you cut the rest of the vegetables into thin (½-inch) slices.
4. Whisk together the sauce ingredients.
5. Towel dry the eggplant slices, and place them on baking sheet. Slip the vegetables between each eggplant slice. Spoon ⅔ of the sauce evenly onto the eggplant fans.
6. Bake for 50–60 minutes or until soft.
7. Before serving, spoon the rest of the sauce onto the eggplant fans.

The deep purple color of **eggplant** comes from anthocyanins, primarily nasunin. The health benefits of eggplant are concentrated in the skin, which is rich not only in nasunin but also fiber, potassium, magnesium, and antioxidants.

Research on eggplant has found that it can block inflammation in the brain and improve blood flow, preventing age-related neurological disorders and improving memory. It also protects the lipids that make up the membranes of the brain cells. The cell membranes are responsible for absorbing nutrients and releasing waste, and nasunin has been found to facilitate these functions as well as protecting the cells from free radical damage.

Eggplant is also rich in chlorogenic acid, a powerful antioxidant found to fight cancer, lower bad cholesterol, and have antiviral properties.

NOTE: For estrogen dominance, limit intake of eggplants because they contain phytoestrogens.

CHAPTER 1: **Hypoglycemia** 19

Teriyaki Chicken with Summer Squash

MEAL 4

CALORIES: 397; Fat: 7 g; Protein: 35 g; Carbohydrates: 49 g

SERVES: 6 | LEVEL: Medium

PART A
1 tbsp. olive oil
4 boneless, skinless, free-range chicken breasts or 5 thighs, cut into 1-inch cubes
1½ cup pearl barley
1 medium-sized carrot
1 garlic clove, snapped and crushed with knife blade

PART B
2 medium-sized zucchini

PART C
1 tbsp. grated ginger
2 tbsp. soy sauce
2 tbsp. honey, maple syrup, or agave nectar
2 tbsp. cold water
1 tsp. cornstarch

PART D
¼ cup fresh mint, finely chopped
½ cup Parmesan cheese (optional)

Recent studies suggest that the fermentation process of **soy sauce** creates unique carbohydrates (called oligosaccharides) that may provide some digestive benefits by supporting the growth of "friendly" bacteria in the large intestine. For people with AFS, soy sauce may provide much-needed sodium to help curb salt cravings and possibly the low blood pressure issues.

1. **PART A:** Cut the carrot diagonally from the small end. Turn the carrot a quarter toward you and slice it diagonally again. Turn the carrot another quarter toward you and slice it again. Continue to slice until you reach the head of the carrot. Do the same for the zucchini, but set the slices aside. In a wok, stir-fry in the olive oil the ingredients for Part A over medium to high heat. Cover and cook, stirring occasionally, about 6–8 minutes.

2. **PART B:** Microwave or steam the zucchini slices for 3 minutes.

3. **PART C:** In a small bowl, mix all the teriyaki sauce ingredients. Stir the teriyaki sauce into the Part A ingredients in the wok. Stir for about 1–2 minutes, until the sauce is thickened. Add in the zucchini.

4. **PART D:** Turn off the heat. Add fresh mint and mix well. Serve over brown rice.

NOTES:
1. People sensitive or allergic to wheat may want to use wheat-free soy sauce.
2. For people sensitive or allergic to soy, research has shown that the fermentation process breaks down the allergy-triggering proteins in soybeans, and therefore the allergenic response is gone.

MEAL 5 — Braised Red Cabbage and Apple

SERVES: 6 | LEVEL: Easy

CALORIES: 161; Fat: 8 g; Protein: 3 g; Carbohydrates: 22 g

1 medium-sized red cabbage, finely shredded
1 large sweet apple, cut in small pieces
1 large red onion, halved and thinly sliced
4 cloves garlic, crushed
4 tbsp. butter, melted
1 tbsp. light brown sugar
3 tbsp. balsamic vinegar
Salt and pepper to taste

1. Preheat oven to 350°F.
2. Mix well all the ingredients in a large ovenproof dish with a lid. Bake 1–1½ hours, stirring every 30 minutes. When done, the cabbage is soft but not slushy.
3. Serve hot or store in the refrigerator and serve cold or reheated.

> **NOTE:** For estrogen dominance and hypothyroid, use romaine lettuce instead of the red cabbage and bake for only 15 minutes, just enough to wilt the lettuce.

Red cabbage gets its bright color from anthocyanins and its sharp flavor from sulfurous compounds. Both substances are known for preventing cancer. The anthocyanins block the formation of plaque in the brain believed to be a primary cause of Alzheimer's disease.

Cabbage is also high in antioxidant vitamins A, C, and E as well as a variety of other vitamins and minerals, for tremendous overall health benefits. Red cabbage has ten times more vitamin A compared with green cabbage.

Cabbage is an age-old remedy for peptic ulcers. Now, scientists know this is because cabbage is a good source of glutamine. It also contains lactic acid, released while cooking or when a bacterium ferments the sugar in the cabbage, which seems to reduce muscle pain.

MEAL 5: Kale Salad with Avocado

SERVES: 6 | LEVEL: Easy

CALORIES: 127; Fat: 8.6 g; Protein: 3.5 g; Carbohydrates: 12.4 g

Avocado seems to be popping up everywhere lately, and not just for its rich flavor and smooth, creamy texture. The monounsaturated fats found in avocados can help to reverse insulin resistance, and its soluble fiber helps to keep blood sugar levels steady. Research has shown that the body uses monounsaturated fats for slow-burning energy, resulting in the feeling of satiety, instead of storing them as fats.

Eating avocados more often can have many health benefits, including a healthier heart, better skin, and weight loss. They can also help you treat or avoid serious health problems such as diabetes and arthritis.

One avocado contains 15 grams of healthy fats. When you add an avocado to a salad or salsa, the fat increases your absorption of several fat-soluble nutrients by as much as 400 percent. Avocados also increase antioxidant absorption from other foods. The fat in avocados primarily is made up of anti-inflammatory phytosterols and oleic acid.

PARTIALLY RAW VERSION

- 1 bunch kale, chopped
- 1 avocado
- 2 tbsp. olive oil
- 1 stalk celery
- 1 tsp. salt
- 2 tsp. lemon juice
- 1 large tomato, chopped
- 10 black olives, chopped

1. Put a little water in a pot and add the salt and kale. Cover and cook until the kale is tender. Drain and chill in the refrigerator.
2. Blend together the avocado, olive oil, celery, salt, and lemon juice until creamy.
3. Mix the kale, tomato pieces, and olives in a bowl.
4. Pour in the avocado mixture, and mix well.

RAW VERSION

- 1 bunch kale, finely chopped
- 2 tsp. salt
- 2 tsp. lemon juice
- 1 large tomato, chopped
- 10 black olives, chopped
- 1 avocado
- 2 tbsp. olive oil
- 1 stalk celery

1. Massage the kale with 1 tsp. salt until it wilts.
2. Add 1 tsp. lemon juice, and massage again.
3. Mix the kale, tomato pieces, and olives in a bowl.
4. Blend the avocado, olive oil, celery, 1 tsp. salt, and 1 tsp. lemon juice until creamy.
5. Pour in the avocado mixture, and mix well.

NOTES

1. For hypothyroid, cooking the kale reduces the goitrogenic properties.
2. For estrogen dominance, substitute mixed green lettuce or baby spinach for the kale.

CHAPTER 1: **Hypoglycemia** 23

Lemon Chicken Breasts

MEAL 5

CALORIES: 389; Fat: 24 g; Protein: 31 g; Carbohydrates: 9 g
NOTE: Nutritional value includes skin.

SERVES: 4 | LEVEL: Easy

¼ cup olive oil
3 tbsp. garlic (9 cloves), minced
⅓ cup dry white wine
1 tbsp. lemon zest (2 lemons), grated
2 tbsp. freshly squeezed lemon juice
1½ tsp. dried oregano
1 tsp. fresh thyme leaves, minced
Kosher salt and freshly ground black pepper to taste
4 boneless, free-range chicken breasts
   (6–8 oz. each), skin on
1 lemon

1. Preheat the oven to 400°F.
2. Warm the olive oil in a small saucepan over medium-low heat, add the garlic, and cook for just 1 minute, but do not allow the garlic to turn brown. Take the pan off the heat. Add the white wine, lemon zest, lemon juice, oregano, thyme, and 1 tsp. salt, and pour into a 9-by-12-inch baking dish.
3. Pat the chicken breasts dry, and place them skin side up in the sauce. Brush the chicken breasts with olive oil, and sprinkle them liberally with salt and pepper. Cut the lemon in 8 wedges, and tuck it among the pieces of chicken.
4. Bake for 30–40 minutes, depending on the size of the chicken breasts, until the chicken is done and the skin is lightly browned. If the chicken is not browned enough, put it under the broiler for 2 minutes.
5. Cover the baking dish tightly with aluminum foil, and allow it to rest for 10 minutes. Sprinkle with salt and serve hot with the juices.

Oregano is a nutrient-dense spice that could be called a super food. Oregano is one of the most potent antioxidants available, more than 40 times more powerful than an apple, 12 times more so than oranges, and 4 times more so than blueberries. It also contains compounds that have antifungal, anti-inflammatory, and potent antibacterial properties. There is evidence that oregano oil can even kill listeria, methicillin-resistant *Staphylococcus aureus* (MRSA), and some varieties of candida.

The antiviral properties of oregano come from compounds known as thymol and carvacrol. Recent research found that oregano can provide immediate and significant relief from symptoms of upper respiratory infections, and it is a better treatment for giardia than the commonly used prescription drug.

Fresh oregano is superior to dry oregano. Dry oregano might be somewhat less expensive than leaves, but if cost is a factor, consider growing some in a small pot in your kitchen windowsill. Then you can snip a few leaves anytime you like!

MEAL 6: Leeks with Lemon and Garlic

SERVES: 4 | LEVEL: Medium

CALORIES: 304; Fat: 27.6 g; Protein: 2.2 g; Carbohydrates: 16.6 g

Related to onions and garlic, **leeks** are delicious, versatile, and easy to use. Leeks are less well researched than their more popular cousins but are high in many of the same nutrients, such as flavonoids and allicin.

Allicin is a sulfur-based compound with a wide range of health benefits. It is antibacterial, antiviral, and antifungal. When digested, it is also converted into one of the most powerful antioxidants known.

Leeks also contain polyphenol and kaempferol, which can fight low-level inflammatory states. Leeks are high in vitamins A, K, and several B vitamins as well as magnesium. The folate in leeks is bioactive and can prevent birth defects.

The nutritional similarity of leeks to onions and garlic suggests that they should provide many of the same benefits. Leeks have a total polyphenol content (TPC) of 33 mg/100 g of the fresh edible portion as compared with the TPC of red bell peppers (at 27 mg) and of carrots (at 10 mg).

PART A
4 leeks

PART B
1 clove garlic, crushed
1 lemon, juice and zest
8 tbsp. olive oil
Salt to taste

PART C
1 cup vegetable stock
2 bay leaves

GARNISH
1 lemon, cut into wedges

1. Preheat oven to 325°F.
2. **PART A:** Prepare the leeks by trimming off the top $1/3$ of the green leaves and cutting off the roots. Split the leeks in half lengthwise. Slightly open the leaves, and thoroughly wash them. Drain.
3. **PART B:** Mix the garlic, lemon juice and zest, olive oil, and salt in a bowl. Brush olive oil on a baking sheet or in a large ovenproof dish. Place the leeks inside, single layer, open like fans. Drizzle the garlic and lemon mixture over the leeks.
4. **PART C:** Pour the vegetable stock over the leeks, and add the bay leaves. Cover the baking sheet or dish with aluminum foil. Bake for 45 minutes.
5. Pour the remaining cooking liquid over the leeks, and serve them on a flat plate. Garnish with the lemon wedges.

> **NOTE:** For weight loss, use half the amount of oil.

Quinoa, Celery and Almond Salad — MEAL 6

CALORIES: 179; Fat: 9.6 g; Protein: 5.4 g; Carbohydrates: 19.3 g

SERVES: 8 | LEVEL: Medium

PART A
- 2 tbsp. olive oil
- 1 yellow bell pepper, cut into small pieces
- 4 stalks spring onions (scallions), thinly sliced
- ½ tsp. crushed red pepper
- 4 cloves garlic, finely chopped

PART B
- 1 cup red quinoa, soaked for 30 minutes
- 1 tbsp. fresh thyme leaves, finely chopped
- 2 cups water

PART C
- 2 medium-sized zucchinis, cut into small cubes

PART D
- ½ cup almonds, coarsely chopped and roasted
- 3 stalks celery, diced
- 1 tbsp. olive oil
- ½ tsp. salt

PART E
- 2 limes, halved

1. **PART A:** In a large saucepan, sauté in olive oil the bell pepper, onions, red pepper, and garlic over medium heat until tender, about 5–7 minutes.
2. **PART B:** Rinse the soaked quinoa under cold running water until the water runs clear. Drain well. Stir the quinoa, thyme leaves, and water into the mixture from Part A. Bring to a boil, cover, and simmer over low heat for 7 minutes.
3. **PART C:** Stir in zucchini cubes; simmer for around 5 more minutes or until quinoa is tender.
4. **PART D:** Remove from heat and stir in the almonds, celery, olive oil, and salt.
5. **PART E:** Cool and drizzle with lime juice.

Quinoa is not technically a grain, though it is a grain crop and still counts as a grain for dietary purposes. Quinoa is actually a gluten-free seed prepared and eaten in much the same way as many grains. It is high in fiber and protein, nutrients essential to regulating blood sugar. Quinoa has a number of nutritional advantages over many grains. It is a good source of complete protein because it contains lysine and isoleucine, two essential amino acids not found in many other grains.

Quinoa is rich in multiple forms of vitamin E, folate, zinc, and phosphorus (largely absent in other grains) as well as the flavonoids quercetin and kaempferol, for a powerful antioxidant punch. Quinoa is also a better source of fat than wheat, providing 50 percent more fat in the forms of oleic acid and omega-3 alpha-linoleic acid. Finally, quinoa is high in fiber, iron, magnesium, manganese, and riboflavin.

MEAL 7 — Lemon Basil Pasta

SERVES: 6 | LEVEL: Easy

CALORIES: 359; Fat: 11.4 g; Protein: 12 g; Carbohydrates: 52 g

Lemons have so many health benefits that they could rightly be considered a super food. Long-distance walkers have long used fresh lemon juice to fight fatigue. Some travelers swear by the ability of lemons to prevent illness from drinking water in some locations.

Lemons are unique in their ability to alkalize the body, despite being quite acidic themselves. This helps restore the body to a neutral pH.

Lemons are especially good for the liver. They work to dissolve uric acid and a variety of toxins, making them easier for the body to remove. Drinking a glass of warm to hot water with a bit of fresh lemon first thing in the morning is a surprisingly effective detoxifier. It also stimulates the digestive tract, helping to eliminate waste, and might be able to kill intestinal parasites.

Parmesan cheese is high in protein and nearly lactose free, making it a good option for those who are lactose intolerant. Parmesan is aged for a long time, so the proteins are broken down, making it very easy to digest because it has essentially been "predigested" for you. It also contains *Bacillus bifidus*, a friendly bacteria found in the gut.

1 14 oz. package gluten-free pasta
Lime wedges for serving

SAUCE
⅓ cup lemon juice
3 tbsp. extra-virgin olive oil
½ cup Parmesan cheese, finely grated
1 cup basil leaves, roughly chopped
½ cup small black olives, roughly chopped
Sea salt and pepper to taste

1. Follow the package directions to cook the pasta. Drain the pasta, and pour it back into the pan.
2. For the sauce, whisk the lemon juice and olive oil in a bowl, and stir in the rest of the ingredients until well mixed.
3. Add the sauce and toss.

> **NOTE:** Some people sleep better when they eat some complex carbohydrates at night. So if you find eating nuts or proteins does not work for you, try eating some comfort food.

CHAPTER 1: **Hypoglycemia** 29

Tomato Eggs

MEAL 7

CALORIES: 179; Fat: 15.6 g; Protein: 6.8 g; Carbohydrates: 3.1 g

SERVES: 4 | LEVEL: Easy

2 ripe, fresh tomatoes, thinly sliced
2 scallions, green parts only, thinly sliced
4 large eggs
3 tbsp. olive or avocado oil
Salt and pepper to taste

1. Beat the eggs; season them with salt and pepper to taste.
2. Heat the oil in a wok or frying pan over a high temperature, and pour in the egg mixture. As soon as the egg mixture has formed a skin over the base of the wok or frying pan, add the sliced tomatoes.
3. Wait until the egg is just cooked and tomatoes just hot. Add the scallions, stir once or twice, and then slide onto a serving plate.

NOTE: This is a very popular Chinese dish and easy to prepare.

Because a medium-sized **egg** contains around 5.53 grams of high quality protein, nutritionists often use eggs as a benchmark to determine whether a food is a good protein source.

Eggs are also a good source of healthy fats at approximately 38 percent monounsaturated fat, 16 percent polyunsaturated fat, and 28 percent saturated fat. Although eggs are high in cholesterol, recent research has shown that, for most people, dietary cholesterol does not translate to increased levels of cholesterol in the blood.

Eggs contain significant amounts of tryptophan, an amino acid necessary for the synthesis of melatonin, serotonin, and other neurotransmitters that help you relax and sleep. Tryptophan is also converted into niacin, a B vitamin that aids digestion, promotes healthy skin, and helps your body convert food into energy. Insufficient levels of niacin can lead to digestive issues, impaired cognitive function, and skin inflammation. Eating eggs can raise your niacin levels.

A word on salmonella and **eggs:** infection occurs in only 0.003 percent of eggs. It is more likely to happen in a commercial kitchen than at home because of cross-contamination when the eggs are broken or use of eggs laid by traditionally raised commercial hens. Pasteurization of the eggs offers no protection against salmonella.

Marinated Carrots with Mint and Garlic

MEAL 7

SERVES: 6 | LEVEL: Easy

CALORIES: 41; Fat: 0.2 g; Protein: 1 g; Carbohydrates: 9 g

Your mother probably always told you to eat your **carrots**; they are good for your eyes. Turns out she was right: carrots are rich in vitamin A. Deficiency in vitamin A causes a variety of issues, including impaired vision and night blindness.

If you are not deficient, you are not going to notice any significant change in your eyesight, but vision is not the only benefit of vitamin A. Vitamin A also helps the liver eliminate toxins and removes excess bile and fat from the liver. The fiber in carrots then binds to the bile and fat and sweeps toxins from the body. Antioxidant phytochemicals found in carrots might be able to reduce your risk of a variety of chronic diseases, including heart disease and certain types of cancer.

Beware of baby carrots. They are actually made by cutting up and shaving down carrots too misshapen to sell as normal carrots. This does not seem like a problem, except they are then washed in chlorine to make them more appealing.

Some research shows that cooking carrots might help to boost their nutritional content, such as beta-carotene and phenolic acids.

PART A
4 cups carrots, sliced

PART B
4 cloves garlic, finely chopped
3 tbsp. apple cider vinegar
Salt and pepper to taste

PART C
¼ to ⅓ cup mint leaves, finely chopped

1. **PART A:** Steam the carrots for 5 minutes, or until just tender. Put them in a serving bowl.
2. **PART B:** Mix in the garlic, apple cider vinegar, salt, and pepper. Marinate them for at least 30 minutes in the refrigerator.
3. **PART C:** Mix in mint. Serve chilled or room temp.

CHAPTER 2

Insomnia

What Is Insomnia? 33
   Sleep-Onset Insomnia 33
   Sleep-Maintenance Insomnia 33
   Keeping Blood Sugar Levels Steady
      throughout the Day 34
   Food Sensitivity 36
   Foods That Promote Sleep................... 36
   Adrenal Breathing and Yoga Exercises 39
   Cereal and Fruit: Not Just for Breakfast 39
   Pair High-Glycemic Foods with
      a Healthy Fat Source..................... 40
   Foods That Might Increase Insomnia........ 41

recipes
   Almond Milk............................... 44
   Apple Carrot Oatmeal 45
   Buckwheat Apple Granola Bar 46
   Chia Coconut Milk Pudding 48
   Dilled Salmon Patties....................... 49
   Nut and Seed Mix 50
   Oatmeal with Walnut and Apple 51
   Presoaked Nuts 52
   Pumpkin Seeds with Almond Milk 53
   Soaked Granola Cookies 54

What Is Insomnia?

The word insomnia conjures up images of tossing and turning in bed, anxiously recounting the day's stressful events, and not being able to fall asleep. For people with Adrenal Fatigue Syndrome (AFS), insomnia does not stand alone; it is often part of a complex web of conditions resulting from the malfunction of the hypothalamus-pituitary-adrenal (HPA) axis.

Sleep-Onset Insomnia

There are two broad categories of insomnia. Sleep-onset insomnia (SOI) refers to the inability to fall asleep, which most healthy people complain of when they are unable to sleep. People with AFS also suffer from SOI, most commonly because medications and natural compounds they take have a stimulatory effect that generates more energy during the day. These range from thyroid medications and testosterone to maca, green tea, ginseng, and other herbs. An overly active mind stimulated by excessive computer-screen work, suspenseful and violent movies, emotional distress, or exercise in the evening (rather than earlier in the day) can contribute to insomnia. Caffeinated or sugary drinks can also be culprits.

Sleep-Maintenance Insomnia

Sleep-maintenance insomnia (SMI) refers to those who experience disturbed sleep because they are easily awakened and have great difficulty falling back to sleep. This inevitably leads to seldom feeling well rested even after a substantial amount of time in bed. The nightly pattern of waking up and being unable to immediately fall back to sleep interferes drastically with the body's ability to recuperate, creating a vicious cycle when one rises in the morning feeling extremely tired and leading to lethargy throughout the day. SMI could be a result of metabolic imbalance, such as problems with blood sugar and insulin regulation. It could also result from excessive neurotransmitter releases from the brain in the advanced stages of AFS, when often the autonomic nervous system is deregulated. The hormones adrenaline and norepinephrine are two of the most common culprits. If the blood sugar drops below a certain threshold during sleep, the body can release adrenaline and norepinephrine, which can contribute to wakefulness. Therefore, to avoid SMI caused by metabolic imbalances, one needs to ensure the stability of the blood glucose level throughout the evening.

A key goal is to achieve continuous balance and stable blood sugar levels throughout the night. We highly recommend avoiding refined white sugar because it has no nutritional value and spikes your blood sugar level too quickly. Do not substitute artificial sweeteners such as aspartame or saccharin. Instead, opt for a natural sweetener such as stevia leaf extract, which does not add to your glycemic load. Avoid all processed fruit and vegetable juices. Whole fruits, such as apples, are acceptable and should be paired with a fat, such as almond butter or a handful of nuts. Complex carbohydrate-rich foods can increase tryptophan availability, thereby inducing sleep.

Keeping Blood Sugar Levels Steady throughout the Day

Those with advanced AFS are already likely to suffer from reactive hypoglycemia during the day. It is prudent to eat every two to three hours, alternating between your main meals and snacks. Do not overlook snacks (see Glycemic Appendix page 210) because they can add a nutritional boost to your diet. Snack on low glycemic foods such as nuts, seeds, turkey, chicken, legumes, and eggs. For sustained energy release, add a small amount of carbohydrate, such as raw carrot sticks. This chapter includes recipes containing pumpkin seeds and almonds, both good sources of protein and fat to stabilize blood sugars and enable slow release of energy throughout the day, ideal for people with AFS. Pumpkin seeds are also rich in zinc, essential for the absorption of micro-nutrients and usually deficient in those with AFS.

Oatmeal with Walnut and apple
page 51

The body's blood sugar levels need to be steady throughout the day to support good health, including sleep. Start your day on the right foot, even if you are tired! Try not to skip breakfast. In fact, it should be the biggest meal of the day, and it need not be a sophisticated, gourmet ordeal. We have included in this book a handful of simple-to-prepare, tasty, and nutrient-dense breakfast recipes that can be incorporated into your daily routine.

Bedtime snacks are especially important—a small amount of protein, a carbohydrate, and a fat. A small snack of protein and fat (e.g., a handful of nuts or cottage cheese) before sleep is beneficial. If you wake up in the middle of the night, have another light snack to normalize blood sugar, thereby allowing you to go back to sleep.

Food Sensitivity

Another food group to avoid is highly allergenic foods because histamine (your body's antiallergenic hormone) is an adrenal stimulant and will therefore likely keep you awake. Depending on your sensitivity, you might have to avoid dairy products, eggs, certain nuts, oranges, strawberries, wheat, or soy. To determine your food sensitivities, see Chapter 4 and attempt the rotational diet. Knowing what to eat and what to avoid will make a huge difference, and you might rest soundly soon enough. See Low Histamine diet (pgs 212–14) for additional help.

Foods That Promote Sleep

The general guideline for pre-bedtime snacks is that they should be high in protein and low in simple carbohydrates. We highly recommend that you incorporate the following foods into a rotational diet to see which ones work well for your individual body and stage of AFS. After you have determined which foods are sleep friendly, you can then incorporate them into a more permanent meal plan.

1. **Bananas.** If you are not sensitive to bananas (as a high-glycemic food—Refer to Appendix page 210) after trying them out on the rotational diet, you can add them to your diet but only once per week. Bananas are full of potassium and magnesium, which can act as a muscle relaxant (but can also worsen your AFS). They are high in vitamin B6, which converts the amino acid tryptophan into serotonin and melatonin, two

hormones that induce sleep. Other foods high in vitamin B6 are raw garlic, pistachio nuts, chickpeas, and tuna. If you have SOI, try eating the Garbanzo Snack (Chapter 8) or Tuna Salad Wraps (Chapter 1).

2. **Almonds.** Almonds are full of protein and magnesium, both of which promote sleep. The protein will help to maintain stable blood sugar levels throughout the night, so you are less likely to wake up and experience SMI. A handful of almonds makes a healthy and convenient snack for bedtime as well as when you wake up in the middle of the night. Almonds can be soaked in water for 12 hours, drained, and stored in the freezer. Thaw just a handful for a few minutes before eating them.

3. **Cherries.** Fresh tart cherries are a great source of melatonin, the hormone responsible for the sleep-wake cycle. Tart cherries, when eaten regularly, can help regulate your sleep. They are one of the very few natural food sources of melatonin and therefore an exception to the rule of avoiding fruit juices. Look for juice made with sour Montmorency cherries, which have six times the melatonin of regular cherries. If you are going to drink the juice, be sure to do so well before bedtime so the extra fluid does not cause you to wake up for a trip to the bathroom. For the most benefit, sip one cup (an eight-ounce glass) in the morning and another cup two hours before bed. One small study showed that people who drank one cup in the morning and one cup in the evening slept better. These cherries are also excellent sources of vitamin C, which is important for converting tryptophan into serotonin.

4. **Honey.** The natural sugar in honey tells your brain to shut off the chemical known to trigger alertness and allows tryptophan to enter the brain more easily. One tablespoon for a good night's sleep is plenty.

5. **Oatmeal.** This hearty grain is a staple in many households; it provides an array of beneficial minerals that promote sleep, such as calcium, magnesium, phosphorus, silicon, and zinc. It does not have to be a breakfast food; have it as a pre-bedtime snack. However, avoid adding sugar or artificial sweeteners; instead you can opt for half a teaspoon of raw honey, sliced almonds or walnuts, or some thinly sliced bananas or tart cherries on top.

6. **Flaxseeds.** These tiny seeds are a powerhouse of rich omega-3 fatty acids and will also work on your mood and help you fall asleep. Try our Flaxseed Soup (Chapter 5) just before bedtime.

Oatmeal with Walnut and Apple
page 51

7. **Calcium.** Calcium helps the brain use tryptophan to manufacture melatonin. Milk, yogurt, kale, spinach, and mustard greens are high in calcium. The Kale Chips (Chapter 8) and the Yogurt Parfait (Chapter 5) would make good pre-bedtime snacks.

Adrenal Breathing and Yoga Exercises

Doing adrenal breathing exercises can greatly help tone down brain activity, improve SOI, and reduce SMI. Please check the *DrLam.com* website, which offers a free adrenal breathing exercise app that can be downloaded onto your smartphone. These exercises can be incorporated into your nightly routine roughly 20 minutes before bedtime. The breathing exercises can also be used for SMI when you are awake in the middle of the night. The practice of adrenal yoga exercise, Sessions 1–4, found on the *DrLam.com* website would help you to relax prior to bedtime as well. Eat a small, high protein snack, do the adrenal breathing or yoga exercises, and find it easier to fall asleep!

Cereal and Fruit: Not Just for Breakfast

You eat it for breakfast, but could a bowl of warm oatmeal help you get more rest? Oatmeal is rich in several minerals known to support sleep, such as calcium, magnesium, silicon, phosphorus, and potassium.

The complex carbs in oatmeal, pretzels, and corn chips trigger insulin production and spike your blood sugar naturally, shortening the time it takes you to fall asleep. Oats are also rich in melatonin, a hormone produced naturally to relax your body and help you fall asleep. In this chapter, we have included recipes containing oatmeal with walnuts and apples, oatmeal with apples and carrots, and oatmeal with pumpkin.

Walnuts contain magnesium and calcium as well as an abundant amount of tryptophan. Walnuts are also an excellent source of protein, which balances out the carbohydrates in the oatmeal. Instead of apples for this recipe, you could substitute tart cherries for improved sleep. The best way to get a good night's sleep is to increase your melatonin intake.

Pair High-Glycemic Foods with a Healthy Fat Source

Never consume high-glycemic foods (e.g., fruit such as watermelon or a banana) without proteins and fats to balance them. For example, eat almond butter with an apple for both protein and a healthy fat.

Carbs are both your best friend and your worst enemy. Quick to digest, simple carbs such as candy and soda are great for a quick boost of energy. Complex carbs, such as whole grains, also tend to spike blood glucose levels, but they can lead to an energy crash after the glucose level drops back down. This is why carbs are great for working out, but you feel sleepy after a huge lunch full of carbs. Adding more protein, such as turkey, and healthy fats to the recipes would help to balance the blood sugar.

Turkey

Some experts say turkey has no effect on sleep, and the annual Thanksgiving food coma is caused by the amount of food you eat and not the bird itself. However, turkey does have tryptophan in it, which metabolizes into serotonin and melatonin, two of the main hormones responsible for your dozing off. Interestingly, elk meat has twice as much tryptophan as turkey breast.

Herbal Teas

Herbal teas such as chamomile, lemon balm, hops, and passionflower have tons of snooze-promoting properties. When you drink chamomile tea, there is an increase in glycine, a chemical that relaxes nerves and muscles and acts like a mild sedative. Researchers found that the Harman alkaloids released in passionflower tea act on your nervous system to make you sleepy. Avoiding all caffeine in the evening hours is key to putting you in sleep mode. Alternatives are caffeine-free teas such as rooibos, which imparts a deep sweet flavor without any additional sugar required. Decaffeinated green tea contains theanine, which helps promote sleep. Experts recommend trying a one cup serving of the hot stuff.

Some herbal teas, such as ginseng, have been shown to act as stimulants, and even though some tea drinkers do not feel their effects, many others experience insomnia and hypertension. If you fall in this category, avoid drinking ginseng tea several hours before bed. It would be more beneficial to drink the herbal teas already mentioned or the Almond Milk or Pumpkin Seed and

Almond Milk recipes in this chapter. Another great bedtime snack is the Chia Coconut Milk Pudding, also in this chapter.

Nuts and Seeds

All nuts and seeds—from almonds and cashews to chia and sunflower seeds—are rich in tryptophan as well as magnesium, a mineral that helps relax your muscles and nerves. In fact, being deficient in magnesium might cause insomnia and Restless Leg Syndrome (RLS).

Almonds contain magnesium, which promotes both muscle relaxation and sleep. They help promote sleep by switching your body from your alert adrenaline cycle to your rest-and-digest cycle. They also supply protein, which can help maintain a stable blood sugar level during sleep.

Almonds also contain tryptophan, which helps to naturally reduce muscle and nerve function while also steadying your heart rhythm; in other words, they relax you. Try this bedtime snack: a tablespoon of almond butter or a one-ounce portion of almonds.

Foods That Might Increase Insomnia

Lack of sleep can be a significant body burden in itself. For example, sometimes low blood sugar overnight is accompanied by nightmares, sudden onset of heart palpitations, anxiety attacks, and cold sweats. For the dinner meal, make sure you eat some low-glycemic-index carbohydrates and avoid the following foods, which can make you toss and turn.

1. **Milk chocolate.** The average milk chocolate bar contains tyrosine, which is converted into a stimulant, dopamine, that causes alertness and restlessness and can keep you up at night. However, eating dark chocolate at night is okay. Dark chocolate contains serotonin, which relaxes your body and mind.

2. **Alcohol.** Alcohol is known as a depressant, but it can keep you up at night. It actually prevents your body from entering the deep stages of sleep.

3. **Processed or smoked meats.** Processed meats contain high levels of tyramine, which makes the brain release a chemical that makes you feel alert.

4. **Spicy foods.** If you are prone to heartburn, lying down after a meal of hot and spicy food only increases its side effects. To prevent a sleepless night, make sure you eat your favorite hot and spicy foods early in the day.

5. **Caffeine and energy drinks.** In addition to avoiding sugary foods (e.g., pastries, cakes, ice cream, and other store-bought, processed desserts), we also suggest restricting your intake of caffeinated and decaffeinated drinks (particularly if you are sensitive to caffeine). Contrary to their labels, decaffeinated drinks do contain caffeine, albeit at a substantially lower concentration. Caffeine has gotten you through countless all-nighters and helped you get going in the mornings. However, caffeine does not actually give your body any energy. Though caffeine does provide you that feeling of alertness, it is a stimulant. The amino acid taurine in many energy drinks increases alertness and elevates heart rate and blood pressure.

6. **Tomato-based sauces.** Tomato-based foods have a tendency to cause acid reflux and heartburn, which might prevent you from having a good night's sleep, so have your pasta at least a few hours before bedtime.

7. **Soy.** Fermented soy products (soy sauce, tofu, miso, and even teriyaki sauce) have some of the highest amount of the amino acid tyramine, which causes alertness.

8. **Aged cheese.** Steer clear of Asiago, Parmesan, Romano, and other hard cheeses if you are planning a nap. Aged cheeses have high levels of the amino acid tyramine, known to keep you up.

In conclusion, insomnia (a disturbed sleeping pattern), brain fog, anxiety, and depression are common symptoms of AFS. Both too-high and too-low nighttime cortisol levels can cause sleep disturbances. The liver is lacking the glycogen reserves needed by the adrenals to keep blood glucose high during the night. When this happens, blood glucose levels might sometimes fall so low that hypoglycemic (low blood sugar) symptoms disrupt sleep during the night. Waking up between 1:00 and 3:00 a.m. often indicates low blood sugar during this time. These recipes help to calm the body by giving it enough protein and healthy fats.

Almond Milk

SERVES: 1 | LEVEL: Easy

CALORIES: 162; Fat: 14.95 g; Protein: 6 g; Carbohydrates: 1 g

½ cup almond milk, homemade or store bought
1 tsp. olive oil
1 tsp. coconut oil
1–2 drop(s) vanilla
1 raw egg

Mix or blend all ingredients together.

CHAPTER 2: **Insomnia** 45

Apple Carrot Oatmeal

CALORIES: 218; Fat: 3.7 g; Protein: 7 g; Carbohydrates: 40 g

SERVES: 2 | LEVEL: Easy

1 cup oatmeal
½ carrot, cut into strips
1 cup rice milk (or hazelnut or almond milk)
½ apple, cut into strips
Salt or sweetener to taste

1. Put the oatmeal and carrot strips into a medium-sized pot. Add enough water to cover the ingredients along with the rice milk, and bring to a boil. Simmer on low heat until carrot is soft (around 10–15 minutes).
2. Add apple strips, and cook until soft (5–10 minutes). Make sure there is enough water so that the oatmeal does not dry out.
3. Turn off the heat. Season with salt or sugar to taste.

With AFS, when you first wake up in the morning, you might experience anxiety, dizziness, or low blood sugar. Having a good, nourishing breakfast makes a big difference. This recipe has the needed ingredients to help balance your blood sugar and might reduce the anxiety. Add nuts as desired.

Buckwheat Apple Granola Bar

SERVES: 20 bars | LEVEL: Medium

CALORIES: 207; Fat: 133.4 g; Protein: 4.2 g; Carbohydrates: 36.82 g

Despite the name, **buckwheat** is not even remotely related to wheat. It is gluten free and packed with nutrition. It is also high in protein and contains no cholesterol or saturated fat, so it can help control blood sugar, aid digestion, and build lean muscle tissue.

Buckwheat is a good source of a variety of minerals, including magnesium and phosphorous, vital for bone and dental health. Magnesium also supports communication between nerve cells, serves as an important part of energy production, and tends to relax the blood vessels to improve circulation. Buckwheat also contains iron, which gives blood its red color and helps transport oxygen to the cells.

The mineral content of this recipe is boosted by apricots, rich in both calcium and potassium, both critical for strong bones. When buying fresh apricots, look for a deep orange or yellow skin, and be wary of any red. Red on apricot skin is the result of an inorganic and potentially harmful sulfur-dioxide preservative.

PART A
1 cup buckwheat, cooked
3 apples, cored and cubed
30 dates, pitted and soaked in water for 15 minutes
¼ cup raw sunflower seeds
½ cup raw honey
1 tsp. salt
1 tsp. cinnamon (optional)

PART B
½ cup cranraisins or tart cherries
1 cup dried apricots
¼ cup raw sunflower seeds
½ cup raw almonds

PART C
1 cup raw rolled oats
1 cup buckwheat, cooked
½ cup raw almonds, coarsely chopped
1 cup raw sunflower seeds
½ cup cranraisins

1. PART A: Follow the package instructions to cook 2 cups of buckwheat. Put 1 cup of buckwheat, the apple cubes, the dates, sunflower seeds, raw honey, salt, and cinnamon in a food processor and grind until smooth. Transfer the mixture to a large mixing bowl.

2. PART B: Put cranraisins or tart cherries, dried apricots, sunflower seeds, and almonds into a blender, and coarsely chop the nuts, seeds, fruit in a few quick pulses. Combine them in the bowl with the mixture of ingredients from Part A.

3. **PART C:** Add the rolled oats, remaining 1 cup of cooked buckwheat, almonds, sunflower seeds, and cranraisins to the mixture, and stir.

4. Form the dough into rectangular bars ½-inch thick. If the dough is too moist, add a pinch more of oats to the mixture. The dough should be sticky but not runny. Place the bars on dehydrator trays and dehydrate at 135 degrees for 4 hours. Flip the bars over and continue dehydrating them for another hour, depending on how chewy and moist you prefer your granola bars. If you prefer very crunchy granola bars, then dehydrate for another 4 hours after flipping.

5. Store them in an airtight container or the freezer.

Chia Coconut Milk Pudding

SERVES: 8 | LEVEL: Medium

CALORIES: 258; Fat: 16.8 g; Protein: 3.8 g; Carbohydrates: 23.3 g

Chia seeds are easier to digest and use than flaxseeds. They are also high in omega-3 fatty acids. Chia seeds can form bulky gel by absorbing 10 times their weight in water, so they have been known to reduce food cravings and help one feel full faster.

PART A
1 can regular coconut milk
1 can water
3-inch ginger root, peeled and slice
6 small sticks cinnamon
3 whole star anise pods
4 whole cloves

PART B
2 tbsp. coconut sugar
2/3 cup golden chia seeds
½ cup cranraisins

1. Put the coconut milk, water, ginger, cinnamon, anise, and cloves in a medium-sized pot, and bring contents to a boil.
2. Simmer the mixture for 15 minutes.
3. Turn off the heat, and let the mixture stand for 10 minutes.
4. Strain out the spices.
5. Stir in the coconut, sugar, chia seeds, and cranraisins, and mix well so that there are no clumps.
6. Refrigerate for 3-4 hours.
7. Spoon the mixture into a small glass. Top with mixed berries (frozen or fresh) as desired.

Dilled Salmon Patties

CALORIES: 121; Fat: 8.7 g; Protein: 9.8 g; Carbohydrates: 0.6 g

SERVES: 4 | LEVEL: Medium

- ½ cup oatmeal
- 2 6-oz. cans wild Alaskan salmon, drained and flaked
- 3 eggs
- ¼ cup dehydrated hash brown flakes
- 1 medium-sized red onion, minced
- 1 clove garlic, minced
- 1 tsp. fresh dill, chopped
- 1 tsp. salt
- Pepper to taste
- Expeller-pressed coconut oil

1. Soak the oatmeal for 30 minutes, then drain thoroughly.

2. In a medium-sized bowl, beat the eggs and add in the rest of the ingredients, including the oatmeal. Mix thoroughly.

3. Heat the coconut oil in a medium-sized skillet over a medium temperature. Use a tablespoon to spoon balls of salmon mixture into the skillet, then flatten each with spatula to form patties. Cook them until golden brown on each side.

The name for **dill** comes from an Old Norse word, *dylla*, meaning "to soothe." The herb is also mentioned in ancient Egyptian texts dating as far back as 3000 B.C. for its use as a soothing medicine. No wonder, then, that it might be a useful remedy for insomnia. In many parts of the world, dill has been steeped into a soothing tea or the seeds chewed. In some cultures, people even place dill over their eyelids to help them sleep. Combine it with chamomile to sleep well all night long.

The soothing properties of dill are not limited to relieving insomnia, however. Dill also contains compounds that can help reduce stomach acid, ease reflux, reduce gas and bloating, ease cramping and belly pain, help expel intestinal gas, and freshen breath.

Nut and Seed Mix

SERVES: 12 | LEVEL: Medium | CALORIES: 191; Fat: 17 g; Protein: 5.6 g; Carbohydrates: 6.5 g

Nuts and seeds have a powerful impact on a diet. They can be key to good nutrition.

PART A

1 cup walnuts, presoaked for 6 hours, water drained
1 cup almonds, presoaked for 6 hours, water drained
½ cup pumpkin seeds, presoaked for 2 hours, water drained
¼ cup sunflower seeds, presoaked for 2 hours, water drained
2 tbsp. flaxseeds

PART B

1½ tbsp. melted butter
1½ tbsp. olive oil
1 tbsp. agave nectar
1½ tsp. cumin
1 tsp. fennel
½ tsp. clove
¾ tsp. cayenne pepper
¾ tsp. black pepper
½ tsp. salt

1. Preheat oven to 250°F.
2. **PART A:** Presoak the nuts and seeds for the time suggested, and drain well.
3. **PART B:** In a medium-sized saucepan, combine butter, olive oil, agave, cumin, fennel, clove, peppers, and salt, and cook for about 1 minute.
4. Add in nuts and seeds and mix well. Spread in a single layer on a baking sheet. Roast until nuts are crunchy (approximately 2 hours).

> **NOTE:** Another option is to dehydrate the nuts and seeds in a dehydrator for 6 hours.

CHAPTER 2: **Insomnia** 51

Oatmeal with Walnut and Apple

CALORIES: 517; Fat: 36 g; Protein: 11.5 g; Carbohydrates: 40.8 g

SERVES: 2 | LEVEL: Easy

- 1 cup rolled oats
- ½ cup presoaked raw walnuts, coarsely chopped
- ½ apple, coarsely chopped
- 2 tbsp. coconut oil
- 2 cups water
- Raw honey to taste

1. Put oats, walnuts, apple, coconut oil, and water into a medium-sized pot. Bring it to a boil, then reduce heat and simmer for 10–15 minutes.
2. When ready to eat, add honey and almond milk.

A study showed that eating **walnuts** along with a Mediterranean diet might protect the brain functions from declining with age. Walnuts have been shown to have more antioxidants than other nuts.

Presoaked Nuts

Presoaking nuts removes the enzyme inhibitors; therefore the nutrients in the nuts are more available for absorption. Presoaking nuts also makes them taste sweeter. Almonds and walnuts are excellent, but avoid peanuts.

1. Cover raw nuts with water, and add 2 cups of water on top of that. After 12 hours, drain the soaked nuts and add new water. Repeat this morning and evening for 1–2 days. When you are finished soaking the nuts, drain all of the water.

2. Nuts can be kept frozen until ready for use, or you can dehydrate the nuts again for convenient storage.

CHAPTER 2: **Insomnia** 53

Pumpkin Seeds with Almond Milk

CALORIES: 17; Fat: 1.25 g; Protein: 0.6 g; Carbohydrate: 1 g

SERVES: 1 | LEVEL: Easy

½ cup almond milk, homemade or store bought
2 tbsp. raw pumpkin seeds, ground

1. Grind enough pumpkin seeds for a one-week supply, and store them in a glass jar in the refrigerator.
2. In a small pot, warm up the almond milk. DO NOT warm it up in the microwave. Remove it from the heat and pour it into a cup.
3. Stir in the ground pumpkin seeds.

NOTE: Another option is to make the recipe and keep it warm in a thermos to drink if you wake up in the middle of the night.

Soaked Granola Cookies

SERVES: 30 cookies | LEVEL: Medium

CALORIES: 222; Fat: 14.3 g; Protein: 3.3 g; Carbohydrates: 23.6 g

Coconuts are amazing and have a surprising array of health benefits. In fact, coconuts were used thousands of years ago in ancient India to boost immunity and for their properties as antifungal, antiviral, and antibacterial. Nearly identical to human blood, coconut milk has even been used for blood plasma transfusions to treat injuries.

Despite the longtime use of coconuts, modern medicine has only recently caught onto the potential of this miracle food. Researchers have found coconuts to have strong antioxidant properties that might be able to help stabilize blood sugar, regulate hormones, and increase thyroid function, all of which can help you to improve your quality of sleep. Coconuts might also be able to kill viruses, bacteria, fungi, and even parasites, helping to improve your overall health.

Pine nuts are rich in several vitamins and minerals, especially magnesium, potassium, and vitamin D, all of which can help you get better sleep. Magnesium deficiency is associated with insomnia and Restless Leg Syndrome (RLS), and potassium deficiency can make it difficult to stay asleep. Vitamin D is associated with daytime sleepiness, which can lead to difficulty falling asleep when you actually want to.

PART A
4 cups rolled oats
2 tbsp. vinegar

PART B
2 cups shredded, unsweetened, dried coconut
1 cup pine nuts
1 cup raw walnuts, soaked and dehydrated, coarsely chopped
½ cup raw sunflower seeds
1 cup dried cranberries or tart cherries

PART C
½ cup melted coconut oil
1 cup honey or less, depending on sweetness and crunchiness desired
2 tbsp. blackstrap molasses
1 pinch sea salt

1. **PART A:** Soak oats in vinegar and water overnight (use enough water to cover the rolled oats, plus a couple of inches, because they will expand). In the morning, place the oats in a colander and let them drain for 1 hour.

2. **PART B:** Mix coconut, pine nuts, walnuts, sunflower seeds, and cranberries or cherries in a mixing bowl. Stir in the oats.

3. **PART C:** In a small saucepan, heat the coconut oil, honey, molasses, and salt at a low temperature. Slowly stir this mixture into the dry mixture from Part B. Form the dough into balls, and flatten them down. Put them on dehydrator trays lined with parchment paper. Dehydrate them for 10–13 hours.

Store them in an airtight container, and they can last 3–4 weeks.

CHAPTER 3

Low Blood Pressure

What Is Low Blood Pressure? 57
The Relationship between Aldosterone
  and Low Blood Pressure 58
Low Blood Pressure and Dietary Guidelines . 58
Adding Salt to Your Diet 60

meal one
Chicken in Basil Cream Sauce 62
Maple Chipotle Corn and Asparagus Salad . . 64
Baked Sweet-Potato Rounds with Pecans 65

meal two
Acorn Squash 66
Apple Walnut Spring Green Salad 67
Lettuce Chicken Cups 68

meal three
Lemon-Tahini Broccoli and Cauliflower 70
Swiss Chard Rolls 72
Roasted Onions with Walnut Crumbs 74

meal four
Couscous with Vegetables 75
Kale Sweet-Potato Chicken Patties 76
Red Cabbage, Romaine
  and Mushroom Salad 78

meal five
Blended Tomato Soup 79
Roasted Brussels Sprouts 80
Honey Teriyaki Salmon 81

meal six
Baked Chicken with Honey-Mustard Sauce . 82
Green Beans, Zucchini and Roasted Garlic . . 83
Potato Onion Frittata 84

What Is Low Blood Pressure?

Blood pressure constitutes one of the vital signs of life. Blood pressure is generated by the heart pumping blood into the arteries and regulated by the response of the arteries to the flow of blood; it is the force exerted by circulating blood on the walls of blood vessels.

Low blood pressure can be indicative of impaired adrenal health and function when accompanied by other symptoms such as fatigue, allergies, frequent influenza, arthritis, anxiety, depression, reduced memory, difficulty concentrating, insomnia, and the inability to lose weight after extensive efforts. Low blood pressure can mean that an inadequate amount of blood is flowing to the organs within your body and in serious cases might result in organ damage.

> **As the adrenals become stronger, the desire for salt decreases.**

In the early stages of Adrenal Fatigue Syndrome (AFS), a person might experience normal to high blood pressure, but if healing of the adrenals is not addressed adequately, then it might progress to low blood pressure. The signs and symptoms of low blood pressure are not necessarily defined by a blood pressure reading at the physician's office but might include dizziness, lightheadedness, orthostatic hypotension, and heart palpitations. For a more complete description of the various stages of AFS, refer to Dr. Lam's *Adrenal Fatigue Syndrome* book.

Being in an upright or standing position can exacerbate the condition and in certain cases cause severe dizziness, which might or might not lead to fainting episodes, called orthostatic hypotension. Ordinarily, the body would be able to compensate for this drop in blood pressure. However, if the autonomic nervous system is not functioning properly as a result of advanced AFS, the blood pressure would not be corrected.

The Relationship between Aldosterone and Low Blood Pressure

Blood pressure regulation for people with AFS is largely influenced by the adrenal hormones aldosterone and cortisol, both at lower levels during the advanced stages of AFS.

Aldosterone is a hormone produced by the adrenal cortex that regulates the amount of sodium and potassium in the body by maintaining the concentration inside and outside the cells. In other words, it will help your body retain salt, which in turn has a direct effect on the amount of fluid in the body and thus controls your blood pressure. It is important to understand the unique interaction of sodium and water within your body, that is, where sodium is present, water will follow. As the concentration of aldosterone rises in the body, the concentration of sodium and water rises; thus more fluid is retained in the body, and blood pressure rises. Conversely, when the level of aldosterone lowers, the amount of sodium and water in the body is reduced. Therefore, the blood pressure goes down.

Low Blood Pressure and Dietary Guidelines

As previously mentioned, aldosterone production is reduced in advanced AFS; therefore, sodium and water retention is also compromised, resulting in low blood pressure. The cells become dehydrated and deficient in sodium, so hydration becomes essential for them. Drinking beverages such as coffee, alcohol, and caffeinated tea during this stage (in fact, consuming these beverages during any stage of AFS) is highly discouraged because this exacerbates the dehydration.

The easiest method of increasing blood pressure is therefore to consume more water and take in more salt by adding salt liberally to your food. Those with low blood pressure might see a temporary increase in blood pressure when sodium is added to their diet. If the adrenals are weak, increasing salt intake will often enhance adrenal recovery.

As the adrenals become stronger, the desire for salt decreases, and excessive salt might make one feel nauseated, especially if the salt is consumed with water rather than by salting your food. In fact, this is one indication that the adrenal functions are improving.

Lettuce Chicken Cups page 68

Adding Salt to Your Diet

When you become more accustomed to listening to your body's reactions, you might notice that when you experience low blood pressure, dehydration, and sodium deficiency, there is a greater tendency for the body to have cravings for salty food and thirstiness that feels unquenchable. Do not go for that sugar-laden, carbonated beverage! Instead, grab a glass of refreshing water with a squeeze of lemon, cucumber slices, or mint leaves to make it more palatable if you are not accustomed to drinking plain water. Plain water can be refreshing, and over time your taste buds will adjust and your body will as well.

It is important to address these cravings with an increase in fluid intake while simultaneously increasing sodium in food as well. If you drink a large volume of water without the extra intake of sodium, the current amount of sodium in your body will be further diluted and can lead to a state called dilutional hyponatremia. Symptoms can include lethargy, fatigue, and in extreme cases, coma.

Another helpful tip to start your day on the right foot is to drink a glass of water with a quarter teaspoon of salt in the morning. If you have a history of being sensitive to salt, then we would recommend starting with a much lower dose and recording your body's reactions before progressing to higher increments of salt. If you find there is some improvement, then drinking another glass in the afternoon might also be beneficial.

Salty Snacks

If adding extra salt to your drinking water or food seems unappetizing to you, there are other creative ways you can increase your daily salt intake. One of the easiest ways to ensure your body obtains the necessary electrolytes it requires is by snacking on savory as opposed to sweet snacks. We have included here a number of recipes to help you kick start this daily habit. My recipes are both nutritionally dense and easy to prepare. If you are a big fan of seaweed, you would be pleased to know that this sea-dwelling algae is rich in both sodium and potassium and makes a great snack. If you have not tried seaweed before, go ahead and begin this new culinary adventure!

Different Types of Salt

Let us now consider some of the different types of salt available on the market, because the dizzying array available can be rather confusing, and discuss which ones are more desirable.

Regular table salt contains mostly sodium chloride and also has anticaking agents added to it, which are not beneficial for your health. It is best to avoid regular table salt on a long-term basis when cooking at home.

Sea salt is better than table salt because it contains trace minerals, which have been removed from table salt. These trace minerals are beneficial for our bodies; however, as a result of the pollution in our oceans and seas, we get the good minerals along with the bad. It is important to know where the salt was harvested.

Himalayan pink salt is mined from ancient sea salt deposits and contains more than 80 minerals and trace elements. There are varying qualities of Himalayan pink salt, and they can be used in a similar fashion as table salt, that is, for cooking, baking, and so on. A few people might experience sensitivities to this salt because of its high mineral content, so be cautious and proceed with small doses and graduate to larger doses accordingly.

Bamboo salt, contrary to what the name might suggest, is not produced by the bamboo tree. Rather, salt is put inside a bamboo trunk, sealed with yellow clay, and roasted for a period of time. Bamboo salt has been used for centuries for medicinal purposes in Korea and was only recently introduced to the North American market. Its makers claim it contains more than 70 kinds of minerals as a result of its production process. Another benefit is that it is highly alkaline because of the high sulfur content in the bamboo trunk, which helps because most of our North American diet is highly acidic because of our consumption of meat and other foods. The only drawback is that bamboo salt is comparatively expensive, and there have not been sufficient long-term studies on its negative effects.

It is important to add more salt in the food you eat when you have AFS, so you might need to sprinkle your food liberally with salt. If you are eating with your family, do not oversalt the food because your family members might not have the same salt requirements you do.

MEAL 1 — Chicken in Basil Cream Sauce

SERVES: 4 | LEVEL: Medium

CALORIES: 310; Fat: 17 g; Protein: 31 g; Carbohydrates: 2 g

A single ounce of **cashews** contains more than 80 mg of magnesium, 20 percent of the amount you need each day. Most of the magnesium in your body is found in the bones. Some of it is used to give bones their structure, and some is stored on the surface of the bone.

Magnesium is also very good for the central nervous system. It keeps calcium from entering the blood vessels and causing them to contract, which can lead to migraines and other ailments. Magnesium also keeps calcium from flooding and hyperstimulating the nerve cells, which can lead to muscle cramps.

Cashews are also high in copper, important for energy production. On top of that, cashews help the body use iron, produce the skin and hair pigment melanin, and eliminate free radicals.

If you have taken milk of magnesia for constipation, you might or might not have noticed that it contains a large amount of magnesium. Making sure you get plenty of magnesium in your diet can help you prevent constipation from becoming a problem in the first place.

- 1 lb. boneless, skinless, free-range chicken breasts or thighs
- 1 tbsp. expeller-pressed coconut oil

CREAM
- 1 cup hot water
- ½ cup raw cashews
- 1 tbsp. pine nuts

SAUCE
- ½ medium-sized white onion, chopped
- 1 tomato, chopped
- 1 tbsp. expeller-pressed coconut oil
- 1 tsp. dried basil
- Salt and pepper to taste

1. Marinate the chicken with salt and pepper, then chill for one hour.
2. Heat a skillet over a medium-high temperature. Add 1 tbsp. of coconut oil. Pan fry the chicken for 5 minutes or until golden brown, then flip it over and cook for another 5 minutes or until golden brown.
3. While the chicken is cooking, put the hot water, cashews, and pine nuts in a blender and blend until creamy. Set aside for use later with the sauce.
4. Heat a saucepan over a medium temperature. Add 1 tbsp. of coconut oil. Stir-fry the onion, tomato, and basil until soft. Add the salt and pepper and enough cream to make it creamy. Add more water as needed to make it saucy.
5. Add the chicken and coat it thoroughly with the sauce. Serve with the sauce to taste over the chicken.

NOTE: Extra cashew cream can be kept in an airtight container in the fridge for one week. You can use the cream in cereal or oatmeal.

Maple Chipotle Corn and Asparagus Salad

MEAL 1

SERVES: 6 | LEVEL: Medium

CALORIES: 115; Fat: 5 g; Protein: 4.5 g; Carbohydrates: 16.5 g

Controversies over high fructose corn syrup (HFCS) and genetic modification of crops have given corn a bad reputation. Despite the reputation, **corn** is actually a highly nutritious food. We are always hearing about corn syrup, especially HFCS, and how bad it is for you. In reality, sweet corn has less than a quarter of the sugar of an apple.

All varieties of corn are loaded with antioxidants and phytochemicals but have different concentrations of myriad nutrients. Yellow corn, for example, is especially high in carotenoids, blue corn is rich in anthocyanins, and purple corn contains protocatechuic acid. Although many fruits and veggies lose much of their nutritional value when cooked, the opposite is true of corn. Its antioxidant strength actually increases with cooking.

PART A
- 2 tsp. expeller-pressed coconut oil
- 1 bunch asparagus, cut into 2-inch strips
- 2 ears fresh corn, kernels shaved off
- ¾ tsp. chipotle powder
- ¼ tsp. salt
- ¼ tsp. black pepper

PART B
- 1 tbsp. fresh lemon juice
- 1 tbsp. Dijon mustard

PART C
- ¼ cup pistachios
- 4 tbsp. cranraisins
- 1 tbsp. maple syrup
- 2 tbsp. nutritional yeast

1. **PART A:** In a medium-sized frying pan, add coconut oil. Heat over a medium temperature. Add in the asparagus. Cover and cook for about 1–2 minutes. Add in the corn, chipotle, salt, and pepper. Cover again and shake the pan to disperse the steam and oil.

2. **PART B:** Add in the lemon juice and mustard. Cook uncovered until the liquid has absorbed into the veggies or steamed off. Stir occasionally.

3. **PART C:** Add in pistachios, cranraisins, and maple syrup. Mix well. Cook for 1 minute or so. Do not overcook the vegetables. Remove from heat and toss with nutritional yeast.

CHAPTER 3: **Low Blood Pressure**

Baked Sweet-Potato Rounds with Pecans

MEAL 1

CALORIES: 325; Fat: 23.4 g; Protein: 8.3 g; Carbohydrates: 23.3 g

SERVES: 4 | LEVEL: Medium

1 big or 3 medium-sized, round sweet potatoes (orange meat) or yams, washed and dried

TOPPING
¾ cup pecans, coarsely crushed
½ cup Parmesan cheese
½ tsp. thyme
⅛ tsp. crushed red chilies
½ tsp. garlic powder
1–1½ tbsp. olive oil
Salt and pepper to taste

1. Preheat oven to 400°F.
2. Slice the sweet potatoes into ½-inch rounds. Make 8 large rounds or 16 medium-sized rounds. Discard the ends.
3. Line a baking sheet with baking paper. Place the sweet-potato slices on the baking sheet. Drizzle them with olive oil.
4. In a medium-sized bowl, mix all the toppings. Add enough olive oil so the mixture sticks together. Spread the topping mixture onto the sweet-potato slices. Press gently. Bake for 40–50 minutes or until the sweet potatoes are tender and the topping is crunchy.

Despite their natural sweetness, **sweet potatoes** have a low glycemic index. This means that the natural sugars are released into the bloodstream slowly, so you do not experience a spike and subsequent crash in blood sugar levels. Instead, you will have a gentler, longer-lasting energy boost.

Sweet potatoes contain high amounts of vitamin D, especially critical during the winter. In many people who experience seasonal affective disorder (SAD), the symptoms arise from a vitamin D deficiency from a lack of sunshine.

Some sweet potatoes have rich purple anthocyanin pigments, which have important antioxidant and anti-inflammatory properties. They might lower the potential health risk from heavy metals and free radicals when passing through the digestive tract.

Another interesting nutrient from sweet potatoes under study now is a group of resin glycosides called batatins and batatosides. These sugar- and starch-related molecules have been shown to have antibacterial and antifungal properties.

MEAL 2 — Acorn Squash

SERVES: 6 | **LEVEL:** Easy

CALORIES: 128; Fat: 4 g; Protein: 1 g; Carbohydrates: 24 g

It is not a coincidence that **acorn squash** ripens just as cold and flu season is getting well under way. Acorn squash is rich in vitamin C, vital for a healthy immune system. Vitamin C stimulates production of white blood cells, the body's first line of defense against pathogens and microbes that would cause illness.

Acorn squash is also high in a variety of antioxidants. In addition to vitamin C, acorn squash also contains beta-carotene (which gives the flesh its orange-yellow color) and omega-3 fatty acids. A single cup of baked acorn squash provides 340 milligrams of omega-3s. This is not as much as you would get from an oily fish, but it is enough to consider acorn squash a good source.

2 medium-sized acorn squash
¼ cup packed brown sugar
2 tbsp. butter
Salt and pepper (optional)

1. Preheat oven to 400°F.
2. Cut the squash in half, and discard the seeds. Place the squash halves flesh side up on a large baking sheet. Place ⅛ cup brown sugar in the middle of each squash half, then place 1 tbsp. of butter on top of the brown sugar (season with salt and black pepper to taste).
3. Roast 25 minutes, until flesh is fork-tender. When squash is done, spoon squash out of the rind, and stir.

NOTE: People with diabetes can substitute stevia for the brown sugar. Acorn squash and other winter squash are higher in sugar content, so limit the intake.

CHAPTER 3: **Low Blood Pressure** 67

Apple Walnut Spring Green Salad — MEAL 2

CALORIES: 182; Fat: 13 g; Protein: 3.8 g; Carbohydrates: 15 g

SERVES: 8 | LEVEL: Medium

- 1 medium-sized red apple, chopped
- 1 medium-sized green apple, chopped
- 1 cup walnuts, chopped
- 10 cups green salad mix or spring mix

DRESSING

- ½ cup fresh apple juice
- 2 tbsp. lemon juice
- 2 tbsp. apple cider vinegar
- 2 tbsp. extra-virgin olive oil
- 1 tbsp. maple syrup
- 3 tsp. brown sugar
- 1 tsp. Dijon mustard
- ¼ tsp. pepper
- ¼ tsp. salt

1. Mix the dressing ingredients in a large salad bowl. Add the apples, toss, and coat well.
2. Add the mixed green salad on top of the apples. DO NOT toss. Cover and put in the fridge.
3. When ready to eat, toss the apples and salad.

NOTE: Always presoak walnuts or pecans for 12 hours to improve the digestibility of the nuts. Walnuts taste sweeter and less bitter after soaking. If you are sensitive to walnuts, you can substitute macadamia nuts, pecans, or hazelnuts.

If you have ever looked at a **walnut** and thought that it looked a little like a brain, it might not surprise you that walnuts are excellent for brain health. This is a result of their abundance of omega-3 fatty acids. A quarter cup of walnuts contains the entire recommended daily intake of omega-3s. Research has shown that omega-3s can prevent or slow cognitive degeneration. Omega-3s can also ease depression, stress, and anxiety.

Walnuts also contain melatonin. In a study on lab animals, their melatonin levels tripled after consuming walnuts. So, if you experience insomnia, consider a handful of walnuts an hour or two before going to bed to help ease your mind and help you fall asleep.

MEAL 2 — Lettuce Chicken Cups

SERVES: 2 | LEVEL: Medium

CALORIES: 276; Fat: 16.4 g; Protein: 23 g; Carbohydrates: 5 g

½ lb. boneless, skinless, ground free-range chicken/turkey or 90 percent lean ground beef

PART A
½ tbsp. olive oil
1 tsp. soy sauce
1 tsp. fish sauce

PART B
1 tbsp. olive or coconut oil
½ red onion, finely chopped
1 clove garlic, finely minced
Fresh chilies, minced (optional)

PART C (premix)
1 tbsp. fish sauce
½ lime, juiced
1 head butter lettuce
Cilantro, cut into tiny strips

1. **PART A:** Marinate the ground meat in olive oil, soy sauce, and fish sauce for 30 minutes in refrigerator.
2. **PART B:** Heat a wok or frying pan over a medium-high temperature and add the olive oil. Add the onion, garlic, and chilies, and stir-fry until lightly browned and fragrant. Push the cooked ingredients to the side of the pan. Add the meat, and stir-fry until golden brown.
3. **PART C:** Mix in the fish sauce and lime juice. Serve in a butter lettuce cup; garnished with cilantro.

The next time you buy a head of **lettuce** for a salad, consider bypassing the iceberg and opting for romaine, butter, or another dark-green variety. The dark green color is a good indicator that these varieties contain significantly more nutrients than their pale green cousin does.

Just 3.5 ounces of butter lettuce give you more than twice the vitamin A you need every day. It is also incredibly rich in copper, iron, potassium, and manganese. Copper and iron are vital to the production of healthy red blood cells, and potassium helps regulate blood pressure and heart rate. Manganese is an antioxidant mineral that can help rid your body of toxins.

When you break open a lettuce leaf, you might notice a bit of white fluid. This fluid is a substance called lactucarium. Lactucarium is very similar to opium, without the side effects. If you have trouble with insomnia, eat a few lettuce leaves before bed to help you sleep. The fluid also has antimicrobial properties and can destroy yeast overgrowths.

Lettuce contains minerals that can help your body rid itself of toxins and maintain your pH levels. Balancing your pH can give you more energy, more restful sleep, and more youthful skin.

Since the Middle Ages, lettuce has been used to treat certain neurological conditions. Recent research suggests that lettuce might be able to ease anxiety.

Lemon-Tahini Broccoli and Cauliflower

MEAL 3

SERVES: 8 | LEVEL: Medium

CALORIES: 101; Fat: 8 g; Protein: 2.2 g; Carbohydrates: 6.9 g

1 cauliflower, cut into florets
2 bunches broccoli, cut into florets

SAUCE
4 tbsp. tahini
3 tbsp. freshly squeezed lemon juice
1 tbsp. apple cider vinegar
4 tbsp. extra-virgin olive oil
1 tbsp. maple syrup
½ tsp. ground pepper
1 tsp. salt
Paprika for garnish

1. Put 1 cup water in a wok and bring it to a boil. Put in the cauliflower and broccoli. Turn down heat to medium. Cover and cook, stirring once or twice. After 2 minutes, uncover and cook until all liquid is gone.

2. Toss the veggies with half the sauce. Before serving, drizzle more sauce over the veggies. Sprinkle paprika over the veggies, and serve hot or cold. (Extra sauce can be used as salad dressing.)

> **NOTES:**
> 1. For estrogen dominance and hypothyroid, substitute mixed green lettuce for broccoli. You should eat cruciferous vegetables twice a week only.
> 2. If you want to use this recipe for a snack to balance hypoglycemia, add more tahini to increase the fat and protein content.

Tahini is a thick paste made from ground sesame seeds and most often used in Middle Eastern dishes such as hummus and baba ganoush. Whole sesame seeds have a hard hull that makes them difficult to digest. Grinding them into tahini breaks down this outer hull, making them easier to digest, which makes it easier to absorb the nutrients they contain. Tahini can be made from either hulled or unhulled sesame seeds. Be sure to choose the unhulled variety because it contains greater concentrations of nutrients.

Tahini is rich in vitamin E, most B vitamins, and a surprising array of minerals, including calcium, phosphorus, magnesium, potassium, iron, and lecithin. Tahini also contains methionine, an amino acid that can help with liver detoxification and is used to protect the liver in the event of acetaminophen poisoning. It also increases the acidity of urine, and evidence suggests that it might be able to protect against urinary tract infections.

Phytosterols are compounds found in plants that have a chemical structure very similar to cholesterol, and when present in the diet in sufficient amounts, they are believed to reduce blood levels of cholesterol, enhance the immune response, and decrease the risk of certain cancers. Sesame seeds have the highest total phytosterol content compared with other nuts.

MEAL 3 — Swiss Chard Rolls

SERVES: 6 | LEVEL: Challenging | CALORIES: 399; Fat: 27.8 g; Protein: 9 g; Carbohydrates: 32 g

If you are not familiar with **Swiss chard,** it is time to give this leafy green vegetable a try. Related to beets and kale, Swiss chard has dark green or reddish leaves and white, yellow, or red leaf stalks, depending on the variety.

A single cup of Swiss chard provides significant amounts of several vital nutrients, including several times the amount of vitamin K you need each day. Vitamin K, calcium, and magnesium help you build strong bones. Along with potassium, vitamin K promotes brain health and can even improve your cognitive abilities. Vitamin K is also an essential component of the myelin sheath, which protects nerves. Swiss chard is also a good source of iron and copper, both of which are essential to preventing anemia.

Swiss chard is loaded with flavonoids, one of which is called syringic acid, shown by recent research to regulate blood sugar by inhibiting the alpha-glucosidase enzymes that help to reduce the carbs to simple sugar. Other phytonutrients found abundantly in Swiss chard are betalains, which have been shown to provide antioxidant, anti-inflammatory, and detoxification support.

PART A
2½ lbs. Swiss chard

PART B
2 white or yellow onions
2 tbsp. olive oil

PART C
1½ cup cooked rice
1 tbsp. parsley, finely chopped
1 tbsp. dried mint
3 eggs
Salt and pepper to taste

PART D
½ cup vegetable stock
½ cup olive oil
2 lemons, juiced

GARNISH
2 tbsp. pine nuts, dry roasted

1. Preheat oven to 400°F.
2. **PART A:** Blanch 20 whole leaves of Swiss chard in boiling water, then plunge into ice water. Drain and set aside.
3. **PART B:** In a medium-sized frying pan, stir-fry the onions in olive oil until they are transparent. Remove them from the heat.
4. **PART C:** Blanch the rest of the Swiss chard and drain. Squeeze out the excess water, and chop it finely. Add the onions from Part B, rice, parsley, mint, eggs, salt, and pepper and mix well. This will be the filling for the rolls.
5. Brush a baking dish with olive oil. Flatten out a parboiled Swiss chard leaf from Part A. Place 1½ tbsp. of filling from Part C at the edge of the leaf and roll it up. Repeat with all the leaves, and place them in the baking dish in a single layer.

CHAPTER 3: **Low Blood Pressure**   73

6. PART D: Pour the vegetable stock, olive oil, and lemon juice over the Swiss chard rolls. Put the rolls in the oven and bake for 20 minutes. Garnish with pine nuts.

> NOTE: If you are in the advanced stages of AFS, ask someone to make a bunch of these rolls ahead of time. You can reheat them easily for snacks.

MEAL 3: Roasted Onions with Walnut Crumbs

SERVES: 8 | LEVEL: Medium | CALORIES: 108; Fat: 9.7 g; Protein: 1.7 g; Carbohydrates: 4.9 g

Love them or hate them (and it is hard to find anyone who is indifferent to them), **onions** are packed with a number of incredibly powerful compounds to protect your health.

Onions are rich in polyphenols, plant compounds with antioxidant properties that might be able to prevent disease. Their polyphenol content is more than that of leeks, carrots, tomatoes, bell peppers, and even garlic. One of the most abundant polyphenols in onions is quercetin, an antioxidant believed to block the release of histamines. Some evidence suggests this antihistamine might be able to support respiratory health and alleviate such cold and allergy symptoms as runny nose, watery eyes, sneezing, and coughing.

Polyphenols in onions tend to be most concentrated in the outer layers, so always be careful to remove as little as possible when peeling them. Unlike many nutrients, quercetin is not degraded by low heat cooking.

2 large, sweet, white onions, cut crosswise into ½-inch thick slices
1 tbsp. extra-virgin olive oil
Salt and black pepper to taste

TOPPING

8 tbsp. walnuts, roasted and ground
2 tbsp. butter, melted
1 tbsp. parsley, finely chopped
1 tsp. garlic, minced
¼ tsp. poppy seeds
1 tsp. sesame seeds
½ tsp. ground oregano
¼ tsp. ground thyme

NOTE: For a good snack for insomnia, almonds have been shown to help. Try substituting almonds for the walnuts in this recipe.

1. Preheat oven to 450°F.
2. On a foil-lined baking sheet, brush the onion slices liberally with oil; season with salt and pepper. Bake until soft and lightly caramelized, about 15 minutes. Turning once, try not to break the onion apart.
3. While the onions are baking, stir together the topping ingredients in a small bowl.
4. When the onions are lightly browned, take them out of the oven. Spread the topping so that all the onion slices have an equal amount of topping. Return them to the oven and continue baking until topping is golden brown, about 15 minutes more.

CHAPTER 3: **Low Blood Pressure** 75

Couscous with Vegetables

MEAL 4

CALORIES: 493; Fat: 21 g; Protein: 12.5 g; Carbohydrates: 65.4 g

SERVES: 4 | LEVEL: Challenging

PART A

2 small eggplants (look for Japanese eggplants), thickly sliced
2 large yellow bell peppers, cut into 1-inch cubes
2 medium-sized red onions, cut into ½-inch wedges
3 tbsp. olive oil
Salt and pepper to taste

PART B

1⅛ cup couscous
1¼ cup cold water

PART C

1¼ cup cherry tomatoes, halved
2 tbsp. Harissa paste
2 tbsp. olive oil

PART D

2 tbsp. roasted pumpkin seeds
1 large bunch fresh cilantro, roughly chopped

1. Preheat oven to 450°F.
2. **PART A:** Put eggplant slices, bell pepper cubes, onion wedges, olive oil, salt, and pepper in a large roasting pan, and mix well. Roast for 20 minutes or until tender.
3. **PART B:** Put couscous and cold water in another roasting pan, and soak for 5 minutes.
4. **PART C:** Stir the cherry tomatoes, Harissa paste, and olive oil into the couscous. Pop the couscous into the oven next to the vegetables, and bake for 4–5 minutes or until warmed through.
5. **PART D:** Mix together the couscous and vegetables. Stir in the pumpkin seeds and cilantro.

> **NOTE:** For estrogen dominance, if you have already eaten some phytoestrogenic food for the week, substitute zucchini or any winter squash for the eggplant.

Pumpkin seeds are a fantastic treat that can be eaten in the shell or by removing the shell as you would with sunflower seeds. Pumpkin seeds are high in zinc, which can protect your reproductive health (both men and women) and cardiovascular health and boost your immune system. The highest concentration of zinc is found in the endosperm envelope, the grayish coating around the actual seed. Sometimes this coating sticks to the shell, so if you remove the shell before eating the seed, be sure you get this part of the seed.

Pumpkin seeds are also a good source of antioxidant vitamin E in a variety of forms, including alpha-tocopherol, gamma-tocopherol, delta-tocopherol, alpha-tocomonoenol, and gamma-tocomonoenol. Most vitamin E supplements contain vitamin E in the form of alpha-tocopherol. Evidence shows there are more health benefits we taken it in multiple forms rather than all at once.

Pumpkin seeds, like pumpkins, are high in tryptophan, which can improve your sleep and boost your mood. In addition, pumpkin seeds seem to be effective in improving an overactive bladder. So, eating pumpkin seeds before bedtime might be a good sleep aid.

MEAL 4 — Kale Sweet-Potato Chicken Patties

SERVES: 4 | LEVEL: Challenging

CALORIES: 235; Fat: 5 g; Protein: 31.3 g; Carbohydrates: 15 g

Scallions, also known as green onions or spring onions, belong to the same family as common onions, but they have a less-developed root bulb. Scallions are milder than common onions and can be eaten raw or cooked. The stem part of the green onion is the medicinal part and might work well as an antipyretic, antibacterial, antifungal, and expectorant. If you suffer colds, chills, or stomach indigestion, you might want to try drinking the stem part of green onion in a tea.

The bacteria in your gut are vital to a healthy immune system, and scallions can directly improve the health of these bacteria. Scallions are high in fructans, a type of complex carbohydrate consisting of soluble fiber. Fructans are not digested in the small intestine, so they nourish the beneficial bacteria in the colon.

Scallions also contain selenium, which lowers inflammation and stimulates the immune system. Studies have found that selenium deficiency can cause immune cells to develop more slowly and function less effectively and that these cells cannot produce protein or transport calcium efficiently.

PART A
- 2 stalks green onion, finely chopped
- 1 tsp. coconut oil
- ½ tsp. sea salt
- ½ medium-sized yam, cut into small cubes
- 1/4 cup water
- 2½ cups kale leaves, finely chopped
- 2 tbsp. coconut flour

PART B
- 1 lb. boneless, skinless, free-range chicken breasts or thighs
- 1 tsp. sea salt
- 1 clove garlic, minced
- 1 tsp. paprika
- ½ tsp. mustard
- 5 stalks Italian parsley
- 1 large egg

1. **PART A:** Heat a large skillet over a medium-high temperature. Add the coconut oil and stir-fry the green onions until tender. Stir in the yam, water, and sea salt. Cover and cook until the yam is almost tender. Add more water as needed. Stir in the kale until wilted. Cook for about 2–3 minutes. Remove from heat and stir in the coconut flour.

2. **PART B:** In a food processor, grind the chicken; you might need to use the pulse from time to time. Then add in the ingredients from Part A along with the sea salt, garlic, paprika, mustard, parsley, and egg. Pulse and mix well in the food processor.

3. Heat a large nonstick skillet over a medium temperature. Use a tablespoon to form balls of the chicken/vegetable mixture and drop them in the skillet. Flatten them with a spatula to make patties. Cook them until golden brown. Flip to the other side and cook until golden and cooked through.

4. Serve the patties with guacamole or chili sauce.

NOTE: This recipe is good for snacks to battle hypoglycemia and sleep-maintenance insomnia. If you are very weak, ask someone to make a bunch ahead of time so that you can reheat them easily.

Red Cabbage, Romaine and Mushroom Salad

MEAL 4

SERVES: 6 | LEVEL: Medium

CALORIES: 142; Fat: 9.8 g; Protein: 2.8 g; Carbohydrates: 12.7 g

If you want a salad with a nutritional kick, go with **romaine lettuce** for the base. The deep green color of the lettuce leaves comes from an abundance of phytochemicals that all help to boost your immune system.

A single serving of romaine lettuce contains 136 micrograms of folate, more than one-third of your daily needs. For pregnant or lactating women, a single serving provides more than one-quarter of the daily needs. Most women of childbearing age are at least aware of the need for extra folate to prevent birth defects, but its benefits go beyond ensuring a healthy pregnancy.

Folate also helps slow the effects of aging on the brain, helping you stay sharp as you grow older. It can also help reduce depression and anxiety. Studies have shown that folate deficiencies can contribute to both depression and dementia.

When you break or cut romaine lettuce leaves, the white fluid you see is called lactucarium. Lactucarium has relaxing and sleep-inducing properties similar to opium but without the strong side effects.

10 button mushrooms, sliced
2 cups red cabbage, coarsely shredded
1 cup parsley, coarsely chopped
2 small heads romaine lettuce, coarsely shredded
1 yellow pepper, thinly sliced

DRESSING

¼ cup hoisin sauce
¼ cup vegetarian oyster sauce
½ lime, juiced
2 tbsp. sesame oil
2 tbsp. extra-virgin olive oil

GARNISH

½ cup pine nuts, raw or roasted

1. Toss all ingredients together.
2. When ready to serve, add the pine nuts.

NOTES:

1. For estrogen dominance and hypothyroid, substitute mixed green lettuce or baby spinach for the cabbage. You should eat cruciferous vegetables only twice a week.
2. For gluten allergies, you might want to eliminate hoisin sauce and vegetarian oyster sauce and use gluten-free soy sauce.
3. For weight loss, do not be afraid of the oil. The oil helps maintain satiety and prevents you from getting hungry until the next meal

CHAPTER 3: **Low Blood Pressure**

Blended Tomato Soup

MEAL 5

CALORIES: 47; Fat: 3.6 g; Protein: 0.8 g; Carbohydrates: 3.7 g

SERVES: 8 | LEVEL: Medium

PART A
1 red onion, cubed
1 large carrot, cubed
2 medium-sized stalks celery, cubed
1 red or yellow bell pepper, cubed
3 medium-sized red potatoes, cubed
1–2 bay leaves

PART B
½ cup presoaked nuts

PART C
4 tomatoes, cubed
1 clove garlic
2 tbsp. olive oil or grape seed oil
Mushroom extract to taste

1. **PART A:** Put the onion, carrot, celery, bell pepper, and potato cubes and bay leaves in a pot. Cover with water, with an additional 2 inches above vegetables. Over medium heat, bring it to a boil. Lower heat and simmer for 30 minutes.
2. **PART B:** Pour the mixture from Part A and presoaked nuts into a blender and blend until smooth.
3. **PART C:** Add the tomato cubes, garlic, oil, and mushroom extract, and lightly blend on low, still leaving chunks.

NOTES:
1. For weight loss, cut down or cut out the oil.
2. For allergies or cancer, substitute sea salt for the mushroom extract. Add more garlic as desired. Use flaxseed oil instead of olive oil.

There is a misconception that choosing a deep red **tomato** is key to getting the highest amount of the antioxidant lycopene, which gives oranges and other pink and red fruits and vegetables their color. However, a small study recently concluded that orange- and tangerine-colored tomatoes contain lycopene in a form more easily used by the body than the lycopene contained in deep red tomatoes. The best way to get lycopene, found in the tomato skin, is through cooked or processed tomatoes.

The most important factor determining the lycopene content in tomatoes might be the variety of tomato. All tomatoes, regardless of variety, color, or growing method (organic or conventionally grown), are rich in lycopene, but some varieties are naturally higher than others. Tomatoes with the highest lycopene content are New Girl, First Lady, Fantastic, and Jet Star. This result also came from a small study, and more research is needed on both of these conclusions, but if you are in the store looking at one of these varieties, go ahead and pick them up.

MEAL 5 — Roasted Brussels Sprouts

SERVES: 4 | LEVEL: Medium

CALORIES: 139; Fat: 10.5 g; Protein: 3.8 g; Carbohydrates: 10 g

1 lb. fresh, whole Brussels sprouts (or cut in half)
2–3 tbsp. olive oil
Salt and pepper to taste
Paprika (optional)

1. Preheat oven to 400°F.
2. Put the Brussels sprouts in a bowl, and mix well with the olive oil, salt, pepper, and paprika.
3. Place the Brussels sprouts on a baking sheet lined with parchment paper.
4. Bake for 25–30 minutes until the outside is crispy and the inside is cooked through.

> **NOTE:** For estrogen dominance and hypothyroid, use this recipe only occasionally.

If you have ever gone on a detox program, whether using a juice fast or a store-bought product, it was probably a waste of time and money. The fact is, detox should be a daily part of a healthy lifestyle, not just a one-time regimen, because toxins will start to reaccumulate as soon as the detox program comes to an end. If you are going to do a detox program, treat it as the beginning of a new lifestyle of healthier habits.

The body's detox system requires ample supplies of sulfur, in which **Brussels sprouts** are rich, to work effectively. Sulfur is in the smell and taste of Brussels sprouts, and when this vegetable is overcooked, the aroma is even stronger. Sulfur-containing nutrients are needed to support Phase 2 of detoxification.

When it comes to continued detox, Brussels sprouts are hard to beat. Evidence from human studies suggests that compounds known as glucosinolates in Brussels sprouts help to regulate the body's immune system to prevent unwanted inflammation, and they can also stimulate certain enzymes in the cells to remove carcinogenic toxins from the cells. Antioxidants in Brussels sprouts break down the toxins pulled from the cells so that they can be more easily eliminated.

Another anti-inflammatory component in Brussels sprouts is omega-3 fatty acids. About 1.5 cups (equivalent to 100 calories) of Brussels sprouts provide about 480 milligrams of the most basic omega-3 fatty acid (called alpha-linoleic acid, or ALA).

CHAPTER 3: **Low Blood Pressure** 81

Honey Teriyaki Salmon

MEAL 5

CALORIES: 225; Fat: 9.5 g; Protein: 23.3 g; Carbohydrates: 10.3 g

SERVES: 4 | LEVEL: Easy

- 1 lb. fresh salmon fillets
- 3 tbsp. soy sauce
- 3 tbsp. mirin (Japanese sweet rice wine)
- 2 tbsp. honey
- 1 tsp. ginger, finely grated
- 2 tsp. olive oil or coconut oil

1. Mix the soy sauce, rice wine, honey, ginger, and oil in a resealable bag. Add the salmon, and shake bag to coat. Refrigerate for 1–8 hours, turning the bag over every 2 hours. Then remove the salmon from the marinade, and save the juice.
2. Heat a frying pan over a medium-high temperature. Add the oil, and sear the salmon for 2 minutes on each side.
3. Turn the heat to low, and pour in the leftover marinade. Cover and cook 2 minutes on each side. Remove the lid, turn up the heat, and cook until all the liquid is gone.

Salmon is a rich source of DHA and vitamin D, both excellent for brain and eye health. One can of salmon contains a full day's worth of vitamin D, especially important in the winter, when most people do not get much sun exposure, and for those who spend a great deal of time indoors.

Several recent studies have found that salmon contains bioactive peptides, small bioactive protein molecules that might provide special support for insulin effectiveness, joint cartilage, and control of inflammation in the digestive tract.

Most of the salmon on store shelves is farm raised. Farmed salmon are typically fed a diet high in corn and soy products, unhealthy both for the fish and the consumer. Corn and soy are two of the most common genetically modified crops and result in fish higher in omega-6 fatty acids and lower in omega-3 fatty acids than wild caught salmon. Omega-6 fatty acids are critical to brain health, but too much omega-6, especially in a high ratio to omega-3, is associated with inflammation.

You might have heard that you should limit your intake of wild caught fish because of the risk of exposure to mercury, pesticides, and persistent organic pollutants. Although this is true, some varieties, especially the Alaskan ones, are known to contain less mercury than many others do.

Baked Chicken with Honey-Mustard Sauce

MEAL 6

SERVES: 4 | LEVEL: Easy

CALORIES: 192; Fat: 8 g; Protein: 20.8 g; Carbohydrates: 9 g

4 boneless, skinless, free-range chicken breasts or 5 boneless, skinless, free-range chicken thighs, lightly salt and peppered
2 sprigs fresh or dried rosemary

SAUCE

2 tbsp. Dijon mustard
2 tbsp. honey, agave nectar, or maple syrup
½ tbsp. olive oil
Salt and pepper to taste

1. Preheat oven to 350°F.
2. Sprinkle salt and pepper on the chicken and lay it on a baking sheet or in a shallow casserole dish.
3. In a medium-sized bowl, mix the mustard, sweetener, and olive oil sauce. Spread the sauce over the chicken. Place the rosemary sprigs between the chicken breasts or thighs. Bake for 45 minutes or until the meat is golden and done.

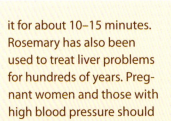

Research has shown **rosemary** to have a variety of benefits for the brain, including improving cognitive performance and memory, preventing premature aging of the brain, elevating mood, and relieving migraine pain.

One component of rosemary oil was found in a study to improve cognitive performance. Another compound, carnosic acid, was found to fight damage from free radicals in the brain. Another study found that carnosic acid might be able to help protect against neurodegeneration in the hippocampus. Some evidence shows that you do not even have to consume rosemary to get some of the brain boosting benefits. In one study, participants in cubicles were given rosemary essential oil to sniff. Their memories were better than a control group, though a little slower. The same participants also had improved mood compared with the control group. Try sniffing some oil of rosemary next time you have a test or mentally demanding task.

If you suffer from migraines, rosemary might be able to help. Boil a handful of rosemary in a saucepan of water. Use a towel over your head to trap the steam, and inhale it for about 10–15 minutes. Rosemary has also been used to treat liver problems for hundreds of years. Pregnant women and those with high blood pressure should exercise caution when consuming rosemary because it might raise blood pressure, and large amounts can trigger uterine contractions.

CHAPTER 3: Low Blood Pressure 83

Green Beans, Zucchini and Roasted Garlic

MEAL 6

CALORIES: 82; Fat: 4.9 g; Protein: 2.7 g; Carbohydrates: 8.8 g

SERVES: 8 | LEVEL: Medium

- 1 lb. green beans, trimmed
- 2–3 green or yellow zucchini, sliced
- 1–2 tsp. of butter
- 1–2 tbsp. extra-virgin olive oil or grape seed oil
- 4–8 garlic cloves, thinly sliced or chopped
- ¼ tsp. salt
- ¼ tsp. black pepper

1. Bring a large saucepan of water to a boil. Add beans, and cook 5 minutes. Plunge beans into ice water, then drain.
2. Repeat with the zucchini.
3. Heat a large skillet over a medium-high temperature. Add the butter and oil; swirl until the butter melts. Add the garlic, and sauté it for 30 seconds. Remove garlic, and set it aside. Add the beans and zucchini; sprinkle with salt and pepper (Johnny's Seasoning Salt is also an option). Cook 2 minutes, tossing frequently. Garnish with garlic.

When we think of bone health, most people think of calcium first, then maybe magnesium, potassium, or even vitamin D. What most people do not think about is silicon. However, silicon is a vital component of connective tissue in general and bone collagen in particular. Collagen provides the structure on which the bones are built. It works by increasing the ability of the bones to absorb and use calcium and vitamin D. **Green beans** are a great source of this little-thought-about mineral.

If you are concerned about the environment, green beans have the added benefit of being an especially sustainable crop. Surveys have found that more than half of all commercially grown green beans are grown right here in the United States, especially in Illinois, Michigan, New York, Oregon, and Wisconsin.

MEAL 6: Potato Onion Frittata

SERVES: 6 | **LEVEL:** Medium

CALORIES: 245; Fat: 17.6 g; Protein: 7.3 g; Carbohydrates: 15 g

Potatoes are a starchy vegetable that has gotten a bad reputation in recent years, but if you can keep them out of the deep fryer, they are actually quite nutritious. Potatoes are high in fiber to aid in digestion along with a variety of compounds that help convert glucose into energy.

Potatoes are an especially rich source of vitamin B6. One medium-sized potato contains more than half a milligram, nearly half of your daily requirements. Vitamin B6 is vital to a number of nervous system functions. Your brain uses vitamin B6 to create various hormones and other substances necessary for proper brain function, including serotonin, melatonin, epinephrine, norepinephrine, and GABA.

PART A
2 large potatoes, quartered lengthwise, then sliced about ¼-inch thick
Salt

PART B
3 tbsp. butter
3 tbsp. olive oil
2 large white or yellow onions, thinly sliced

PART C
¼ to ⅓ cup fresh thyme leaves
3 cloves garlic, crushed with salt

PART D
6 eggs, beaten
Salt and pepper to taste

1. **PART A:** Bring a pot of water containing salt to a boil. Blanch the sliced potatoes for 3 minutes, leaving them crunchy. Drain and cool them.

2. **PART B:** In an ovenproof frying pan, heat the butter, olive oil, and onions over a medium temperature for 5 minutes, stirring occasionally.

3. **PART C:** Add the thyme leaves and garlic. Cook for 2 minutes. Add the blanched potato slices. Stir until they are all coated. Cook for 5 minutes.

4. **PART D:** Pour in the eggs, then salt and pepper to taste. Cook over low heat until the frittata starts to come away from the side of pan. Place the pan in oven, and broil the frittata until golden.

> **NOTE:** If you want to make this into a complete meal, add diced chicken and green peas.

CHAPTER 4

Food Sensitivities

What Is a Rotational Diet?	89
Food Sensitivities.	90
The Major Culprits	90
Rotational Diet Protocol	93

What Is a Rotational Diet?

A rotational diet is essentially a well-thought-out meal plan in which foods are rotated every seven days so that you do not eat those same foods more than once in that period. Meal plans are not based on specific food items per se but rather on biological similarities within the food group. For example, almonds are a type of tree nut that also belongs to the same family as apples, pears, and a few other fruits. Another example is that of cashews and mangoes, which are related. If you eat cashews on Day 1, you would not then be eating mangoes on Day 2. Instead, you would wait until the whole rotational period is over and incorporate mango in your meals on Day 1 of the second seven-day rotational cycle.

> **The primary goal in using a rotational diet is to space out the time your body is exposed to cetain types of food groups.**

Some people choose to do a shorter rotation of four days, and this might work as well depending on how thorough you desire your results to be. Because foods in the same family are apt to cause similar allergies or sensitivities in the body, the entire food family is avoided during the rest of the food rotation if you have already included it in Day 1.

The primary goal in using a rotational diet is to space out the time your body is exposed to certain types of food groups and to accurately record how your body reacts to what you are eating. It is important to listen to how your system is responding. Learn how to take your pulse before and after your meals, and record everything accurately because this will give you a great understanding of how your system is reacting to certain foods. If there is no significant increase in your heart rate, then in all likelihood this food does not cause your body any sensitivity. If after your meal you find that your pulse has increased, then it is an indication that the body had to work extra hard during the meal, and something in the meal is causing problems. Other signs to look out for are joint inflammation, aches and pains, itchy skin, impaired cognition (also known as brain fog), and fatigue.

Food Sensitivities

Food sensitivities are less obvious than food allergies, which sometimes can show up as hives, itching in the mouth or throat, swelling of the lips, wheezing, or vomiting. These easily distinguished signs show up because your immune system is responding to the food or its additives as a perceived attack on the body, and it begins to release histamine. Excessive histamine release is associated with symptoms ranging from mild to severe allergic responses that can often be life threatening, such as anaphylactic shock. Reactions to food allergies tend to be very quick in nature, within minutes to an hour of touching, smelling, or ingesting a certain food. You can find out more about low histamin diet in Appendix page 000,

Food sensitivities are much more complex and not as easily identifiable because the response is often delayed, and symptoms sometimes do not show up until four days after consumption. They tend to arise from certain molecules within foods that your digestive system is unable to break down and properly digest. Often times the undigested molecules will be allowed to permeate the gut lining and leak into the bloodstream, causing an array of problems for your body that can be physical, emotional, and psychological. The symptoms of food sensitivities are wide ranging and can include, but are not limited to:

1. **gastrointestinal problems,** such as vomiting, diarrhea, constipation, bloody stools, gassiness, bloating;
2. **dermatological disorders,** such as eczema, acne, skin rashes, urticarial;
3. **nerve and muscle problems,** such as rheumatoid arthritis, aches, and pains; and
4. **adrenal fatigue,** lethargy, mood swings, anxiety, migraines, and eating disorders.

Because of the subtlety of the reactions and the delayed response of the body, one way to help identify hidden food sensitivities is to follow a rotational diet.

The Major Culprits

Many people are not even aware of what foods might cause sensitivities, we will list here the major culprits, but bear in mind that each of you has an individual genetic makeup and constitution. Knowledge is a powerful tool, and this list will serve as a good starting point into your healing regime.

1. **Wheat** (and other gluten-containing foods such as barley and rye) might seem a difficult food to live without, especially if you are accustomed to your daily breakfast of toast. However, there are many gluten-free alternatives now available on the market, such as rice bread or buckwheat bread. Ezekiel bread is another option in which the grains are sprouted so the gluten protein structures are changed, though it is not 100 percent gluten free.

2. **Cows' milk** contains more than 25 different molecules identified as having the potential to elicit an allergic food response. The protein casein in cow's milk is the most common allergen. This is possibly another daily staple that would be difficult to live without. Try almond milk or rice milk, and you might be pleasantly surprised. Other alternatives are goat and camel's milk, but they have overpowering flavors.

3. **Hens' eggs** are added to many processed foods, so you need to be aware and read the labels. Foods to look out for include salad dressing, mayonnaise, cakes, pastries, pastas, and soups.

4. **Peanuts and other tree nuts** (walnuts, almonds, pistachios, Brazil nuts, cashews, pecans, etc.)

5. **Soy,** including soy milk, edamame, tofu, and texturized vegetable protein (TVP)

6. **Fish**

7. **Shellfish,** such as shrimp, prawns, lobster, and crab

Rotational Diet Protocol

The key to success in following the rotational diet protocol is planning. For the purposes of those with Adrenal Fatigue Syndrome (AFS), we have formulated a modified rotational diet plan. We did not pay special attention to the same food species but made sure all the foods were not repeated for the seven-day period. Because most people with AFS are sensitive to certain foods, not allergic, severe restriction is not necessary. Following the guidelines in our rotational menu plan will help reduce inflammation within your body and give your immune system the opportunity to rest up for the body to heal.

We have taken the hard work out for you and provided a one-week menu plan. You can use this until you are more comfortable in formulating your own meal plan. It is best to prepare the food as simply as possible, using methods such as steaming and stir-frying. Avoid casserole dishes that have too many ingredients that might not be in your rotational plan for the day. Stay away from sauces and dressing. Salt and pepper are not included in our rotational diet plan, so you can use them in your food. We did not include oils, herbs, or spices in the rotational diet plan. If you do choose to add them, it is better to use different types of oils, herbs, and spices from day to day.

Another benefit of having a structured rotational meal plan is that by allowing your system time to heal, you are actually preventing new sensitivities from developing and eventually increasing the nutritional availability within your overall diet.

If you do not already keep a food journal, now would be a good time to start keeping a record of the food you eat, when you eat it, and any reactions your body experiences. Review and peruse this journal after your first week on the rotational diet, and see if you notice anything significant. If not, just continue with the rotational diet protocol. The best case scenario is that you can confirm you have no sensitivities. If you find that you do have a list of foods that cause you a reaction, try to eliminate those foods from your diet until your body heals itself. Then try that food on a rotational basis once more to determine if you are still sensitive to it.

This is a modification of food rotation for those with AFS. It does not follow the food family rotation, in which you do not repeat the same food family group in four to seven days. An example of a food family is the grass family—where most of the grains belong. As a result, you will only eat grains once every four to seven days.

Food Types	Day 1	Day 2	Day 3	Day 4	Day 5	Day 6	Day 7
Proteins	Turkey Pheasant Eggs	Lamb/Goat Shrimp	Freshwater fish	Beef Venison	Chicken Duck Eggs	Pork Scallops	Saltwater fish
Veggies	Spinach Green beans Chard Beets Beet greens String beans Alfalfa Rhubarb	Zucchini Cucumber Mushrooms Pumpkin Squash Okra Lettuce Endive Truffles	Broccoli Brussels sprouts Radishes Mustard greens Cabbage Collard greens Taro Bok Choy	Eggplant Tomato All peppers Potato	Celery Parsnips Fennel Water chestnuts Carrots Parsley Lettuce Chicory Artichokes	Bamboo shoots Sweet potato Yam Jicama Cactus (prickly pear)	Turnips Kale Cauliflower Napa cabbage Watercress Garlic Chives Onions Leeks Asparagus
Grains	Buckwheat	Millet Oat Rye Spelt	Arrowroot Ezekiel bread	Rice	Quinoa	Corn Ezekiel bread	Barley Teff Amaranth Kamut (khorasan wheat)
Nuts	Almonds Flaxseeds Chia seeds	Sesame seeds Chestnuts Pumpkin seeds	Hazelnuts Pine nuts	Walnuts Pecans	Macadamia nuts Sunflower seeds	Pistachios Cashews	Butternut Brazil nuts
Legumes Beans	Lentils Mung beans	Pinto beans Peas	Lima beans	Chickpeas (garbanzo beans)	Black-eyed peas	Navy beans	Kidney beans
Fruits	Cherries Plums Peaches Nectarines Apricots Prunes	Avocados Pineapple Grapes	Oranges Grapefruit Lemons Tangerines Coconut	Apples Kiwis Pears	Pomegranates Dates Figs Mulberries	Mangoes Blackberries Strawberries Raspberries Gooseberries	Papayas Guavas Cranberries Blueberries Huckleberries Persimmons

CHAPTER 5
GI Disturbances

What Is a Digestive Imbalance? 97
Irritable Bowel Syndrome (IBS) 98
Foods to Avoid 98
FODMAP Diet 100
Foods to Consume 101
GAPS: A Healing Diet 104
AFS Diet for Digestive Issus 105

recipes Cucumber Mint Yogurt 106
Flaxseed Soup 107
Miso Dressing 108
Mushroom Millet Porridge 109
Red Bean and Black Sesame Seed Porridge . 110
Yogurt Parfait 111

meal one Roasted Bell Pepper Soup 112
Spaghetti Squash Edamame Casserole 113

meal two Acorn Squash Kale Soup 114
Cucumber Lime Cod Salad 115

meal three Korean Cold Noodles 116
Rice and Celery Soup 117

meal four Almond Meal Pizza 118
Bok Choy Pineapple Salad 120

meal five Pesto, Garbanzo and Zucchini Salad 121
Stir-fried Bean Sprouts and Sugar Snap Peas 122

meal six Green Beans with Cherry Tomatoes 123
Salmon with Ketchup-Ginger Glaze 125

meal seven Baked Lemon-Almond Cod 126
Asparagus with Ginger-Miso Butter 127

meal eight Spinach Patties 128
Sautéed Asparagus with Thyme 129

meal nine Pearl-Barley Risotto 130
Grated Zucchini Basil Soup 132

What Is a Digestive Imbalance?

In the previous chapters, we discussed metabolic system imbalances such as hypoglycemia (low blood sugar) and food sensitivities. Now we will turn to Adrenal Fatigue Syndrome (AFS) digestive imbalances such as irritable bowel, constipation, slow movement, and low production of digestive enzymes. They can lead to bloating, indigestion, delayed food sensitivity, cramps, and gastric discomfort.

AFS manifests in myriad ways. Whereas one might experience a musculo-skeletal system breakdown, another might be going through a metabolic system imbalance. The further along your AFS is, the more your organs are affected because multiple organs are involved when your body down-regulates during a crash or as AFS worsens and the body returns to a simple state.

> **Contrary to popular belief, having fruit in your diet is not a necessity.**

Poor digestion is a common sign of AFS. As the thyroid is affected, constipation will ensue as the body attempts to reduce the basal metabolic rate to conserve energy. The gastrointestinal tract also tends to slow down, and the assimilation of food becomes a greater burden on the body. Processed foods become more difficult to digest, and complex foods are less readily absorbed. The indigestion is further exacerbated as digestive enzymes and acid-release production are reduced. Gallbladder function might be compromised because bile flow slows or is not regular. Liver congestion is common, leading to inadequate metabolic breakdown. This in turn leads to brain fog as toxin buildup accelerates. Dysbiosis and pH imbalance can be a problem, with systemic candida and other gastric dysbiosis retarding the recovery process.

On a few occasions, the signs and symptoms of poor digestion could actually be a paradoxical effect from taking supplements to address your AFS. If this happens to you, please consult your natural healthcare specialist, who will be able to review your supplement protocol and might recommend a change in supplements or dosage.

Irritable Bowel Syndrome

Irritable bowel syndrome (IBS) occurs when your colon muscles are not functioning as they should be, which could result in chronic constipation or cramping and bloating after a meal. IBS can be effectively managed through dietary protocols. Certain foods might trigger IBS symptoms, and the most effective way of discovering these culprits is through the rotational diet found in Chapter 4. By keeping a detailed journal of the various foods you eat and how they affect your IBS symptoms, over a period of time you will be able to determine which foods to avoid. Many people who suffer from IBS go on a FODMAP diet, which we will discuss below.

Foods to Avoid

People with AFS should avoid dairy products because they can cause inflammation. Inflammation can lead to a whole host of other health problems such as joint pain, respiratory diseases, and heart disease. However, after your AFS improves to either Stage 1 or 2, you can resume dairy in the form of yogurt or dairy kefir, which can be added to smoothies. This chapter includes some smoothie recipes to get you started on this healthy and filling drink, which can also be substituted for a convenient lunch. The ingredients are very forgiving, and you can add or subtract different food items depending on your food preferences and sensitivities.

Another food group to avoid is fruits. Contrary to popular belief, having fruit in your diet is not a necessity; only vegetables need to be a staple. It has been estimated that up to 30 percent of the population has some sort of sensitivity to the fructose sugar contained in fruits, and this can contribute to IBS. Another sign or symptom of fructose sensitivity is bad breath not caused by poor dental hygiene, because the fruit has fermented in the gut as a result of the bacteria feeding on the fructose. Going on a FODMAP diet will assist with avoiding certain fruits until you realize how your body reacts to them.

You should also avoid certain oils. The process of extracting oil from a fruit or nut varies based on the type of oil. Cold-pressed oils are simply pressed out of soft fruits and nuts, such as olives, avocados, and walnuts. No heat or solvents are used. Harder fruits, nuts, and seeds might require some steaming or other heat treatment to extract the oil prior to pressing. Use of solvents depends on the manufacturer.

Many mass-produced oils are extracted using hexane or other toxic solvents. The oils are then treated to remove the solvent, heated, and strained. This results in a uniform oil lacking in flavor, aroma, and nutrition. Regardless of processing method, oils might be refined or unrefined. Unrefined oils are filtered to remove particles, and some might look cloudy or have some sediment. This is not an indicator of poor quality. Unrefined oils have more distinct flavor, color, and aroma and greater nutritional value. They also have a shorter shelf life and lower smoke point. Unrefined oils are best for salads and lower-heat cooking.

Refined oils go through more filtering and might be heated. This gives the oil a greater shelf life and higher smoke point but reduces nutrients, flavor, and aroma.

Exposure to air, light, and heat can cause oil to become rancid, possibly increasing your risk of cancer and heart disease. Your oil should taste and smell fresh. If you are not sure, throw it out. To get the most out of your oils and to keep them from going rancid, you should keep a few things in mind. First, do not buy oil in quantities larger than you can use quickly. Second, store your oil in a cool, dry place. Unless you expect to use it within a month or so, refrigeration is preferred.

Finally, do not heat your oil until it smokes because this can damage the oil and create cancer-causing compounds. If you do inadvertently heat your oil until it smokes, discard it, clean the pan, and start over. Straining and reusing oil is not recommended because this can degrade the oil.

FODMAP Diet

The FODMAP diet is essentially about avoiding a group of carbohydrates that can cause irritation to the bowels. These carbohydrates are called fermentable oligosaccharides, disaccharides, monosaccharides, and polyols (FODMAP). It has been found that these foods are not absorbed well by the small intestine, which results in the foods being fermented in the gut. The result is bloating, abdominal pain, and gassiness.

Foods that fall within this group include wheat, beans, peas, onions, dairy, fruits, honey, sugar snap peas, cauliflower, dandelions, and mushrooms. More comprehensive lists can be easily located on the Internet under a search for FODMAP diet.

Is it necessary that you avoid all of these foods? Absolutely not! The point is to first realize that even foods clearly healthy for you might not actually be good for your body at this stage in your life. Each individual will react to the foods differently, and depending on your stage of AFS, you might be able to tolerate certain foods after your condition improves. The FODMAP diet, when used in conjunction with the rotational diet, will give you a guideline to the foods likely to be problematic and the foods you can freely consume. Over time, as your condition improves and digestive enzyme production is greater, you might be able to reintroduce certain foods into your rotation and determine whether they are now suitable for you to consume.

Foods to Consume

Although there is a list of foods above to avoid so as not to further exacerbate digestive issues, one can be eating certain foods to help oneself along in the healing journey. Unbeknownst to many people in today's society, many foods are filled with hormones, pesticides, and toxins that could be underlying contributors to countless diseases and illnesses. As we eat inorganic substances, our immune system is put into overdrive, trying to combat the artificial sludge coming through, thus causing many of the food allergies and intolerances seen today. That is why it is important to eat whole organic foods, especially organic meats such as poultry. Not only will the taste and flavor be more fragrant but the natural nutrition in the food will be better for you.

Depending on where you shop, organic products can be a bit more expensive than many other products, but the difference they can have on your health is tremendous. Most people are aware that organic meat is grown without chemicals, but that is not the only difference between organic and conventional meat. Food grown naturally is more nutrient rich and has less fat than chemically altered food. Some differences between organic and conventional meats are outlined below.

Lamb

A study performed in Spain found that organic suckling lamb meat had lower saturated fat and higher polyunsaturated fat when compared with conventionally fed lambs. Similarly, in a study performed in the United Kingdom, organic lamb loin chops were found to have higher levels of linoleic acid and total omega-3 fatty acids when compared with conventional lamb loin chops. This study analyzed 360 samples from three major UK supermarket chains.

Chicken

Two separate studies have shown that chickens fed organic diets have more polyunsaturated fat and less saturated fat than conventionally fed chickens. In addition, their eggs provide significantly more beta-carotene; omega-3 fatty acids; and vitamins D, E, and A than their conventional counterparts. They also contain less cholesterol and saturated fat.

Beef

There has been minimal research on cows fed an organic diet, but multiple studies have shown that beef from grass-fed cows contains more beneficial fatty acids and more of vitamins A and E than cows fed conventionally. In addition, cows fed an organic diet are not fed animal by-products, so mad cow disease is virtually unheard of in organic beef. Not only is the beef from organically raised cows healthier but also their milk has been shown to contain more healthy fatty acids. In addition to being better for you, organically grown meat is better for the planet and more humanely grown than conventional methods.

When it comes to cooking, it is also important which kind of oil is healthiest for you. Oil is oil, so we should be able to buy the least expensive, right? Not so fast. All oil is not created equal. Some oils are healthier than others, some oils maintain their health benefits at higher temperatures, and some can be stored longer. Here is some basic information on six of the best cooking oils.

Butter
Butter earned a bad reputation for its saturated fat, but real butter (not margarine) is good for you—even better if it comes from grass-fed cows. Butter contains vitamins A, E, and K as well as beneficial fatty acids. However, butter does contain proteins and sugars that can burn, and clarifying it removes these molecules so that butter can be used at higher temperatures.

Canola Oil
The neutral flavor and high smoke point of canola oil make it highly versatile, but it is also highly refined, so it lacks many of the health benefits of some other oils. Canola is also one of the most commonly genetically modified crops, though it is possible to find non-GMO products.

Grape Seed Oil
Most grape seed oils have a mild flavor, though some might taste a bit like the grapes from which they were extracted. With a medium smoke point, grape seed oil can be used in a variety of cooking methods, such as sautéing, low temperature baking, and sauces.

Coconut Oil
With a low to medium smoke point (depending on whether it is unrefined or refined) and loads of health benefits, coconut oil is a great choice for nearly any purpose.

Sesame Oil
The rich nutty flavor of sesame oil makes it a staple in Asian cooking. With a slightly lower smoke point than some of the other oils discussed, it should be reserved for lower temperature cooking.

Olive Oil
Olive oil has a good flavor, making it one of the best choices for use on salads, and light/refined olive oil has a medium to high smoke point that makes it a good choice for a variety of other uses. Extra-virgin olive oil is made by pressing the oil from olives without heat or chemicals, but it has a low smoke point and should not be used to cook. Other varieties of olive oil might be processed using either heat or solvents.

Smoke Point
Oils with a high smoke point include almond, safflower, rice bran, and refined olive oil. These oils are good for most uses, including searing, browning, and deep frying.

Oils with a medium-high smoke point include canola, peanut, soybean, and sunflower. These are suitable for baking, stir-frying, and oven cooking.

Oils with a medium to low smoke point include sesame, grape seed, and coconut. These oils should be used for sautéing, low-heat baking, and sauces.

Oils with a low smoke point include butter, unrefined coconut oil, and extra-virgin olive oil. These oils are suitable for salad dressings or low heat cooking.

Fermented Foods
Food fermentation is an ancient practice known to many cultures throughout the world, from Japanese miso, Korean kimchi, and Vietnamese fermented fish sauce to German sauerkraut, English sourdough, Greek yogurt, and traditional American pickles and relish. Each region of the world has its own unique fermented cuisine that is a staple at most meals, and there is good reason for this practice.

Fermentation promotes digestion and absorption of nutrients because the process breaks down the food into its more basic components, thereby making the food more readily absorbed by the body. Fermentation unlocks unique nutritional benefits that can heal the gut because raw, fermented foods are rich in enzymes, probiotics, antioxidants, vitamins, organic acids, and minerals that all promote the presence of good bacteria in the gastrointestinal tract. As the body ages, its supply of enzymes deteriorates; thus there is a greater need for enzymes to aid in the digestion and absorption of food. Poor adrenal function is often associated with the inability to digest food.

Other fermented foods quickly gaining popularity are kefir beverages and milk kefir. Kefir is a cultured and microbial-rich food that helps to restore the balance of bacteria in our gastrointestinal tract and is rich in many strains of probiotics. For those in the earlier stages of AFS, dairy kefir is acceptable. The only precaution with kefir beverages is that the fermentation process does produce a very slight level of alcohol to which some people might experience sensitivity. By including kefir beverages in your rotation diet, you will be able to determine whether kefir products are acceptable to you.

Although fermented foods are both beneficial for you and also healing, they are also potent. If you are not accustomed to eating fermented foods, start slowly with the recipes included in this book, and look out for any adverse reactions.

GAPS: A Healing Diet

The designers of the gut and psychology syndrome diet (GAPS) claim that it has a great effectiveness for healing the gut. People following this diet avoid foods that irritate the gut while simultaneously consuming foods that nourish and heal it. The GAPS diet also includes fermented foods to repopulate the gut with beneficial bacteria and detoxify the body of yeast, bad bacteria, fungi, and parasites.

Grated Zucchini Basil Soup page 132

The GAPS diet practitioners recommend starting on a liquid and "soft" diet—that is, rich broth of chicken, beef, and fish—then gradually adding in nonstringy vegetables that are easy to digest. Consuming lots of broth (with the fat included) coats the stomach lining (a compromised stomach lining led to leaky gut syndrome in the first place). The diet strictly excludes dairy products along with sugars and starches, including potatoes, rice, pasta, bread, and wheat-flour products.

The GAPS diet protocol is a healing one if followed with caution. It is a stringent diet regimen, and we do not recommend that those with AFS pursue it 100 percent because it is labor intensive. Like the other diets we have introduced in this book, use it as a guideline to which foods might cause you sensitivity in any form, be it IBS or otherwise. Put that food on the rotational diet, and record the reactions in your food journal.

AFS Diet for Digestive Issues

All of these steps you are taking toward your healing journey will culminate in you having a greater understanding of your body. Use the many recipes we have included in this chapter to help you along with your digestive issues, and be on your way toward adrenal healing and health! In summary, digestion issues such as diarrhea, constipation, gastritis, acid reflux, and IBS are common in people with AFS. This can be for many reasons, including lack of food assimilation as well as internal dysbiosis. Here are some suggestions by stage of AFS:

1. **Stage 1:** Make a big pot of soup so you can use it for meals and snacks. Also include two cups of chicken broth in your diet every day.

2. **Stage 2:** After you feel better, gently introduce more solid food. Avoid eating raw food for a month or so. Continue to drink two cups of chicken broth every day.

3. **Stage 3:** Go on a diet that is easy on the stomach for a week. This will give the digestive tract some time to heal. Eat our Flaxseed Soup (included in this chapter), and take one digestive enzyme before each meal. Avoid food that might cause more gas and bloating, such as cruciferous vegetables and onions.

Cucumber Mint Yogurt

SERVES: 4 | LEVEL: Easy | CALORIES: 71; Fat: 3.6 g; Protein: 2.7 g; Carbohydrates: 6 g

1 cup whole-milk plain yogurt
½ English cucumber, finely chopped
3 tbsp. finely chopped fresh mint
Sea salt and pepper to taste

1. Mix all ingredients together.
2. Keep chilled in refrigerator.

NOTES:
1. Snack: You can eat this yogurt along with some crackers, carrot sticks, or celery sticks.
2. Topping or sauce: You can use this as a sauce for a lamb dish.
3. Meal: This is a great light dish for dinner with some walnuts or pistachios added to it.
4. For weight loss, use nonfat plain yogurt.

Probiotics, such as those commonly found in live-culture yogurt, are a vital part of restoring healthy gut flora. A great deal of research has been done on live-culture yogurt in the digestive tract and has found that the bacteria in yogurt can promote healthy digestion and improve the absorption of nutrients. Bacteria in yogurt also convert sugars into short-chain fatty acids, which fuel the cells in the large intestine, improving function in this section of the digestive tract.

Probiotics are living bacteria that become metabolically active in the gut and aid in absorption of nutrients. The live cultures in the yogurt break down the lactose into easily absorbed by-products. The digestive tract is able to move food with steadiness and prevent issues such as diarrhea, bloating, and constipation. Yogurt from grass-fed cows is especially rich in minerals, B-complex vitamins, proteins, omega-3s, and phytonutrients.

If you have avoided yogurt because of lactose intolerance, this might not be necessary. The bacteria in yogurt feed on the lactose (a type of sugar) in milk. One-half cup of grass-fed cow's milk contains five to six grams of lactose, but the bacteria cut this amount by about one-third, giving you only three to four grams of lactose in a half cup of yogurt.

Mint is another powerful digestive aid. Mint stimulates the appetite and promotes gastric emptying. Simply chewing a few mint leaves can alleviate nausea, stimulate the salivary glands and the glands that release gastric juices, and jump-start the digestive process. There are approximately 15–20 different varieties of mint, each of which has a unique flavor, but all of them offer similar benefits. Mint is very easy to grow and is therefore a great plant to place in your kitchen window for use anytime.

Flaxseed Soup

CALORIES: 77.7; Fat: 4.3 g; Protein: 1.9 g; Carbohydrates: 9.2 g

SERVES: 1 | LEVEL: Easy

1 tbsp. flaxseeds
1 cup water
¼ tsp. cinnamon (optional)
1 tsp. honey to taste (optional)
Whey powder (optional)

1. Put the water and flaxseeds into a small pot. Cook them over low heat until the liquid thickens. Add one serving of whey powder if you wish. Add honey to taste.
2. Stir the soup as best as you can (the whey powder will become lumpy because it does not mix well).

For constipation we always recommend the Flaxseed Soup. Although it might not sound appetizing, it tastes great.

> **NOTE:** Make the soup in the morning. Split into three portions, and store the leftover portions in the refrigerator. Eat one portion before each meal or before bed. For people with digestion issues, *do not add* the whey powder. If you cannot consume whey, you can skip it or substitute your preferred protein powder.

Miso Dressing

SERVES: 10 | LEVEL: Easy

CALORIES: 82; Fat: 6.7 g; Protein: 1 g; Carbohydrates: 5 g

Healthy intestines are home to trillions upon trillions of beneficial bacteria known collectively as gut flora. These bacteria help you digest your food, extract nutrients, produce vitamin K, and process and eliminate indigestible fiber. When you are ill or when you take antibiotics, a portion of these bacteria might die, leading to digestive issues.

Miso paste is made by fermenting soy with microorganisms similar to the bacteria found in healthy intestines. Eating miso introduces these bacteria into your digestive tract, helping to recolonize your intestines. The length of fermentation directly influences both the flavor of the miso and the number of microorganisms it contains. The fermentation process also makes miso easier to digest because the microorganisms have already begun the process of "digesting" the soy.

¼ cup raw almonds, presoaked
¼ cup fresh lemon juice
¼ cup cold-pressed sesame oil
½ cup water
½ white sweet onion, chopped
2 tbsp. miso
1 tbsp. soy sauce
2 tbsp. maple syrup

1. In a blender, mix almonds, lemon juice, and oil until smooth.
2. Add the remaining ingredients and blend until very smooth and no lumps remain.

> **NOTE:** Keep in an airtight glass container in the refrigerator. It should keep for 2 weeks. If you are sensitive to almonds, use cashews.

CHAPTER 5: **GI Disturbances** 109

Mushroom Millet Porridge

CALORIES: 280; Fat: 2.8 g; Protein: 8 g; Carbohydrates: 55.3 g

SERVES: 2 | LEVEL: Easy

½ cup fresh mushrooms, sliced
¼ cup brown rice, soaked overnight
½ cup millet, soaked overnight
1 spring onion, chopped
Salt to taste

1. Pour boiling water over the mushroom slices; drain.
2. In a medium-sized pot, add 4 cups water, the rice, and the millet. Bring them to a boil over high heat. Turn down the heat and simmer until rice is cooked. Add more water if needed.
3. Add mushrooms and salt. Cook 5 more minutes. Add chopped spring onion.

> **NOTE:** For the catabolic state of AFS, this is a very nourishing and easy-to-digest porridge. You can stir some marinated ground beef into the porridge after it is boiled, then turn off the heat to finish cooking it.

Millet might be a staple in birdseed, but it packs a nutritional punch for people as well. Depending on how it is cooked, millet has a consistency like that of mashed potatoes or fluffy rice, with a nutty sweet flavor. Millet might well be one of the most easily digested grains and among those least likely to cause an allergic reaction.

Millet is a good source of phosphorus, an essential mineral for bone strength. It also contains a molecule known as adenosine triphosphate (ATP) produced by the cell's mitochondria, used by the cell for energy. In addition to its beneficial fiber content, millet functions in the intestines as a prebiotic. This means it feeds the beneficial bacteria in your gut, improving both digestion and your body's ability to absorb nutrients.

Millet does not contain gluten, but it is still wise to eat it in moderation because it does contain compounds known as goitrogens that impair the function of the thyroid gland and can lead to enlargement of the thyroid, a condition known as goiter.

Red Bean and Black Sesame Seed Porridge

SERVES: 4 | LEVEL: Easy

CALORIES: 396; Fat: 12.4 g; Protein: 13.2 g; Carbohydrates: 61 g

Traditional Chinese medicine held black **sesame seeds** to be a virtual fountain of youth, and there might be something to that reputation. Black sesame seeds are high in B-complex vitamins and iron. Deficiencies of either of these nutrients can lead to premature aging.

Black sesame seeds contain oil that can lubricate the intestines. This, with the fiber content, can help improve digestion. Soaking the seeds overnight before eating them reduces oxalic acid, making the calcium they contain easier for your body to absorb and use.

Black sesame seeds are high in calcium and zinc, both essential for strong bones. They also contain vitamin E, which promotes healthy skin. Even if they cannot stop the clock, black sesame seeds can help to keep you beautiful and strong.

¾ cup red beans, soaked overnight
½ cup brown rice, soaked overnight
¾ cup black sesame seeds, roasted
¼ cup brown sugar

1. Drain the red beans and brown rice.
2. In a nonstick pan, stir-fry the black sesame seeds over medium heat until they are fragrant/done.
3. Put the red beans, brown rice, brown sugar, and enough water to cook in a large pot. Cook over high heat until done. Check the water level every 15 minutes.
4. When ready to serve, add the black sesame seeds.

CHAPTER 5: **GI Disturbances**   111

Yogurt Parfait

CALORIES: 300; Fat: 2.9 g; Protein: 10.6 g; Carbohydrates: 61.6 g

SERVES: 4 | LEVEL: Easy

- 1½ cups of sugar-free strawberry yogurt (or any flavor you choose as long as it is sugar free)
- 2 cups granola
- 1 cup fresh strawberries, sliced
- 1 cup blueberries

1. In each of 4 parfait glasses, alternate layers of yogurt, granola, strawberries, and blueberries. You can use raspberries or apples as well.
2. Eat as a late afternoon snack or for dessert.

NOTE: You can also use plain whole-milk yogurt and add your own sweetener or flavor.

Berries of all kinds, particularly strawberries and blueberries, are packed with antioxidant phytochemicals that can help boost your immune system.

Strawberries are loaded with vitamin C, a powerful antioxidant, well-known immune booster, and fiber provider that stimulates digestion. Strawberries also contain anthocyanins, and there is some evidence that they can boost your short-term memory as much as 100 percent.

Blueberries contain more antioxidant power than nearly any other fresh fruit. One of the most powerful, yet little known, compounds in blueberries is gallic acid. Research has shown that gallic acid can protect the brain against degeneration and oxidative stress. Other research has shown that gallic acid might be able to slow cognitive decline and improve memory.

Blueberries are also a good source of both soluble and insoluble fiber, both of which stimulate digestion and promote a healthy digestive tract. Wild blueberries have also been shown to act as prebiotics, which nourish the friendly bacteria found in the intestines.

MEAL 1: Roasted Bell Pepper Soup

SERVES: 6 | LEVEL: Medium

CALORIES: 150; Fat: 2.7 g; Protein: 4 g; Carbohydrates: 29 g

Bell peppers are delicious and a great source of many nutrients, including vitamins C and E and more than 30 distinct carotenoids. They are low in fat but provide just enough to facilitate absorption of vitamin E. Red bell peppers are a good source of magnesium and vitamin B6, a combination shown to decrease anxiety related to premenstrual symptoms.

To get the most nutrient value from bell peppers, allow them to ripen before eating them. As they ripen, bell peppers increase their vitamin C and carotenoid content and their antioxidant power. Most green peppers, but not all, will turn red over time, but they can be optimally ripe before they change color. To find the ripest bell peppers, look for peppers that are heavy, firm, and vividly colored. Many of the nutrients in bell peppers are heat sensitive, so either enjoy them raw or limit cooking to low heat and short cooking times.

1 red bell pepper
1 yellow bell pepper
1 orange bell pepper
1 large onion
3 celery stalks, cut into small pieces
4 red potatoes, cubed
1 tsp. garlic salt
1 tsp. mushroom extract
¼ tsp. cayenne pepper
1 tbsp. olive oil

GARNISH
Pimiento pieces
Salt and pepper to taste

1. Preheat oven to 400°F.
2. Wash and halve the bell peppers, and take out the seeds. Remove the skin and ends of the onion and cut in 6 pieces. Put these vegetables in a baking dish, and bake for 20 minutes.
3. Put the celery stalks, red potatoes, and 6 cups water or broth in a large pot. Bring to a boil.
4. Add the baked vegetables to the pot. Boil again for 10 minutes.
5. Put the contents of the pot in a blender, and blend on a low speed. Stir in garlic salt, mushroom extract, cayenne pepper, and olive oil.
6. Pour the contents of the blender back into the pot and bring to a slow boil. Season with salt and pepper to taste. Garnish with the pimiento.

Spaghetti Squash Edamame Casserole

MEAL 1

CALORIES: 234; Fat: 14 g; Protein: 8 g; Carbohydrates: 24 g

SERVES: 10 | LEVEL: Medium

1 medium-sized spaghetti squash

PART A

1 medium-sized leek, white and light green part, thinly sliced

1 cup frozen edamame

1 tbsp. cold-pressed coconut oil

PART B

1 tbsp. cornstarch

1 cup almond milk

½ tsp. basil leaves

1 cup raw cheese (reserve ¼ cup for topping)

Salt and pepper to taste

GARNISH

Chopped green onion (optional)

Preheat oven to 400°F.

1. Cut the spaghetti squash lengthwise in half. Scrape out the seeds. Place the squash halves face down in a large baking dish, and bake for 40–60 minutes. Scrape the pulp from the rind; it should flake off easily in strings. Set the squash aside.

2. **PART A:** Heat a medium-sized saucepan over medium heat. Stir-fry the leek and edamame in the coconut oil until tender.

3. **PART B:** Mix cornstarch, almond milk, basil leaves, ¾ cup cheese, salt, and pepper in a bowl. Pour the mixture into the saucepan. Add the squash pulp, and mix well.

4. Pour the contents of the pot into a baking dish. Sprinkle the remaining cheese on top. Broil until the cheese turns golden brown. Garnish with chopped green onion.

It is difficult to cut through the tough rind of **spaghetti squash,** so the best approach is to bake or boil it whole. After it is cooked, use a fork to separate the flesh into strands.

A gluten-free alternative to pasta, spaghetti squash is packed with vitamins and minerals. It is especially high in vitamin C, known to support the immune system, and vitamin B6, required for more than 100 different enzyme reactions in the body, including energy metabolism and hemoglobin production.

Spaghetti squash also contains small amounts of nearly every essential vitamin and mineral needed for good health. Potassium is an especially important mineral component of spaghetti squash. Potassium is vital for metabolizing carbohydrates, building muscle, and maintaining muscle function.

Spaghetti squash contains only 10 grams of carbohydrates, 2 of which consist of dietary fiber, which can help regulate digestion, alleviate constipation, and lower cholesterol.

MEAL 2: Acorn Squash Kale Soup

SERVES: 6 | **LEVEL:** Medium | **CALORIES:** 175; Fat: 5 g; Protein: 5 g; Carbohydrates: 33 g

Acorn squash is a great food for relieving constipation. It is high in dietary fiber; a single serving provides nine grams, more than one-third of what you need each day. Dietary fiber can ease constipation by softening and adding bulk to stools and pushing waste through the intestines. Be careful with foods such as acorn squash if you do not currently consume a high-fiber diet. Introducing too much fiber into your diet too quickly can lead to gas and bloating as your body struggles to adapt to the change in your diet.

COOKED OPTION

- ½ onion, cubed
- 1 carrot, cubed
- 1 apple, cubed
- 10 kale leaves, sliced
- ½ cup presoaked nuts
- 1 tbsp. mushroom extract
- 1 tsp. nutmeg, cinnamon or thyme
- 1 tsp. nutrition yeast
- 2 tbsp. olive oil
- Sea salt to taste

GARNISH

- 6 sprigs of mint (optional)

1. Preheat oven to 400°F.
2. Bake the whole acorn squash for 1½ hours. When done, set it aside.
3. Put the onion, carrot, apple, and kale in a soup pot and cover with water plus 2 inches. Bring to a boil, then lower heat to simmer until the kale is soft. Pour the contents of the pot into a blender and mix on low speed. Add presoaked nuts, mushroom extract, nutmeg, nutritional yeast, olive oil, and sea salt to taste, and mix lightly so that the nuts are still in chunks.
4. Pour the soup into a serving bowl. Spoon the squash pulp out of the rind and stir it into the soup. Garnish with mint.

PARTIALLY RAW OPTION

Do not boil the carrots and apples; add these two raw to the cooked soup in the blender.

NOTES:

1. For diabetes, use the raw version rather than the cooked version; cut down half the carrots. You might also add more cinnamon to the soup.
2. For estrogen dominance and hypothyroid, substitute spinach or Swiss chard for the kale. You should eat cruciferous vegetables only twice a week.

CHAPTER 5: **GI Disturbances** 115

Cucumber Lime Cod Salad

MEAL 2

CALORIES: 148; Fat: 9 g; Protein: 20 g; Carbohydrates: 16 g

SERVES: 4 | LEVEL: Easy

400 grams cooked cod fillet or sashimi fish (Japanese raw fish)

SALAD

2 English cucumbers, thinly sliced
½ cup lime juice
1 tbsp. fish sauce
2 tbsp. light brown sugar
1 cup shredded jicama or white radish (daikon)
⅓ cup shredded fresh mint leaves
⅓ cup fresh cilantro leaves, torn into pieces

GARNISH

4 lime wedges

1. Poach the cod in water until just done. Use a fork to separate the meat into smaller pieces.
2. Put all the salad ingredients in a bowl and toss. Let stand for 30 minutes.
3. When ready to serve, add the fish and garnish with lime wedges.

NOTE: For diabetes and metabolic syndrome, use ¼ tsp. stevia powder instead of brown sugar.

Cucumbers are a great source of the two things most vital to digestion: water and fiber. The flesh of cucumbers contains soluble fiber, which takes on a gel-like consistency in the digestive tract. This has the tendency to slow digestion, so that you are able to absorb nutrients more effectively, and to soften the stool so it is easier to pass.

To balance the digestion-slowing effects of the soluble fiber in the flesh of the cucumber, the skin and seeds contain a high amount of insoluble fiber. Insoluble fiber tends to move food through the digestive tract more quickly and can relieve constipation.

MEAL 3 — Korean Cold Noodles

SERVES: 8 | LEVEL: Challenging | CALORIES: 267; Fat: 3.6 g; Protein: 1.5 g; Carbohydrates: 58.7 g

The key to **seasoning** in Asian cooking is to adjust the seasonings to your taste. The seasoning here is a suggestion. You need to add enough so that the Korean glass noodles are totally coated.

1 package Korean glass noodles
2 tbsp. sesame oil
2 tbsp. vegetarian oyster sauce
1 tbsp. Kecup Manis (Indonesian dark, sweetened soy sauce)
1 tbsp. Amino Soyu
1 tsp. Maggi Soy Sauce
½ cabbage head
2 stalks green onion, shredded
1 package needle mushrooms
1 carrot, shredded

GARNISH
Japanese rice sprinkles
Vegetarian mushroom floss

1. Follow the package directions to cook the noodles, and let them cool. Add the sesame oil, oyster sauce, Kecup Manis, Amino Soyu, and Maggi Soy Sauce.

2. Shred the cabbage, and lightly cook it in a little water or steam it. Add salt to taste. Turn off the heat, and stir in the green onions, mushrooms, and carrot. Mix in the noodles.

3. Before serving, add the Japanese rice sprinkles and vegetarian mushroom floss.

NOTES:

1. For estrogen dominance and hypothyroid, substitute romaine lettuce or spinach for the cabbage. Mix in the lettuce after you turn off the heat.

2. For blood sugar balance problems, glass noodles are low in starch, but you might want to add more oil, mixed greens, shredded cucumbers, and green onions. Also, adding beef or chicken strips would help stabilize your blood sugar.

3. For gluten sensitivities, use gluten-free soy sauce and vegetarian oyster sauce; omit the Kecup Manis and Maggi.

CHAPTER 5: **GI Disturbances** 117

Rice and Celery Soup

MEAL 3

CALORIES: 257; Fat: 12.5 g; Protein: 3 g; Carbohydrates: 36 g

SERVES: 6 | LEVEL: Easy

PART A
2 tbsp. olive oil
3 tbsp. butter
8 oz. celery stalks, finely chopped
2 tbsp. fresh parsley, finely chopped
1 bay leaf

PART B
5 cups vegetable stock
Salt to taste

PART C
1¼ cup short-grain rice

GARNISH
Parmesan cheese

1. **PART A:** In a large soup pot, simmer the celery, parsley, and bay leaf in the olive oil and butter over low heat until tender, around 10–15 minutes. Stir often.
2. **PART B:** Add the vegetable stock and salt. Bring to a boil, then reduce to low heat. Cover and simmer for 5 minutes.
3. **PART C:** Add the rice and simmer until tender, about 15 minutes. Remove the bay leaf. Garnish with the Parmesan cheese.

Celery has long been used in Hungary to relieve indigestion. Commission E, Germany's agency for evaluating medicinal herbs, has approved celery for relieving dyspepsia.

Celery contains 24 different pain-relieving compounds, even more anti-inflammatory compounds, a similar number of sedative compounds, 11 compounds that inhibit formation of ulcers, and 3 compounds that prevent the buildup of gas and facilitate expulsion of accumulated gas. All of these compounds support healthy digestion and relieve painful conditions in the gut.

In addition to these compounds, celery contains pectin polysaccharides shown in lab animals to protect and improve the stomach lining, control gastric secretions, and decrease the incidence of gastric ulcers. Further studies should be done to confirm these effects in humans, but existing research is quite promising.

MEAL 4 — Almond Meal Pizza

SERVES: 10 | LEVEL: Challenging | CALORIES: 237; Fat: 12.5 g; Protein: 9.4 g; Carbohydrates: 26 g

Almond meal is a gluten-free alternative to processed flour that contains the same nutritional value as whole almonds. No matter how you eat them, almonds have the highest nutritional value of any tree nut.

Almonds are naturally cholesterol free, and a quarter cup of almond meal contains seven grams of healthy fats, three grams of fiber, and five grams of protein. Almond meal is also rich in vitamin E and the B vitamins folate and niacin.

Despite the nutritional value of almonds, they also contain some substances that might not be so healthy. Almond meal is high in omega-6 fatty acids. Although these are healthy fats, they should be balanced with omega-3s. You can do this by eating plenty of seafood. Almonds are also high in oxalates. Oxalates tend to bind with certain minerals so the body cannot absorb them. You can counter this by eating more fruits and vegetables, especially those high in calcium.

The final reason to exercise moderation

CRUST
2 cups almond meal
2 medium-sized eggs
¼ tsp. baking soda
3 tbsp. olive oil
1 tsp. garlic powder
Fresh rosemary

MARINARA SAUCE
3 tbsp. olive oil
1 medium-sized onion, chopped
1 tsp. Italian seasoning
1 6-oz. can tomato paste
1 8-oz. can tomato sauce

TOPPINGS
½ cup mushrooms, sliced
1 zucchini, thinly sliced
½ Japanese (long) eggplant, thinly sliced
1 yellow squash, thinly sliced
1 tomato, thinly sliced
Fresh basil leaves
Mozzarella cheese (optional)

1. Preheat oven to 350°F. Lightly grease a pizza sheet with olive oil.

2. **CRUST:** Use a spoon to mix all crust ingredients until the dough becomes very thick. Form the dough into a ball. Place the ball of dough in the center of the pizza sheet. Using a large piece of plastic wrap on top of the pizza dough, flatten

it and gently push it outward toward the edges of the pizza pan. Make the dough as thin as possible so that it covers the entire sheet with 1 inch to spare all around. Bake for 20 minutes.

3. **SAUCE:** Heat a frying pan and add oil, onion, Italian seasoning, and tomato paste. Fry until oil turns red. Add in the tomato sauce. Cook for 5 more minutes. Put aside one cup for the pizza and refrigerate the rest for future use.

4. **TOPPINGS:** After the crust is done, remove from the oven and evenly spread the marinara sauce over it. Add evenly over the sauce, and bake it again for 25–30 minutes.

when consuming any form of almonds is that they contain cyanogenic glycosides, which convert to highly toxic hydrogen cyanide when digested. The herb bitter almond contains 40 times more cyanogenic glycosides than sweet almonds. Soaking, fermenting, or drying almonds will reduce the levels of hydrogen cyanide through the action of plant enzymes and subsequent leaching.

MEAL 4 — Bok Choy Pineapple Salad

SERVES: 4 | LEVEL: Medium | CALORIES: 116; Fat: 9.7 g; Protein: 1.6 g; Carbohydrates: 7 g

Bromelain is a protein digestive enzyme made up of proteolytic enzymes. These enzymes aid in the digestion and absorption of proteins. For many years, scientists doubted the efficacy of enzymes such as bromelain because they thought the enzymes were destroyed early in the digestive process. New research on lab mice, however, has found that the enzymes might actually survive all the way to the colon.

A large part of your immune system is found in your digestive tract, and if it is unhealthy, the rest of your body will suffer. The fiber and bromelain in **pineapple** can both help to improve gut health and repair damage from free radicals because they contain vitamin C.

Most of the fiber in pineapple is the soluble variety, which absorbs excess moisture in the intestines, slowing the process of digestion and allowing more of the nutrients in your food to be absorbed and used.

2 cups bok choy, chopped
½ cup pineapple chunks, drained
½ cup cherry tomatoes
½ tsp. ginger, chopped

DRESSING
2 tbsp. extra virgin olive oil
1 tsp. sesame oil
1 tbsp. hoisin sauce
1 tbsp. vegetarian oyster sauce

GARNISH
Presoaked and dehydrated sunflower seeds

1. Mix the bok choy, pineapple, tomatoes, and ginger in a bowl. Stir the olive oil, sesame oil, hoisin sauce, and vegetarian oyster sauce in a separate bowl, then add the dressing to the salad and toss it.
2. Garnish with sunflower seeds, and serve in chilled bowls.

NOTES:
1. For estrogen dominance and hypothyroid, substitute mixed green lettuce for the bok choy. You should eat cruciferous vegetables only twice a week.
2. For weight loss, do not be afraid of the oil. The oil helps maintain satiety and prevent you from getting hungry until the next meal.
3. For sensitivity, substitute gluten-free soy sauce or garlic salt, maple syrup, or honey for the hoisin sauce and vegetarian oyster sauce. Add according to your taste.

CHAPTER 5: **GI Disturbances**

Stir-fried Bean Sprouts and Sugar Snap Peas

MEAL 5

CALORIES: 66; Fat: 2.6 g; Protein: 3.7 g; Carbohydrates: 8.5 g

SERVES: 4 | LEVEL: Medium

8 oz. bean sprouts
8 oz. sugar snap peas or snow peas, slivered

PART A
1 tsp. soy sauce
1 tsp. fish sauce
½ tsp. sesame oil
Dash black pepper, finely ground

PART B
2 tsp. olive oil
3 slices of ginger

GARNISH
2 tsp. white sesame seeds

1. **PART A:** Mix the soy sauce, fish sauce, sesame oil, and pepper. Set aside.
2. **PART B:** Heat a wok over a medium temperature. Stir-fry the ginger in the olive oil briefly. Add the bean sprouts and peas. Stir-fry for 2 minutes.
3. Add the sauce from Part A and stir well. Cover and simmer for 2 minutes. Remove the lid, and stir-fry until all the liquid is gone. Garnish with sesame seeds.

NOTE: You can cook this dish until very tender or leave it crispy by not covering it. You might want to serve it as a salad by adding some lemon juice to the sauce. Turn off the heat when you add the sauce from Part A, and keep the dish in the refrigerator until ready to serve, then add the sesame seeds.

Seeds, beans, grains, and legumes (for the sake of brevity, we will just use the word seeds) are all loaded with nutrients, but many of them also contain phytic acid and other antinutrients that bind to the nutrients, making them difficult to absorb. Soaking and sprouting the seed wakes up the dormant plant so that it is no longer a seed but a living plant. This process neutralizes the phytic acid as well as enzyme inhibitors, making the seed easier to digest. Some studies have shown that, aside from neutralizing the antinutrients and making the nutrients easier to absorb, sprouting seeds actually increases the amount of certain vitamins and minerals, in some cases significantly.

Soaking and sprouting causes other changes in a seed as well. It breaks down some of the fat content, dense vegetable protein, and complex carbohydrates into forms easier to digest and assimilate. This process makes the seeds easier to digest and reduces the accumulation of uncomfortable gas and bloating. Research has shown that enzymes in sprouts could be 100 times the amount in raw fruits and vegetables. Furthermore, the protein in seeds improved in nutritional value after sprouting.

MEAL 5: Pesto, Garbanzo and Zucchini Salad

SERVES: 4 | LEVEL: Medium

CALORIES: 156; Fat: 3 g; Protein: 13.7 g; Carbohydrates: 19 g

4 oz. cooked chicken meat, cut in cubes
1 small zucchini, thinly sliced
2 celery stalks, thinly sliced
1 15-oz. can chickpeas (garbanzo beans), rinsed and drained
2 tbsp. basil pesto
2 tbsp. freshly squeezed lemon juice
2 tbsp. Italian parsley, chopped
Salt and pepper to taste

1. In a bowl, mix all the ingredients.
2. Serve over a bed of mixed spring salad.

If you thought **parsley** was only good as a restaurant garnish, think again. According to the U.S. Department of Agriculture, a half cup of parsley gives you 10 percent of the iron you need each day. It also contains vitamin C, without which iron is difficult to absorb and use. Iron is vital to a variety of physiological processes, including healthy immune function. Parsley also contains vitamin A, crucial to the tissues lining your lungs and gastrointestinal tract. Teeming with immune cells, this tissue is your first line of defense against airborne and foodborne pathogens.

Anti-inflammatory properties and antioxidants in parsley can reduce the type of inflammation associated with many chronic conditions, including cancer, Alzheimer's disease, and Parkinson's disease. An essential oil, eugenol, in parsley has been found to reduce blood sugar and has been used as a local anesthetic and antiseptic agent for teeth and gum disease.

Nibbling or chewing parsley several days before menstruation can help increase urination and reduce bloating or water retention. The healing compounds in parsley, myristicin and apiole, help increase urine flow, which can remove infection-causing bacteria from the urinary tract and prevent kidney stones. Parsley juice has been shown to help improve female hormonal issues and speed up wound healing.

Green Beans with Cherry Tomatoes

MEAL 6

CALORIES: 65.2; Fat: 3.6 g; Protein: 1.8 g; Carbohydrates: 7 g
Nutritional value is based on 4 servings.

SERVES: 2–4 | LEVEL: Easy

- 1 lb. green beans, trimmed
- 1 cup (5 oz.) cherry tomatoes, cut in half
- 3 tsp. olive oil or coconut oil
- 1 large clove garlic, crushed
- 3 tbsp. flat-leafed parsley, chopped
- Salt and pepper to taste

1. Fill a large frying pan with water, and add salt. Bring to a boil. Add the green beans, and bring to a boil for 1 minute; drain well. Set green beans aside.
2. In a wok or large frying pan, stir-fry the garlic in the oil over medium-high heat until slightly golden. Add the green beans and tomatoes, and stir-fry 2–3 minutes or until the green beans are tender and cherry tomatoes are beginning to soften.
3. Stir in parsley and season with salt and pepper.

You would not know it by looking at them, but **green beans** are a great source of carotenoids such as beta-carotene, lutein, and zeaxanthin, in amounts comparable to carrots and tomatoes. The reason they are not orange is they contain high levels of chlorophyll. They are also rich in flavonoids such as quercetin, kaempferol, catechins, and epicatechins. All of these substances are known to have strong antioxidant properties. In fact, studies have shown that green beans have antioxidant and anti-inflammatory properties greater than many other similar foods. The carotenoids in green beans are especially good for eye health. Beta-carotene is used to synthesize vitamin A, vital to night vision. The lutein and zeaxanthin absorb blue light, which can damage eyes.

CHAPTER 5: GI Disturbances

Salmon with Ketchup-Ginger Glaze

MEAL 6

CALORIES: 218; Fat: 9.2 g; Protein: 29 g; Carbohydrates: 3 g
Nutritional value is based on a 4 oz. cooked salmon steak

SERVES: 4 | LEVEL: Easy

4 salmon steaks (each 8 to 10 oz. and 1-inch thick)
Salt and pepper to taste

SAUCE

1 tbsp. fresh orange juice
1 tbsp. ketchup
1 tbsp. vegetarian oyster sauce
⅛ tsp. grated fresh ginger
1 tsp. honey

1. Season both sides of the salmon steak with salt and pepper for 30–60 minutes.
2. In a small bowl, whisk together the orange juice, ketchup, vegetarian oyster sauce, ginger, and honey.
3. Preheat the oven broiler. Lay the salmon on a baking sheet lined with aluminum foil. Baste the salmon with the sauce. Broil the salmon about 4 inches from the heat source for 2 minutes.
4. Turning the salmon over, baste with the sauce again, and broil for 2 minutes. Basting once more, broil for another 2 minutes.

Ketchup is a common part of the modern American diet, but not a sauce most people think of as "healthy." However, it is a rich source of lycopene, an antioxidant phytochemical found in tomatoes and other red fruits and vegetables such as watermelon, grapefruit, and papaya.

Unlike nutrients destroyed by processing and cooking, lycopene is actually increased and converted into a form more easily absorbed and used. Lycopene is fat soluble, which means it should be consumed with a bit of fat (such as the salmon in this recipe) to make it even easier for the body to absorb and use it.

For all the health benefits of lycopene, and the abundance of the phytochemical in tomato sauces, it is still important to exercise moderation and look at labels when purchasing. Most brands of ketchup (even organic varieties) contain as much as 25 percent sugar, much of which is in the form of high fructose corn syrup (HFCS). Also remember that ketchup is most often consumed with fried foods and other non-nutritious foods. So do not be afraid to enjoy ketchup when the occasion calls for it, but do not make it an everyday habit.

MEAL 7: Baked Lemon-Almond Cod

SERVES: 4 | LEVEL: Medium

CALORIES: 236; Fat: 14.2 g; Protein: 23.6 g; Carbohydrates: 4 g

Fish is high in protein and easily digested compared with other types of meat. It is high in omega-3 fatty acids and essential nutrients. However, many fish and shellfish contain traces of mercury that accumulate in humans who consume large amounts of seafood. Mercury is toxic and damages the central nervous system and the ability to metabolize epinephrine. A general rule for fish and high mercury levels is to consume seafood at the top of the food chain that lives longer.

Shark, marlin, king mackerel, ahi tuna, and tilefish have the highest mercury levels and should be avoided. Canned albacore tuna, sea bass, and grouper have high mercury levels and should not exceed three servings per month. Canned chunk light tuna, Alaskan cod, halibut, mahi mahi, and perch have moderate amounts of mercury and should not exceed six servings per month. Seafood that can be enjoyed at any time because of low mercury levels includes anchovies, crab, herring, mackerel, oysters, salmon, sardines, scallops, shrimp, sole, tilapia, trout, and whitefish.

4 cod fillets

PART A
¼ cup butter, melted
4 tbsp. lemon juice
1 piece of lemon peel

PART B
½ cup almond meal
1 tsp. salt
½ tsp. pepper
Paprika for dusting

GARNISH
Parsley
Lemon wedges

1. Preheat oven to 350°F.
2. **PART A:** Melt the butter in a small saucepan over low heat. Add the lemon juice and lemon peel. Remove from heat.
3. **PART B:** Mix almond meal, salt, and pepper on a plate. Dip each fillet into the mixture from Part A, then coat it with the mixture from Part B.
4. Place all the fillets in a baking dish. Pour the rest of the butter and lemon over the top of the fish fillets. Spoon the remaining almond meal over the top of each fish fillet. Dust each fillet with paprika for color.
5. Cook the fish until it becomes flaky, usually 25–30 minutes. Garnish with parsley and lemon wedges.

CHAPTER 5: **GI Disturbances** 127

Asparagus with Ginger-Miso Butter

MEAL 7

CALORIES: 119; Fat: 7.6 g; Protein: 5.7 g; Carbohydrates: 10.5 g

SERVES: 2 | LEVEL: Easy

1 lb. asparagus tips
½ cup water

SAUCE
1 tbsp. butter
1½ tsp. white miso
½ tsp. ginger, grated
1 medium-sized clove garlic, finely chopped
½ tsp. sesame oil

1. Put water in a 10-inch frying pan. Bring it to a boil. Add the asparagus, cover, and cook for 5 minutes. Drain the water.
2. In a smaller frying pan over low heat, stir-fry the ginger and garlic in the butter until fragrant. Add the miso and mix well. Stir in the sesame oil.
3. Pour the ginger-miso butter onto the asparagus.

Ginger is well known for its ability to ease nausea, especially in pregnant women and in cancer patients undergoing chemotherapy. Perhaps less well known is that it has antimicrobial and antiviral properties. Consuming ginger daily, especially during flu season, can help ward off illness when everyone around you is getting sick or help you fight it off faster if you do succumb.

Ginger also helps to stimulate secretion of digestive juices to aid digestion. It has been shown to ease symptoms of irritable bowel syndrome (IBS), and it does not seem to make much difference how it is consumed. So go ahead—cook it, steep it in tea, candy it, or eat it fresh. You will get the benefits.

MEAL 8 — Spinach Patties

10 PATTIES
LEVEL: Challenging

CALORIES: 122; Fat: 5.7 g; Protein: 7.8 g; Carbohydrates: 10 g

- 2 cups frozen spinach, thawed
- 1 cup oatmeal, soaked and drained (can use gluten-free oatmeal)
- 4 eggs
- 1 cup sweet white onion, finely chopped
- 1 cup raw cheese (you can use cottage cheese)
- ½ tsp. crushed red pepper
- 1 tsp. nutritional yeast
- 1 tsp. garlic powder
- 2 tbsp. cold expeller-pressed coconut oil
- Salt and pepper to taste

1. Soak the oatmeal in water for 1 hour. Drain well.
2. Squeeze all the water out of the frozen spinach. Mix the spinach, oatmeal, eggs, onion, cheese, pepper, yeast, and garlic powder. Form the spinach mixture into burger-sized patties.
3. Heat a large frying pan over a medium temperature. Fry the patties in the coconut oil until golden brown, around 4–6 minutes on each side.

> **NOTE:** Serve as a main dish or as a sandwich filling. For the catabolic state of AFS, you can make a bunch of these patties ahead of time and reheat them for snacks.

Eggs have often been vilified because of their high cholesterol. Although this is true, eating eggs does not raise cholesterol levels in most people. Eggs are an excellent source of tryptophan and a variety of healthy antioxidants.

If you have looked at egg labels, you have probably noticed a number of confusing terms such as cage free, free range, organic, and vegetarian. Cage-free birds, as the term implies, are not kept in cages. Rather, they are housed in an open barn with pine shavings or other bedding material as well as perches and nests. Depending on the farm, they might still be fairly crowded and might not have access to the outdoors. Free-range hens have access to the outdoors for at least part of the day. Organic eggs are laid by hens fed an organic diet. They are not given vaccines, hormones, or antibiotics. To qualify as organic, the feed must be grown on land that has not had fertilizer or pesticides used on it for at least three years. Genetically modified crops do not qualify. Typically, these hens are cage free, but not necessarily. You will probably notice that the yolks of organic eggs have a deep orange color; this indicates they are rich in carotenes. Vegetarian eggs are laid by hens fed a strict vegetarian diet. These hens are kept indoors, sometimes in cages, so they do not eat grubs or worms.

Pasteurization of eggs involves heating them to 140 degrees for three and a half minutes. The heat is enough to kill bacteria without cooking the egg. Be sure to use pasteurized eggs for any recipe calling for raw eggs. Except for pasteurizing, none of these terms have anything to do with how safe the eggs are to eat; any of them could be contaminated with salmonella. Check eggs for cracks and refrigerate them as soon as you get them home.

Sautéed Asparagus with Thyme

MEAL 8

CALORIES: 56; Fat: 3.6 g; Protein: 2.6 g; Carbohydrates: 5.2 g

SERVES: 4 | LEVEL: Easy

- 30 asparagus spears (frozen or fresh)
- 3 sprigs fresh thyme
- 1/3 to 1/2 cup water
- 1 tbsp. olive oil
- Mushroom extract

1. Add the asparagus and thyme to water in a skillet over high heat. Cover and bring to a boil; cook until water is gone. Turn off the heat.
2. Stir in the olive oil and mushroom extract.

> **NOTES:**
> 1. For people with allergies or cancer, use flaxseed oil instead of olive oil, and substitute sea salt for the mushroom extract.
> 2. For people taking blood thinner, do not eat too much asparagus.

Asparagus is a good source of inulin, a dietary fiber used by some plants to store energy in place of starch. In the digestive tract, inulin survives intact until it reaches the large intestine. In the large intestine, it is used as a prebiotic to nourish and encourage the growth of the beneficial bacteria critical to efficient digestion. In addition to inulin, asparagus contains significant amounts of both soluble and insoluble fiber and protein. Both fiber and protein keep the digestive tract functioning and food moving along at a healthy rate, not too slow as to cause constipation nor too fast as to cause diarrhea.

MEAL 9: Pearl-Barley Risotto

SERVES: 6 | LEVEL: Medium

CALORIES: 362; Fat: 9.9 g; Protein: 13 g; Carbohydrates: 57 g

Barley is rich in beta-glucan, a specific type of dietary fiber that can lower the glycemic index of other foods, helping improve control of blood sugar levels and lowering insulin response. Beta-glucan is also found in high concentrations in oats, but at least one study has found barley superior to oats at controlling blood sugar.

Barley is also high in other types of soluble and insoluble fiber, both of which support gastrointestinal health in different ways. Some of the soluble fiber is used to nourish gut flora as a kind of prebiotic that can improve bowel health. Sprouted barley is being studied as a potential treatment for ulcerative colitis because of its ability to soothe intestinal mucous.

PART A
2 tbsp. olive oil
1 tbsp. butter
1½ cups pearl barley
3 leeks, thinly sliced

PART B
½ cup cooking wine
2 cups water
3 cups vegetable stock
Salt and pepper to taste

PART C
2 cups frozen peas
1 lb. asparagus, cut into 2-inch pieces

PART D
¼ cup fresh mint, finely chopped
½ cup Parmesan cheese (optional)

1. **PART A:** Cook the barley and leeks in the oil and butter in a large frying pan; stir until the vegetables start to soften, about 5–7 minutes.

2. **PART B:** Add wine and stir until evaporated, around 5 minutes. Add water, salt, and pepper, and bring to a boil. Reduce heat and simmer until liquid is absorbed, about 10 minutes. Add vegetable stock, and cook over medium heat until barley is almost tender, about 10 minutes.

3. **PART C:** Add the peas and asparagus; cook until tender and all liquid is gone, about 5 minutes.

4. **PART D:** Stir in the mint and Parmesan cheese.

NOTE: For gluten sensitivity, barley is not gluten free. The only gluten-free grains are buckwheat, corn, millet, quinoa, and rice. You can substitute quinoa for the barley.

MEAL 9 — Grated Zucchini Basil Soup

SERVES: 6 | LEVEL: Medium

CALORIES: 167; Fat: 7 g; Protein: 5.3 g; Carbohydrates: 23 g

Zucchini is an excellent vegetable that fills you up, encourages healthy digestion, and detoxifies your body. Zucchini is high in fiber, which cleanses the digestive tract, particularly the intestines. The fiber in zucchini is a mild laxative, so it clears out the intestines and prevents toxins from building up in the colon.

Zucchini is especially useful for managing blood sugar levels. Metabolizing sugar requires adequate intake of many B vitamins, including B1, B2, B3, B6, folate, and choline, most of which are found in high amounts in many varieties of summer squash. Zinc, magnesium, and omega-3 fatty acids are also vital to stabilizing blood sugar, and all of them are found in zucchini. It is important to eat the skin, seeds, and flesh of zucchini to get the full antioxidant benefit. The fiber in zucchini includes pectin and other polysaccharide fibers. Recent studies have shown that these polysaccharides can help balance metabolism of insulin and sugar.

PARTIALLY RAW VERSION

- 1 red onion, cubed
- 1 large carrot, cubed
- 2 medium-sized celery stalks, cubed
- 1 red or yellow bell pepper, cubed
- 3 medium-sized red potatoes, cubed
- ½ cup presoaked nuts
- 1 clove garlic
- 2 tbsp. olive oil or grape seed oil
- Mushroom extract to taste
- 4 zucchini, grated

GARNISH

Fresh basil, slivered

1. Add to a pot enough water to cover the vegetables plus 2 inches. Bring to a boil. Add the onion, carrot, celery, bell pepper, and potato cubes to the pot. Cook for 30 minutes on medium-low heat. Turn off heat, and let sit for 15 minutes.
2. Pour the contents of the pot into a blender. Add the nuts, garlic, oil, and mushroom extract, and blend until smooth.
3. Add the zucchini and the basil to the blended mixture. Garnish with the basil slivers.

COOKED VERSION

1. Put onion, carrot, celery, bell pepper, and potato cubes into a pot. Cover with water plus 2 inches above the vegetables. Bring to a boil over medium heat, then lower heat to simmer for 30 minutes.
2. Pour the contents of the pot into a blender. Add the nuts, garlic, oil, and mushroom extract and blend well.
3. Put the mixture back into the pot, add the zucchini, and bring to another boil. Turn off the heat. Garnish with the basil slivers.

NOTES:

1. For people with allergies or cancer, substitute sea salt for the mushroom extract and add more garlic as desired.
2. For weight loss, do not be afraid of the oil. The oil helps maintain satiety and prevents you from getting hungry until the next meal.

CHAPTER 6

Toxin Overload

	Why Do I Need to Detox?	135
	Detox Instructions	136
	Soup	138
	Tea	138
	Supplementing with Probiotics and Enzymes	139
general	Cleansing Juice Recipes	140
	Detoxifying Beet Soup	144
	Garlic Tea	146
	Garlic Ginger Lemon Drink	147
	Strawberry Green Smoothie	148
meal one	Broccoli Leek Soup	149
	Cucumber Tomato Red Onion Salad	150
meal two	Carrot Thyme Soup	151
	Napa and Red Cabbage Salad	152
	Spinach Strawberry Salad	153
meal three	Stir-fried Baby Bok Choy	154
	Green Bean Potato Pine Nut Salad	155
	Vegetable Chowder	156
meal four	Barley Date Asparagus Salad with Mint Dressing	158
	Curried Butternut Squash and Apple Soup	159
	Roasted Cauliflower	160

Why Do I Need to Detox?

The human body is constantly bombarded with the toxins from our environment in the form of chemicals, such as pesticides, industrial waste, preservatives, and so forth. Unfortunately, some of these chemicals go into our food supply, and we eventually ingest them.

Changing our lifestyles with diet and exercise and choosing to use natural products in our homes and on our bodies are a great start toward detoxification. However, these actions alone cannot completely eliminate the toxins stored and accumulated in our bodies because our fat cells store toxins that cannot be metabolized or eliminated by either diet or exercise. Fat cells have the ability to shrink but also have the ability to grow again.

When detox is done correctly, it has numerous benefits; it cleanses the body from long-term buildup of toxins, enhances the immune system, reduces the burden on the liver, supports healthy adrenal function, increases metabolism (and therefore assists with weight loss), reduces the free radicals in our body, and restores balance to the body!

> **Get sufficient rest when detoxing.**

Several methods can be used for cleansing yourself of the buildup of toxins in your body, but we will concentrate primarily on how this can be achieved through proper diet and nutrition in a gentle way that suits people with Adrenal Fatigue Syndrome (AFS). Aggressive detoxification is not recommended because it can worsen AFS and trigger adrenal crashes. Never considered doing a detox before? Follow our gentle method of detoxing mainly through nutrition, and your body might thank you yet.

The more advanced the AFS, the more care should be considered before embarking on any form of detoxification therapy, even the gentle ones we suggest here. Each individual will respond differently, and the weaker the body is the more congested the detoxification organs. When you detox this can lead to a massive release of internal toxins that the body is unable to excrete sufficiently and quickly enough, which might result in unpleasant side effects such as heart palpitations, fever, dizziness, insomnia, joint pain, nausea, chills, and etcetera.

Detox Instructions

We recommend starting on a one-day juice fast, and depending on your body's reaction, then moving up to the four-day juice fast protocol if you are in the early stages of AFS, in which symptoms are mild to moderate. These juice fasts are gentle enough that they should not cause your body to crash and have any major paradoxical reactions, but they are sufficiently powerful to significantly cleanse your body. However, as with all things new to your body, proceed with caution and consult an expert. Juice fasts are not recommended in advanced stages of AFS unless under proper guidance.

The ideal seasons in which to detox are the spring and summer, and if you live in moderate climates, the fall is also acceptable. Winter is traditionally not recommended because the body is focused on rebuilding, staying warm, and keeping illness at bay rather than cleansing.

It is important to get sufficient rest when detoxing, so common sense dictates that you do not begin a detox when starting out on a new or stressful job. Ideally, you would begin your cleanse on a weekend and give yourself ample time and a freed-up schedule to listen to your body's rhythm and reactions. You should expect not to feel well while your body is cleansing because the toxins are making their way out of your body. However, after the juicing cleanse, you should feel a renewed sense of energy and clarity.

We have included a gentle juicing protocol in this chapter that will get you started on cleansing your body of toxic buildup. Remember to always use fresh organic fruits and vegetables when possible because you do not want to load your body with pesticides and other harmful chemicals sprayed on the surface of produce to make it last longer and appear more presentable on grocery store shelves. When possible, shop at your local farmers' market, where you are able to ask the farmers about their produce and farming practices.

Stop the protocol if after one day on the juice fast you feel that your symptoms are 30 percent worse than your baseline condition. In this situation we advise an even gentler method of cleansing your body—nourishing and nutrient-dense soups.

Garlic Tea
page 146

Soup

Our soup recipes are so nourishing that they can be used throughout your AFS recovery period, when your body is recovering from an illness, during winter months to keep your immunity high and sickness at bay, and so forth. Nutrients are easy to assimilate through the gut, and soups are easier to digest than other foods. Nurturing soup is supportive of AFS recovery at all stages. The more severe the AFS, the more benefit soups can provide if properly used. Soups should definitely not be used just for cleansing and revitalizing your system; eat these soups all the time! Not only are they full of vitamins and minerals that will bind themselves to the chemicals and chelate them out of your body but also they will simultaneously give your body much needed nutrients.

The most basic recipe and the most versatile is our chicken broth recipe. Homemade chicken stock is so simple to prepare in advance and freeze in quart jars that after you get into the habit of preparing this broth on a regular basis, you should no longer be buying MSG- and preservative-laden commercial chicken broth unlikely to be of benefit to your body. Homemade chicken broth provides macronutrients the body craves, especially in the advanced AFS recovery stages, but if consumed earlier on in your recovery, it will yield even better results. The vital ingredients are found in the chicken bones and the marrow within, which contain key nutrients easily assimilated by the gastrointestinal tract.

When possible choose organic, free-range/pastured chickens because they are free from antibiotics and genetically modified chicken feed; otherwise, you will be consuming the chemicals and hormones to which the chicken was exposed.

Many people with AFS might find that they also have salt cravings as well as fluid depletion. Drinking chicken broth helps with the fluid depletion because volume is restored, and adding salt to the chicken broth is an excellent way to replenish the sodium supply in the body because of aldosterone dysregulation. There is no restriction on the amount of salt being added, provided that there are no signs of edema or high blood pressure and upon approval of your physician. Remember to take your adrenal supplements along with the chicken broth to help the recovery process.

Tea

Other alternatives for detoxing include teas, probiotics, enzymes, and specialized water such as H2Nano water. These alternatives might also be used concurrently with the juice/soup cleanse.

Detox teas are generally herbal teas and contain little, if any, caffeine. Detox teas contain a blend of herbs (usually senna leaf, peppermint leaf, stevia leaf, buckthorn bark, damiana leaf, RED peel, chamomile flower, and uva ursi leaf) that have unique cleansing properties.

These teas can be consumed throughout the day on a regular basis because they are gentle on the body, although the ideal time to drink detox teas is after the evening meal because they might have a laxative effect. If you experience increased bowel movements or slight cramping in the first few days, do not be alarmed because this is a result of the initial cleansing of the digestive system and is to be expected. Reduce steeping time accordingly. If you are in advanced stages of AFS, in which there is an electrolyte imbalance and a catabolic state, detox teas are not recommended because the body is already weak and can decompensate quickly.

Supplementing with Probiotics and Enzymes

In Chapter 5 we already covered the numerous benefits of the probiotics found in fermented foods. Probiotics are also available as a supplement and can be taken as part of your detox regime because they can help to decrease the amount of pathogenic bacteria and fungi that produce their own toxins in the body.

Acidophilus supplements are widely available in health food stores and drugstores. Selecting from among the numerous brands and product varieties might appear a daunting task. Examine the labels, and you will discover a variety of useful bugs including *Lactobacillus acidophilus, Bifidobacterium bifidum, Bifidobacterium longum, Bifidobacterium breve, Lactobacillus thermophilus, Lactobacillus casei, Lactobacillus bulgaricus,* and *Streptococcus faecium.* Some products might contain fructo-oligosaccharides, sugars that nourish beneficial bacteria to make them colonize faster. All of these ingredients are acceptable, and any combination of them can be taken. Excessive probiotic use can lead to constipation for some. Reduce probiotic use in such a case.

Enzymes are naturally occurring in many fruits and vegetables in varying quantities, helping the body to break down and absorb the foods we eat. If you take digestive enzymes while detoxing, it will help you absorb the nutrients from the soup and juices better, helping your body along with the increased minerals you are consuming. Excessive enzyme use can lead to diarrhea. Reduce as indicated.

Cleansing Juice Recipes

Benefits of juicing:

1. Easier to digest and absorb.
2. Enzymes, vitamins, minerals, and phytochemicals remain intact and active in much larger quantities than if the piece of vegetable is eaten whole.
3. Flushes out acid wastes and detoxifies the liver to improve clearance of by-products.
4. Restores and rebuilds the body.
5. Improves the immune system.
6. Rich in chlorophyll.
7. Cleansing, rejuvenating, and energizing.

Preparation Tips for Vegetable Juicing

1. Do not buy more than a week's worth of fresh fruits and vegetables because they might spoil before you use them.
2. Buy organic produce.
3. Thoroughly wash produce before juicing. Use a vegetable brush to remove any residue and waxes. (You might also want to use the vegetable washes found in health food stores.). Let the produce sit in a tub of clean water filled with activated charcoal for 20 minutes. Store the cleaned vegetables in containers to keep their freshness.
4. Stems and leaves of most vegetables can be left intact when juicing; however, carrot and rhubarb greens must be removed.
5. As a general rule, do not mix vegetables and fruits when juicing.

Juicing Machine

The best juicing machine is the cold-press machine, that is, the Green Machine, Omega, or Champion brands. However, for the AFS recovery process, if budget is a concern, a regular centrifuge juicer will serve the purpose.

Recipe 1 — SERVES: 1 | LEVEL: Easy

CALORIES: 80; Fat: 0.7 g; Protein: 3.5 g; Carbohydrates: 16.4 g

- ½ red bell pepper
- 1 cup lettuce (spring mix)
- 2 medium-sized celery stalks
- ½ medium-sized cucumber
- ½ medium-sized carrot

Recipe 2 — SERVES: 1 | LEVEL: Easy

CALORIES: 119.4; Fat: 0.7 g; Protein: 6.7 g; Carbohydrates: 27.3 g

- 1 cup lettuce (spring mix)
- 1 large celery stalk
- ½ medium-sized beet root
- 5 stalks beet greens
- ½ medium-sized cucumber
- ¼ medium-sized lime

Recipe 3 — SERVES: 1 | LEVEL: Easy

CALORIES: 90; Fat: 0.6 g; Protein: 3.3 g; Carbohydrates: 22

- ½ cup red cabbage
- ½ medium-sized cucumber
- 1 large celery stalk
- 1 cup lettuce (spring mix)
- ½ medium-sized carrot
- ¼ lime

Recipe 4 — SERVES: 1 | LEVEL: Easy

CALORIES: 82.9; Fat: 0.5 g; Protein: 3.4 g; Carbohydrates: 18.2 g

- 1 cup red cabbage
- ½ medium-sized cucumber
- ¼ red pepper
- 1 large celery stalk
- ½ medium-sized beet root
- ¼ lime

NOTES:

1. *Do not start juicing on your own without consulting with your coach.*
2. Those who have estrogen dominance or hypothyroid should avoid cruciferous vegetables.
3. Stop the juicing if you feel more tired or wired, and report this to your coach.

Detoxifying Beet Soup

SERVES: 8 | LEVEL: Medium   CALORIES: 148; Fat: 6.6 g; Protein: 3.9 g; Carbohydrates: 19.7 g

The rich red color of **beets** comes from a pigment known as beta-lain. Beta-lain enhances the production of glutathione and superoxide dismutase in the liver. Both of these substances are important parts of the detoxification process. Superoxide dismutase is a molecule found in the mitochondria that protects against free radicals produced during generation of energy. Glutathione binds with toxins and makes them water soluble so they can be excreted from the body.

The choline in beets is also well known for detoxifying and strengthening the liver, gallbladder, and kidneys. It can help heal a variety of liver-related ailments, including jaundice, hepatitis, and damage done by years of excessive alcohol consumption.

PARTIALLY RAW VERSION
(Cooked version next page)

PART A
- 1 red onion, cubed
- 1 large carrot, cubed
- 2 medium-sized celery stalks, cubed
- 1 red or yellow bell pepper, cubed
- 3 medium-sized red potatoes, cubed

PART B
- 1 bunch beet greens, chopped
- 1 beet root, cubed
- ½ cup presoaked nuts
- 1 clove garlic
- ½ tsp. ginger, chopped
- 2 tbsp. olive oil or grape seed oil
- Mushroom extract to taste
- 1 tsp. whole-milk yogurt or cashew cream

CASHEW CREAM (optional)
- 1 cup hot water
- ½ cup raw cashews
- 1 tbsp. pine nuts

1. **PART A:** In a stockpot, boil enough water to cover the vegetables plus 2 inches and add the onion, carrot, celery, bell pepper, potato. Turn down to medium heat and simmer for 30 minutes. Remove the pot from the heat and let it sit for 15 minutes.

2. **PART B:** Pour the contents of the pot into a blender. Add the beet greens, beet root, nuts, garlic, ginger, oil, and mushroom extract. Blend on a low speed (does not need to be smooth). Add whole-milk yogurt before serving.

3. **CASHEW CREAM:** In a blender, put the hot water, raw cashews, pine nuts. Blend until smooth. Store in glass jar. Can keep 3-4 days in refrigerator.

COOKED VERSION
(Partially raw version previous page)

PART A
1 red onion, cubed
1 large carrot, cubed
2 medium-sized celery stalks, cubed
1 red or yellow bell pepper, cubed
3 medium-sized red potatoes, cubed
1 beet root, cubed

PART B
1 bunch beet greens, chopped
½ cup presoaked nuts
1 clove garlic
½ tsp. ginger, chopped
2 tbsp. olive oil or grape seed oil
Mushroom extract to taste
1 tsp. whole-milk yogurt or cashew cream

CASHEW CREAM (optional)
1 cup hot water
½ cup raw cashews
1 tbsp. pine nuts

NOTES:
1. For people with diabetes, use natural whole-milk yogurt. Add more beet greens and mixed green lettuce into the raw version.
2. For people with allergies or cancer, substitute sea salt for the mushroom extract and use cashew cream instead of yogurt.
3. For weight loss, do not be afraid of the oil. The oil helps maintain satiety and prevents you from getting hungry until the next meal.

1. **PART A:** In a stockpot, add enough water to cover the onion, carrot, celery, bell pepper, potato, and beet cubes plus 2 inches and bring them to a boil. Lower to medium heat and simmer for 30 minutes.
2. **PART B:** Add in beet greens, nuts, garlic, and ginger. Cook for 5 minutes, then immediately turn off the heat.
3. Pour the contents of the pot into a blender. Add the oil, and mushroom extract. Blend on a low speed (does not need to be smooth). Add whole-milk yogurt before serving.

Garlic Tea

SERVES: 1 | LEVEL: Easy

CALORIES: 118; Fat: 0.2 g; Protein: 1.3 g; Carbohydrates: 31.1 g

Garlic is packed with antioxidants as well as zinc and selenium, which can help ward off wrinkles caused by exposure to ultraviolet radiation from the sun. When you are in the sun, your body produces enzymes that break down connective tissue, causing wrinkles. Allicin and other antioxidants in garlic inhibit the action of these enzymes.

Garlic is also high in vitamin C, with more than twice as much as a similar amount of fresh tomatoes. Vitamin C promotes collagen production, further boosting the antiaging properties of garlic. Garlic is also excellent for removing heavy metals from the body. In one study of employees at a car battery plant who experienced excessive lead exposure, garlic was found to reduce levels of lead in the blood by nearly 20 percent over four weeks.

PART A
4 large garlic cloves, roughly chopped
1 cup boiling water

PART B
½ lemon, juiced
1 tbsp. apple cider vinegar
Honey to taste

1. PART A: Put the garlic cloves in the cup of boiling water, cover, and steep for a few minutes.
2. PART B: Add the lemon juice, vinegar, and honey. Sip slowly. The garlic can also be eaten to boost your immune system.

CHAPTER 6: **Toxin Overload** 147

Garlic Ginger Lemon Drink

CALORIES: 37.7; Fat: 0.1 g; Protein: 0.6 g; Carbohydrates: 10.9 g

SERVES: 1 | LEVEL: Easy

1–3 medium/large garlic cloves
Ginger root (same size as garlic cloves)
½ lemon (large) or 1 lemon (small)
Pinch of cayenne pepper powder

1. Into a cup, grate the garlic cloves and ginger root and squeeze the lemon juice. Mix with warm water.
2. Drink immediately after fixing first thing in the morning on an empty stomach.

Strawberry Green Smoothie

SERVES: 2 | LEVEL: Easy

CALORIES: 158.5; Fat: 6.3 g; Protein: 5.2 g; Carbohydrates: 23 g

Both **strawberry** and **spinach** are high in vitamin C, much-needed nutrients for the adrenal glands to make cortisol.

2 tbsp. flaxseeds
2 cups fresh or frozen strawberries
½ frozen or fresh banana
3 cups fresh baby spinach
1 cup unsweetened almond milk, oat milk, or rice milk
¼ tsp. vanilla

1. Grind the flaxseed in a grinder. Do not use flaxseed meal.
2. Blend the flaxseed with the strawberries, banana, spinach, milk, and vanilla until smooth.

CHAPTER 6: **Toxin Overload** 149

Broccoli Leek Soup

MEAL 1

CALORIES: 135.3; Fat: 6.8 g; Protein: 3.1 g; Carbohydrates: 17.5 g

SERVES: 4 | LEVEL: Easy

2 medium leeks, white and light green parts, thinly sliced
1 garlic clove, thinly sliced
3 cups broccoli, stems and florets separated
1 tbsp. grape seed oil
1 tbsp. butter
1 medium-sized sweet potato, cubed
Salt and pepper to taste

GARNISH
Chives, chopped

1. In a stockpot, stir-fry leeks, garlic, and broccoli stems in oil and butter over medium heat for 5 minutes, stirring constantly. Add broccoli florets and sweet potato. Add enough water to cover all the ingredients, bring to a boil, and then simmer for 5 minutes.

2. Transfer the soup into a blender, and blend until smooth. Reheat soup in stockpot. Garnish with chives.

> **NOTE:** For people with estrogen dominance or thyroid issues, limit the use of broccoli to two times per week.

Every day you are exposed to a variety of toxins in the food you eat and the air you breathe. These toxins, along with poor diet and exposure to allergens, lead to the body's inflammatory system going into overdrive.

We think of inflammation as unhealthy, but the reality is that inflammation is part of the body's healing process. Problems arise when inflammation is constant, which often happens when the flood of toxins is so great that the body cannot effectively rid itself of them. Chronic inflammation can damage DNA over time.

Broccoli contains a number of phytonutrients, specifically glucoraphanin, gluconasturtiian, and glucobrassicin, that support all stages of the body's detoxification process.

MEAL 1: Cucumber Tomato Red Onion Salad

SERVES: 6 | LEVEL: Easy

CALORIES: 45; Fat: 0.35 g; Protein: 2 g; Carbohydrates: 10 g

Cooling and soothing, **cucumbers** can help you stay hydrated, flush toxins from your digestive system, boost your immune system, and boost your energy.

Cucumbers are more than 90 percent water, important for hydration and flushing toxins from your system. If you are not a big fan of drinking water, or if you are just looking for something a little different, try munching on a few slices of cucumber. Better yet, add a few slices of cucumber to your water for extra flavor and hydration.

Cucumbers are a good source of a number of vitamins, including vitamin C. Most of the vitamin C found in cucumbers is located in the skin, so leave it on for the biggest boost. Cucumber is also rich in B-complex vitamins, which can increase your energy levels.

3 cucumbers, peeled and sliced
½ red onion, chopped
4 tomatoes, cubed

DRESSING

2 tbsp. white wine vinegar
Extra-virgin olive oil or grape seed oil to taste
Sea salt to taste
Pepper to taste

1. Put cucumbers, onion, and tomatoes in a bowl and toss.
2. Mix the vinegar, oil, salt, and pepper and then add to salad.

> **NOTE:** You can use another type of vinegar such as apple cider vinegar, but you might need to adjust the quantity of the vinegar.

CHAPTER 6: **Toxin Overload** 151

Carrot Thyme Soup

MEAL 2

CALORIES: 117; Fat: 3.7 g; Protein: 2.3 g; Carbohydrates: 19.5 g

SERVES: 8 | LEVEL: Easy

- 3–4 carrots, cubed
- 1 red onion, cubed
- 2 medium-sized celery stalks, cubed
- 1 red or yellow bell pepper, cubed
- 3 medium-sized red potatoes, cubed
- ½ tsp. thyme
- ½ cup presoaked nuts
- 2 tbsp. olive oil or grape seed oil
- Mushroom extract to taste
- 1 tsp. cream

RAW VERSION

1. Put all ingredients in a blender, cover with hot water, and blend on low speed (does not need to be smooth). Add more hot water if needed.
2. Before serving, swirl cream into each bowl as decoration.

COOKED VERSION

1. In a stockpot full of water, bring the carrots, onion, celery, bell pepper, potatoes, and thyme to boil. Cook for 30 minutes, then immediately turn off heat. Let stand for 15 minutes.
2. Pour the contents of the stockpot into a blender. Add the nuts, oil, and mushroom extract. Blend on a low speed (does not need to be smooth).
3. Before serving, swirl cream into each bowl as decoration.

Long before refrigeration existed, people used herbs and spices to preserve foods and prevent microbial contamination. A study published in the journal *Food Microbiology* in February 2004 found that thyme essential oil could not only prevent contamination from a variety of pathogens such as *Shigella* and *E. coli* but also could decontaminate food already infected with these organisms.

Washing produce in a solution containing 1 percent thyme essential oil can reduce foodborne pathogens to a level where they are undetectable. Adding fresh thyme to your food, especially salads and other foods eaten raw, can help you avoid illness.

NOTES:

1. For weight loss, do not be afraid of the oil. The oil helps maintain satiety and prevents you from getting hungry until the next meal.
2. For diabetes, use the raw version rather than the cooked version. Cut down to 1–2 carrots and add mixed green lettuce instead.
3. For allergies or cancer, substitute sea salt for the mushroom extract and substitute flaxseed oil for the olive oil.

MEAL 2 — Napa and Red Cabbage Salad

SERVES: 6 | LEVEL: Easy

CALORIES: 264; Fat: 14.3 g; Protein: 9 g; Carbohydrates: 35.3 g

Cilantro is most well known for its ability to rid the body of toxic heavy metals such as lead, mercury, and aluminum in a process known as chelation. This is because cilantro contains unique chemical compounds that bind with these metals to free them from tissue so they can be excreted. Some of the most common sources of heavy metal toxicity include eating certain types of fish, cooking with aluminum, smoking, wearing deodorant, taking certain medications, having silver fillings, and getting vaccines.

Many people exposed to mercury have reported a reduction in symptoms of mercury poisoning after eating large amounts of cilantro. In lab studies, cilantro given to rats was found to protect them against lead accumulation. Because of these properties, cilantro is being studied for its potential as a natural water purifier.

Cilantro contains high concentrations of chlorophyll, a great detoxifier that flushes the liver and removes excess bacteria. These bacteria typically colonize the armpits and feet, causing odor. By keeping bacteria under control, chlorophyll acts as a natural deodorant. Cilantro also has some muscle-relaxing qualities that help to calm the nerves and relieve anxiety.

- 2 cups Napa cabbage, chopped
- 1 cup red cabbage, chopped
- 1 cup presoaked/sprouted wheat berries
- 3 tbsp. chopped cilantro
- ½ cup pineapple tidbits

SAUCE
- ¼ cup oil
- 2 cups apple cider vinegar
- 2 tbsp. sesame oil
- 1 tbsp. sugar
- ¼ tsp. pepper
- 1 tsp. mushroom extract

GARNISH
Pine nuts

1. Mix both kinds of cabbage, the wheat berries, the cilantro, and pineapple tidbits in a bowl.
2. Mix oil, vinegar, sugar, pepper, and mushroom extract for the sauce. Add half of sauce and toss. Store extra sauce in refrigerator. Garnish with pine nuts.

NOTES:
1. For estrogen dominance and hypothyroid, substitute mixed green lettuce or romaine lettuce for the cabbage. You should eat cruciferous vegetables only twice a week.
2. For allergies or cancer, substitute sea salt for the mushroom extract and substitute flaxseed oil for the olive oil.

CHAPTER 6: **Toxin Overload** 153

Spinach Strawberry Salad

MEAL 2

CALORIES: 92.2; Fat: 7.5 g; Protein: 2.7 g; Carbohydrates: 5 g

SERVES: 8 | LEVEL: Easy

DRESSING
3 tbsp. seasoned rice vinegar
2 tbsp. grape seed oil
2 tbsp. agave nectar
1 tbsp. soy sauce
2 tbsp. orange juice
1 tbsp. poppy seeds
1 tbsp. toasted sesame seeds
$\frac{1}{8}$ tsp. paprika

SALAD
8 oz. baby spinach
8 large strawberries, thinly sliced crosswise

GARNISH
½ cup sliced almonds, toasted (optional)

1. Whisk together the vinegar, oil, agave, soy sauce, orange juice, poppy seeds, sesame seeds, and paprika. Set aside.
2. Half an hour before serving, mix the dressing, spinach, and strawberries in a large bowl. Refrigerate. Just before serving, garnish with the toasted almonds.

This recipe is high in vitamin C, which will help you absorb much more of the iron in the **spinach**. Iron is essential to transporting oxygen from your lungs to your cells, and a deficiency can cause fatigue.

Research has found that spinach contains more than a dozen different flavonoid compounds, many of which have anti-inflammatory and antioxidant properties. Spinach is especially rich in lutein and zeaxanthin, antioxidants vital to several parts of the eye, particularly the retina and macula, and might be able to protect against age-related vision problems.

Many nutrients found in fruits and vegetables are diminished by heat, but cooking spinach can actually triple the amount of nutrition you get from it. This is because spinach contains nutrients in forms difficult for the body to break down and absorb. Spinach leaves stored under direct sunlight have been found to contain more nutrients than those stored in the dark.

Even better than cooking, though, is blending. Run a handful of spinach leaves through a blender or juicer with some other veggies and an apple for a power-packed beverage. You should buy organic spinach: otherwise the leaves are heavily sprayed with pesticides that normal washing does not remove.

MEAL 3: Stir-fried Baby Bok Choy

SERVES: 4 | LEVEL: Easy

CALORIES: 43; Fat: 3 g; Protein: 1.8 g; Carbohydrates: 3.2 g

Rich in vitamin C, carotenoids, manganese, and zinc, **bok choy** is an antioxidant powerhouse. The antioxidant properties are increased by a variety of phytonutrients, including flavonoids and phenolic acids.

Different types of antioxidants can all help prevent and repair oxidative damage, but they do the job in different ways. With bok choy (as with many fresh, whole foods), the whole is greater than the sum of the parts because the unique combination of antioxidants is much more powerful than any single antioxidant supplement you could take.

Most of the antioxidants found in bok choy also have anti-inflammatory properties. Bok choy also contains omega-3 fatty acids and vitamin K for extra inflammation fighting. The inflammatory response is critical to efficient healing, but constant inflammation causes a variety of ailments. The anti-inflammatory properties of bok choy can help prevent many of these conditions.

1 lb. baby bok choy

PART A
2 tsp. olive oil
2 garlic cloves, finely minced
2 slices ginger root

PART B
2 tbsp. water
½ tsp. salt
½ tsp. sesame oil
¼ tsp. fish sauce (optional)

1. Wash the bok choy and cut in half lengthwise.
2. **PART A:** In a wok or frying pan, stir-fry the garlic and ginger in the olive oil over medium heat. When the garlic and ginger become fragrant, add the bok choy. Stir to coat the bok choy with oil.
3. **PART B:** Add the water, salt, and fish sauce. Cover and cook for 4–6 minutes until the bok choy is tender. Turn off the heat. Drizzle the mixture with sesame oil before serving.

> **NOTE:** This is a good basic recipe for stir-frying all kinds of vegetables, such as spinach, Swiss chard, Yiu Chai, cabbage, broccoli, and so forth. Make sure you limit the intake of cruciferous vegetables if you have estrogen dominance or thyroid issues.

CHAPTER 6: **Toxin Overload**

Green Bean Potato Pine Nut Salad

MEAL 3

CALORIES: 146; Fat: 14 g; Protein: 2.25 g; Carbohydrates: 5.1 g

SERVES: 6 | LEVEL: Medium

1 cup green beans
1 cup red cabbage, chopped coarsely
3 purple unpeeled potatoes, cubed

DRESSING

1 tbsp. hoisin sauce
1 tbsp. vegetarian oyster sauce
2 tbsp. olive oil
2 tsp. sesame oil

GARNISH

½ cup pine nuts

1. In a pot, parboil the green beans for 1 minute, then chop them coarsely. Refrigerate to cool.
2. Steam the cubed potatoes until cooked. Refrigerate to cool.
3. Mix the green beans, cabbage, and potato cubes.
4. Whisk together the hoisin sauce, vegetarian oyster sauce, olive oil, and sesame oil, add to the salad, and toss. Garnish with pine nuts before serving in chilled bowls.

> **NOTES:**
> 1. For weight loss, do not be afraid of the oil. The oil helps maintain satiety and prevents you from getting hungry until the next meal. You can use sesame seeds or sunflower seeds in addition to or to replace the pine nuts.
> 2. For gluten allergies, use gluten-free hoisin sauce and vegetarian oyster sauce.

Purple potatoes owe their deep color to an abundance of an antioxidant flavonoid known as anthocyanin. Purple potatoes actually contain about four times the amount of antioxidants as white potatoes. The darker the purple color, the greater the concentration of anthocyanins.

Along with their antioxidant properties, anthocyanins are considered to have strong anti-inflammatory properties. Research suggests that they might be able to help fight chronic inflammation and protect against a variety of conditions, including heart disease, diabetes, dementia, and more.

Other evidence suggests that anthocyanins might have a direct protective effect on the brain. A study conducted on rats found that those given anthocyanins suffered less memory loss and less motor-function degradation than those that did not receive the flavonoid. The majority of the power-packed nutrients are found in the potato skin. It is best to use unpeeled whole potatoes in this recipe.

MEAL 3: Vegetable Chowder

SERVES: 8 | **LEVEL:** Medium

CALORIES: 278; Fat: 7.1 g; Protein: 6.8 g; Carbohydrates: 50.4 g

This chowder is great to have on a cold night. If your digestion is poor or you are in a catabolic state, you can blend all the vegetables in the soup to help improve the absorption. When blended, this soup is easy on the digestion.

PART A
- 1 tbsp. olive oil
- 2 tbsp. butter
- 1 large white or yellow onion, diced
- 2 medium-sized red bell peppers, diced
- ½ tsp. dried thyme

PART B
- 3 cups almond milk
- 2½ lbs. potatoes, peeled and cubed
- 5 cups vegetable stock

PART C
- 4 cups corn (fresh or frozen)
- Salt and pepper to taste

PART D
- 1 lb. green beans, trimmed and cut to 1½-inch length

1. **PART A:** In a large soup pot, cook the onion, bell peppers, and thyme in the olive oil and butter over medium heat until the vegetables are softened, 8–10 minutes. Stir occasionally.

2. **PART B:** Add the almond milk, potatoes, and vegetable stock. Bring to a boil, then reduce to low heat. Cover and simmer until the potatoes are almost tender, 8–10 minutes.

3. **PART C:** Add corn, salt, and pepper. Simmer until the corn is tender, 3–5 minutes. Transfer 4 cups of the soup to a food processor or blender, and blend until smooth. Return to pot. Balance of soup is not processed.

4. **PART D:** Add the green beans. Simmer and cook until the green beans are tender, 5–8 minutes.

Barley Date Asparagus Salad with Mint Dressing

MEAL 4

SERVES: 8 | LEVEL: Medium

CALORIES: 406; Fat: 30.3 g; Protein: 4.2 g; Carbohydrates: 34.6 g

Dates have a unique ability to alleviate symptoms of both constipation and diarrhea. Dates contain both soluble and insoluble fiber. Soluble fiber absorbs water and takes on a gel consistency to soften stools, whereas insoluble fiber does not absorb water and adds bulk to help keep things moving through the digestive tract. These actions can also help prevent hemorrhoids.

When ripe, dates also contain potassium, which can help to relieve diarrhea. The soluble fiber also helps to absorb excess liquid, helping to restore normal bowel movements. Surprisingly, dates also contain small amounts of nicotine, which might be able to relieve many other intestinal issues. Eating dates on a regular basis can inhibit the growth of disease-causing organisms, allowing beneficial gut flora to thrive. Amino acids found in dates can stimulate digestion and help you absorb nutrients from food more effectively. Organic sulfur, not commonly found in foods but present in dates, has been shown to reduce allergic reactions and seasonal allergies.

2 cups pearl barley, cooked
18 large asparagus stalks, trimmed 1 inch from bottom

DRESSING
¾ cup olive oil
2 tbsp. mint leaves, minced
3 tbsp. lemon juice
1 tsp. salt
1 tsp. pepper

SALAD
5 Madjool dates, pitted and chopped
⅔ cup cranraisins
1 cup walnuts, roughly chopped
2 tbsp. mint leaves, minced
1 tbsp. lemon zest

1. Follow the package instructions to cook the barley.
2. Put water in a large frying pan, and bring to a boil. Add the asparagus. Drain after 2 minutes (or if you prefer it well done, leave it to cook longer). Let cool and cut into 1-inch pieces.
3. For the dressing, add olive oil, mint, lemon juice, salt and pepper in a glass jar. Shake it well. Let stand for 30 minutes or keep overnight for the flavors to develop.
4. In a large bowl, mix the barley, asparagus, dates, cranraisins, walnuts, mint, and lemon zest, and toss. Make sure the dates are evenly spread throughout the salad. Keep it in the refrigerator until ready to serve.
5. At least 30 minutes before serving, add the dressing to the salad and toss.

NOTE: This salad can be prepared the night before serving. It can be eaten as is or served over mixed green salad or spring salad mix.

Curried Butternut Squash and Apple Soup

MEAL 4

CALORIES: 151; Fat: 9.5 g; Protein: 2 g; Carbohydrates: 17.6 g

SERVES: 8 | LEVEL: Medium

- 1 medium-sized onion, chopped
- 2 tbsp. grape seed oil
- 2 tbsp. butter
- 1 tsp. curry powder
- 2 medium-sized apples (do not use tart apples), cubed
- 5 cups butternut squash, cubed
- ½ tsp. crushed red chilies
- Salt and pepper to taste
- 2 cups water
- ¼ cup pine nuts

1. In a large pot, stir-fry the onion in the oil, butter, and curry powder over medium heat until the onion is soft.
2. Add the apples, butternut squash, chili, salt, pepper, and water. Bring to a boil, cover, and cook for 30 minutes.
3. Transfer the soup to a blender, and add the pine nuts. Blend until smooth.

Curry is not actually one spice but rather a blend of spices used in many Asian countries to give food a very distinct flavor. Curry is made with turmeric, coriander, and cumin. Other spices are typically added, depending on the region.

Curcumin, a compound found in turmeric, has been found in animal studies to suppress the expression of genes associated with many liver issues, including tumor growth. The studies suggest that eating turmeric can help protect against both liver diseases and liver toxicity.

Other studies have shown that coriander might be able to help remove lead, mercury, and other heavy metals from the body in a process known as chelation. Research at UCLA found that taking vitamin D3 with curcumin might trigger the immune system to remove amino acids known to form plaque in the brain, protecting against Alzheimer's disease.

The most common ingredients of curry powder are turmeric, coriander, sweet basil, cardamom, cumin, and red pepper. These spices can help the digestive system when consumed in moderation. Because of the turmeric in curry, some people can experience some digestive issues such as reflux.

MEAL 4: Roasted Cauliflower

SERVES: 6 | LEVEL: Easy | CALORIES: 121; Fat: 9.6 g; Protein: 3.3 g; Carbohydrates: 8 g

Cauliflower is a surprisingly effective food for helping you to detox in two ways. First, cauliflower contains a variety of antioxidants that support Phase 1 detoxification. In Phase 1, toxins are converted into a more water-soluble form. However, Phase 1 detox can actually make some toxins more harmful. This is why Phase 2 detox is vital.

Cauliflower is also rich in nutrients that contain sulfur, important to Phase 2 detox. Phase 2 is the phase in which the liver actually processes the toxins and excretes them. Nutritional deficiencies, excessive alcohol consumption, tobacco use, and toxic overload can all impair the liver's ability to carry out this phase. Cauliflower and other cruciferous vegetables can support the liver so it can carry out these activities.

1 small to medium-sized head cauliflower, florets separated
1 head broccoli, florets separated

SEASONING
3 tsp. minced garlic
½ tsp. crushed, dried red chilies (grind in a coffee grinder)
1 tsp. curry powder
Salt to taste
4 tbsp. extra-virgin olive oil

GARNISH
½ lime, juiced
1¼ cup cilantro leaves, chopped

1. Preheat oven to 325°F.
2. Put the cauliflower and broccoli in a mixing bowl.
3. Whisk together the garlic, chilies, curry powder, salt, and olive oil. Sprinkle over the cauliflower and broccoli; toss gently to coat well.
4. Spread the seasoned florets on a baking sheet. Roast until tender, stirring occasionally. Depending on the oven, it might take 45 minutes to 1 hour and 25 minutes. If you like your vegetables crunchy, you can take them out at 30–45 minutes. It is much faster with a convection oven. When done, remove from oven.
5. Stir in the lime juice and garnish with cilantro.

NOTE: If you have estrogen dominance or thyroid issues, you need to limit intake of cauliflower and broccoli.

CHAPTER 7

Catabolic State

What Is the Catabolic State? 163
Digestive System Breakdown 164
Smoothies, Soups, Stews, and Broths 167
Immune-Boosting Foods 168
Foods to Avoid 169

recipes
Baked, Stuffed Pumpkin Bowl 171
Asparagus with Lemon-Basil-Yogurt Sauce .. 172
Brown Rice with Edamame 173
Brown-Sugar Garlic Chicken 174
Butternut Squash Edamame Casserole 175
Chicken Hash-Brown Casserole 176
Dr. Lam's Chicken Broth 177
Dr. Lam's Beef Broth 180
Festive Butternut Squash Soup 181
Gluten-free Macaroni and Cheese 182
Grilled Apple 183
Kelp Mung-Bean Porridge 184
Millet Jujube Porridge 185
Potato Pea Soup 186
Pumpkin Oatmeal 187
Roasted Garlic 188
Spinach with Eggs 189
Spinach Fennel Soup 190
Vanilla Pears 192
Vegetable Pesto Pasta 193

What Is the Catabolic State?

This chapter focuses on the advanced stages of Adrenal Fatigue Syndrome (AFS), in which the body is left with impaired metabolic, clearance, and detoxification pathways; many at this stage will find themselves housebound or bedridden. The damage in this stage of AFS is referred to as late Stage 3C and 3D in Dr. Lam's *Adrenal Fatigue Syndrome* book, and it often gives rise to paradoxical, unpredictable, and exaggerated reactions and outcomes. Therefore, any healing protocol suggested will be very gentle and slow, and you should be perceptive to the way your body is reacting to any changes in lifestyle and diet to determine the healing pathway best suited for your circumstances.

The nutritional and dietary advice contained here is also applicable to Stage 4, in which the body is continuing to deteriorate regardless of interventions and might ultimately collapse because the adrenals have become totally exhausted. The neuroendocrine response mechanism is in its final effort and might surrender, creating in this process a catabolic state that can be clinical or subclinical. If not reversed, it can naturally progress to catabolic wasting or cachexia.

> **The goal is to slowly and gently build up your body to return it from a catabolic state to a metabolically neutral state.**

Many will find that at this stage it is difficult to eat regular meals, and thus they become weaker and begin to lose weight. Despite higher intake of calories, weight does not increase easily compared with when the body is in a healthy state. Furthermore, the high levels of cortisol being produced in the body will result in excessive breakdown of collagen and protein without sufficient replenishment. The body is cannibalizing its muscle for energy. Food passes through the gastrointestinal tract poorly digested, and assimilation is diminished. Bloating, gastric irritation, pain in the abdominal area, and constipation are common.

Our goal is to slowly and gently build up the body to return it from a catabolic state to a metabolically neutral state in which catabolic and anabolic processes are balanced. After this is accomplished, the diet can help to propel the body into an anabolic state to make up for lost weight and muscle mass, including in internal organs. With this catabolic state diet, we stop the deterioration from developing any further.

Digestive System Breakdown

As the collagen structures of the internal organs break down, their functions are compromised, and the gastrointestinal tract motility (movement) and contraction are reduced. The body's acid production might be insufficient to help break down digested foods, resulting in further digestive problems. Therefore, the diet at this stage should consist of simple and easily digested foods so as not to place an extra burden on the digestive system.

The Extracellular Matrix

The extracellular matrix (ECM) is a network of nonliving tissues located outside the cells of our body, hence the term extracellular. The ECM provides structural support to the cells as well as cell adhesion, migration, and proliferation. Essentially, the ECM provides the physical scaffolding for our 70 trillion internal cells to roam and thrive, connecting all the spaces within the body; without its proper functioning, our bodies suffer. When the ECM begins to break down, your health can be severely threatened. Deteriorating ECM may eventually lead to depletion of the body's nutritional reserves, which can result in cellular dysfunction and organ failure. In contrast, rehabilitation of the ECM can vastly improve the outcome of chronic diseases because within the ECM the healing begins.

Diet and the Extracellular Matrix

An increase in water consumption plays a major role in healing the ECM because fluid intake carries the toxins to the kidneys and liver for processing and excretion. It is important for people with AFS to balance the extra fluid intake with electrolytes, especially sodium and potassium, to avoid any imbalances. The ideal water to drink is room temperature spring water; avoid cold water, sugary drinks, and caffeinated beverages. For greater detail on the ideal type of water to drink, refer to Dr. Lam's *Adrenal Fatigue Syndrome* book.

Detoxifying Beet Soup
pages 144–145

Millet Jujube Porridge
page 185

Smoothies, Soups, Stews, and Broths

Smoothies, soups, stews, and broths are extremely nourishing for those at this stage of AFS. Not only are these foods simpler to cook for those that have weakened energy reserves and cannot labor in the kitchen for a prolonged amount of time but they are also easier to digest and therefore create less work for the digestive tract.

Smoothies can provide much-needed enzymes because the ingredients are raw and have not been exposed to the cooking process whereby enzymes can be destroyed by the heat. The ingredients used in the smoothies should ideally be organic and made up of nonhormonal components, especially when it comes to dairy products. Yogurt may be added into the smoothies if you are able to tolerate dairy products.

For an even gentler diet ideal for those who are bedridden at this stage, the most nourishing food is soup because it is easy to digest, and therefore the much-needed nutrients are better absorbed by the body.

Traditional Chinese medicine consistently prescribes soups as a staple food for those with illnesses because the yin and yang are delicately balanced by the various ingredients used to make the soup. Beef, pork, and chicken are cooked for approximately six hours so the meat is extremely tender, and it is eaten along with the broth for a good source of protein. Meat broths (not including bone-only broths) should not be cooked for longer than six hours because the nutritional value of the meat and protein can be destroyed.

If you prefer, you can blend the entire contents of the soups and consume them as thick broths or pureed soups. The soups should be consumed at warmer than room temperature but not above 120°F because prolonged consumption of extremely hot soups may lead to cancer of the esophagus. While drinking soups and smoothies, it is important to continue "chewing" because this activates the saliva enzymes, which will lighten the burden on the gastrointestinal tract of digesting the food.

In order to get healthy fats into the body at this stage, it is a good idea to add extra-virgin olive oil to the soup. Other alternatives can include avocado oil, flaxseed oil, and expeller-pressed coconut oil (does not contain the strong coconut flavor). Put these different oils on a rotation to observe how your body reacts to them.

Bone-only broths are great for anti-aging regimens and calcium replenishment. In order for the calcium and other minerals to leach from the bones into the broth, add one tablespoon of apple cider vinegar to the pot of water and bones, and let it sit for 30 minutes before cooking.

Fish broth does not need to be cooked as long as other meats, and the omega-3 fatty acids in the fish will greatly assist those with respiratory illnesses such as asthma and bronchitis. Cooking the fish in broth for 30 minutes will be sufficient.

Chicken broth is famous for helping with colds and flus. Adding some kelp or mushroom into the broth when cooking will help improve thyroid function.

Lamb or mutton soup is good for the winter months because it is considered an internally "hot" soup, according to traditional Chinese medicine, and should not be used when you are weak. Lamb soup can help with circulation for those with cold hands and feet.

If you are vegetarian, fresh vegetable broths have great detoxing properties and can be used instead of meat broths. For added protein, blending in soaked cashews, almonds, or tofu can create a creamy texture. If you can tolerate dairy, you can add organic cheese or cream.

As a general rule when making meat or bone broth, you should be adding lots of alkaline foods (mostly dark green leafy vegetables) to offset the acidic meat proteins. Root vegetables can be added simultaneously with the meat, but leafy greens are generally best added at the end of the cooking process to preserve the nutrients. Salt should be added later as well, because as the soup reduces in liquid, it may get too salty. For a list of benefits of the various types of salt available, refer to Chapter 3 of this cookbook.

Immune-Boosting Foods

The foods we recommend that have the greatest immune-boosting properties for those in the catabolic state are onions, turmeric, garlic, ginger, oregano, and thyme. These herbs and spices can be added to broths you are cooking or steeped and consumed as a tea-like beverage.

Your food should largely be nonprocessed, fresh, and organic. Meats should be from grass-fed sources, truly free range, with no hormones either given to the animal itself or put in its food.

Opt for simple cooking methods such as steaming or cooking in liquids, which will ensure that you retain the maximum amount of nutrition that aids in digestion. Avoid deep-frying your food because the heat changes the hydrogen-bond structure, turning the good fats into bad fats, which can trigger inflammation and histamine release that pollute the ECM.

The current raw food movement gaining mainstream attention can be beneficial for those who have a strong gastrointestinal tract and can digest raw foods in large amounts. However, for those in a catabolic and weakened state, it is best to avoid raw food.

As with all our advice provided thus far, take precautions and go slowly. Do not make drastic changes to your diet, not even if it is toward better nutrition. Your body will react not only to what foods you put into it but also to nutrition of which it is deprived. You will also mentally feel the changes you are making, which is why we recommend taking baby steps. Begin by decreasing the amount of sugar in your diet, and be wary of any "hidden" sugar, such as that in the "healthy" whole-grain muffin you just purchased. If you feel the need for a snack, opt for a handful of soaked nuts and a small amount of fruit to curb that sweet tooth.

Foods to Avoid

The foods to avoid are similar to the ones mentioned in the previous chapters, such as refined white sugar, bleached white flour, and dairy (although, if yogurt is tolerable for you at this stage, then it is acceptable). Yogurt from pastured, or grass-fed, cows (organic yogurt) is your best choice.

Nuts can be difficult to digest; however, if you soak them for 10–12 hours you will have started the sprouting process, and this will make them easier to digest. After soaking, they must be kept refrigerated (for one or two days) or kept in the freezer and defrosted before consuming. Soaked nuts are prone to spoiling quite easily, and any mold spores will not yet be visible to the naked eye but might have a detrimental effect on your health.

We hope the knowledge we have shared with you has empowered you to be creative and pursue better nutrition for yourself and your loved ones. Realize that you have the potential to change your health and well-being by implementing the advice and recipes in this book, and do it slowly. It could well be a long and narrow path, but it certainly is well worth it. Rest assured that you are fueling your body with what it needs, and it in turn will repair itself and function the way it was designed to do.

Bon appetit!

Baked, Stuffed Pumpkin Bowl

CALORIES: 166; Fat: 7.8 g; Protein: 4.2 g; Carbohydrates: 23.3 g

SERVES: 8
LEVEL: Challenging

PART A
1 pumpkin (3–4 lbs.)

PART B
2 tbsp. olive or coconut oil
2 leeks, chopped
2 garlic cloves, crushed
2 tbsp. fresh thyme leaves, chopped
2 tsp. paprika
1 tsp. ground turmeric

PART C
2 cups cooked long-grain rice
2 tomatoes, seeded and roughly chopped
½ cup cashews, roasted and roughly chopped
Salt and pepper to taste

1. Preheat oven to 350°F.
2. **PART A:** Cut the stem and 2 inches off the top of the pumpkin to use as a lid when baking. Scoop out the seeds and discard them or save them for roasting. Scrape out the rest of the pumpkin flesh with a knife and spoon. Cut the pumpkin flesh into small pieces to be used later.
3. **PART B:** In a large frying pan, stir-fry the leeks, garlic, thyme, paprika, and turmeric in the oil for 10 minutes over medium heat. Add the pumpkin flesh, and cook another 10 minutes. Stir frequently to prevent sticking.
4. **PART C:** Mix in the rice, tomatoes, cashews, salt, and pepper. Spoon the mixture into the pumpkin shell. Cover it with the lid and cook it in the oven for 1¼–1½ hours, until the pumpkin skin turns brown. Remove it from the oven and let it stand for 10 minutes, then cut it into wedges to serve.

Pumpkins get their bright orange color from carotenoids, which the body uses to synthesize vitamin A, essential to good vision especially in dim light. A single cup of pumpkin provides nearly twice as much vitamin A as you need each day, along with three grams of fiber, for only 50 calories.

Pumpkins can help you sleep better and boost your mood. This is because they are high in L-tryptophan, an amino acid that cannot be synthesized in the body. Consuming foods high in L-tryptophan, such as Thanksgiving turkey and many other high-protein foods, increases levels of serotonin in the brain, helping you to relax. Serotonin is, in turn, converted into melatonin, which can help you sleep better.

Asparagus with Lemon-Basil-Yogurt Sauce

SERVES: 4 | LEVEL: Medium

CALORIES: 57; Fat: 0.2 g; Protein: 4.2 g; Carbohydrates: 11.5 g

Asparagus contains glutathione and asparagine, two substances that support the detoxification process in different ways.

Glutathione converts toxins, carcinogens, and free radicals into a water-soluble form so they can be excreted from the body. Glutathione is one of the primary antioxidants produced by the cells and is directly responsible for neutralizing free radicals inside cells as well as maintaining levels of vitamins C and E outside cells. Asparagine is an amino acid that functions as a diuretic, helping to flush excess salts and retained water from the body via the kidneys. Asparagine is vital to maintaining balance in the nervous system, keeping you from being too stimulated or too calm.

1 lb. asparagus tips
½ cup low-fat Greek yogurt
3 tbsp. fresh basil, chopped
½ tsp. lemon zest
2 tbsp. fresh lemon juice
1 tbsp. honey, maple syrup, or agave nectar
¼ tsp. salt
¼ tsp. freshly ground black pepper

1. Bring a pot of water to boil, add the asparagus, and cook it for 2 minutes or until tender, then drain. Immediately put the asparagus into ice water, then drain again.
2. Combine the yogurt, basil, lemon rind and juice, sweetener, salt, and pepper. Pour over the asparagus.

CHAPTER 7: **Catabolic State** 173

Brown Rice with Edamame

CALORIES: 192; Fat: 4.4 g; Protein: 6.6 g; Carbohydrates: 32.3 g

SERVES: 4 | LEVEL: Medium

PART A
¾ cup long-grain brown rice
1½ cup lightly salted water

PART B
1¼ cup frozen, shelled edamame

PART C
3 stalks spring onions, thinly sliced diagonally
2 tbsp. fresh-squeezed lime or lemon juice
1½ tsp. toasted sesame oil
1 tsp. honey
Salt and pepper to taste

1. **PART A:** In a medium-sized pot, bring the water and rice to a boil. Cover, reduce heat, and simmer for around 30 minutes.
2. **PART B:** Add in edamame, cover, and continue to simmer until the rice is done, around 15–20 minutes. Make sure you add more water if needed.
3. **PART C:** Whisk together the onion, citrus juice, oil, honey, salt, and pepper. Stir into the rice.

NOTE: For estrogen dominance and hypothyroid, substitute edamame with green peas or other legumes.

Protein is vital to rebuilding muscle, and cooked brown rice contains 5 grams of protein per cup. This recipe contains a whopping 6.6 grams per serving. **Brown rice** is not quite a complete protein because it lacks lysine, but the edamame makes up for this with more than 1 gram per cup.

Brown rice can help increase your levels of natural growth hormone, vital to building lean muscle and helping you regain your strength. Brown rice also contains more than 50 grams of carbohydrates per cup, but it is very dense and digests slowly, so it does not produce a spike in insulin levels, giving you a gentle energy boost that lasts for hours.

Brown-Sugar Garlic Chicken

SERVES: 4 | LEVEL: Easy

CALORIES: 212; Fat: 8 g; Protein: 20.4 g; Carbohydrates: 14.1 g

4 boneless, skinless, free-range chicken breasts or thighs
1 tsp. salt
½ tsp. pepper
2 tsp. expeller-pressed coconut oil
2 tsp. minced garlic
4 tbsp. brown sugar

1. Preheat oven to 400°F.
2. Tenderize the chicken with the salt and pepper for 1 hour or more in the refrigerator.
3. In a small saucepan, melt the coconut oil, and add the minced garlic. Sauté until the garlic is tender. Remove from heat and stir in the brown sugar.
4. Dip the chicken in the brown sugar and garlic mixture. Place the coated chicken in a greased casserole dish. Make sure most of the brown sugar and garlic mixture is on top of the chicken pieces. Bake 30 minutes until golden brown.

Coconut oil is a superfood when it comes to relieving symptoms of AFS. It can actually lower the glycemic index of other foods, which helps to regulate blood sugar and provide sustained energy levels.

Coconut oil also helps to speed up your metabolism and nourishes your mitochondria. The mitochondria are the structures within your cells responsible for generating energy. In these ways, coconut oil boosts your energy and helps you lose weight.

Coconut oil has few nutrients of its own, but it helps your body to more efficiently absorb nutrients such as calcium, which helps to calm your nerves; magnesium, which aids in energy production within the cells; B-complex vitamins, which are key in both energy production and lowering stress levels; and vitamin E, which supports adrenal function.

CHAPTER 7: **Catabolic State** 175

Butternut Squash Edamame Casserole

CALORIES: 300; Fat: 12.6 g; Protein: 13 g; Carbohydrates: 36 g

SERVES: 8 | LEVEL: Medium

- 2 cups butternut squash
- 6 cups dehydrated hash browns (rehydrate per package instructions)
- 3 cups frozen edamame beans, thawed
- 1 cup shredded cheese (optional)
- 2 eggs, beaten
- 1/8 tsp. crushed red chilies
- 2 tbsp. extra-virgin olive oil
- Salt and pepper to taste

1. Preheat oven to 350°F.
2. Put the butternut squash in a blender, add ½ cup water, and blend roughly. Pour into a mixing bowl. Add the hash browns, edamame, 3/4 cup of the cheese (save ¼ cup for topping), eggs, chilies, oil, salt and pepper, and mix.
3. Spread the mixture into a casserole dish. Sprinkle the remaining cheese on top. Bake for 50 minutes or until golden brown.

Edamame may well be the ideal midday snack. If you have never had it, it is a young soybean harvested while still tender. Edamame is a good source of iron, providing a full fifth of your daily needs in one serving. Iron helps your body to use energy more efficiently, and iron from plant-based foods may improve fertility in women of childbearing age.

As a soy food, edamame shares many of the same benefits as tofu and other soy foods. These include decreased risk of osteoporosis and easing symptoms of menopause. The calcium and magnesium in edamame may be able to relieve PMS and reduce the number and severity of migraines in those who experience them.

Although soy is one of the most common genetically modified crops, the National Soybean Research Laboratory reports that edamame does not come from genetically modified soy. If you are concerned about GMO soy, look for the "Non-GMO Project Verified" seal.

As with other soy foods, if you are estrogen dominant or you suffer from certain thyroid conditions, enjoy edamame in moderation.

Chicken Hash-Brown Casserole

SERVES: 6 | LEVEL: Medium   CALORIES: 288; Fat: 9 g; Protein: 15.3 g; Carbohydrates: 37.6 g

Potatoes are high in alpha-lipoic acid, an enzyme that helps convert nutrients into energy. Some evidence exists that this enzyme can also help control blood sugar levels, improve circulation, and help protect brain and nerve tissue.

Potatoes are also rich in vitamin B6, which stimulates energy metabolism by helping the body break down complex carbohydrates into glucose and proteins into amino acids. Potatoes are also a great source of potassium, copper, vitamin C, phosphorus, niacin, pantothenic acid, manganese, and dietary fiber along with several antioxidant phytonutrients, including carotenoids and flavonoids. So ignore the naysayers who tell you potatoes are not nutritious. They are—just keep them out of the deep fryer.

6 cups dehydrated hash browns (rehydrate per package instructions)
4 boneless, skinless, free-range chicken thighs, cubed
1 tsp. soy sauce
2 tsp. cooking wine
½ tsp. salt
½ tsp. pepper
2 tbsp. olive oil
½ large sweet onion, chopped
½ tsp. paprika
½ tsp. thyme
¼ tsp. crushed red chilies
Salt and pepper to taste

1. Preheat oven to 350°F.

2. Marinate the chicken for 30 minutes in the soy sauce, wine, salt, pepper, and olive oil.

3. In a large mixing bowl, stir together the hash browns; the chicken in its sauce; and the onion, paprika, thyme, chilies, salt, and pepper to taste. Pour into a baking dish. Bake for 30 minutes or until the chicken is done.

Dr. Lam's Chicken Broth

The following recipes are simple and excellent. Do not replace these ingredients with commercial, off-the-shelf products because many of them contain MSG and are too diluted to have any significant clinical impact. Try to make the chicken broth fresh every morning, ready to be consumed from midday onward for the rest of the day.

Homemade chicken broth provides vital, foundational macronutrients sorely needed in advanced AFS recovery. It is part of a complete program including lifestyle changes, dietary adjustments, and micronutrients such as vitamins. Of vital importance are the chicken bones, which provide key nutrients easily assimilated by the gastrointestinal tract and thus bioavailable to the cells when delivered in a liquid form such as chicken broth.

continued next page

Each cup (8 ounces) provides 10 calories, 0 grams of fat, 1 gram of protein, 2 grams of carbohydrates, and no cholesterol. The nutritional value goes far beyond what meets the eye. The key lies in the bone marrow. Bone marrow is the essence of all mammals. It contains all of the necessary nutrients for the human body, such as proteins, B-complex vitamins, and minerals (calcium, magnesium, and zinc). Bone marrow also contains lecithin and methionine. It has been used as a whole food source since early civilization. Studies show it helps maintain healthy cholesterol levels, reduces inflammation, and promotes a strong immune system tied to the adrenal glands.

Most people with AFS have salt cravings as well as fluid depletion. Consuming chicken broth helps with fluid depletion because volume is restored. Adding salt to chicken broth provides an excellent way to replenish the sodium deficiency in the body resulting from aldosterone dysregulation. Chicken broth accomplishes both purposes. There is no restriction on the amount of salt added, provided there are no signs of edema or high blood pressure and upon approval of your private physician.

Those who have a tendency to urinate in the middle of the night should watch and restrict fluid intake in the evening to avoid excessive fluid buildup and urine retention in the bladder, which can exacerbate this.

We recommend that you consume chicken broth twice a day. The best times are midmorning and midafternoon. This is usually the time when the body runs out of steam. Chicken broth at these times will be of great benefit to recharge your body. If you can only do it once a day, then consume it when you experience your worst "low" of the day. For most people, this can be midmorning, midafternoon, or immediately after work. You can consume extra chicken broth after exercising, even on top of the recommended amount.

A good routine is to do adrenal exercises (such as adrenal breathing, adrenal restoration, and adrenal rebuilding) midmorning, followed by the chicken broth and a small healthy snack.

Those who need a more aggressive nourishment protocol should consume the broth five times a day, preferably in the morning right after waking up, midmorning, at lunch, in the early afternoon (two hours after lunch), and in the late afternoon (4–5 p.m.). For maximum effectiveness, do short sessions of adrenal breathing exercises before eating (8–24 breaths lasting one to three minutes), which are designed to help stimulate the parasympathetic nervous system and prepare the gastrointestinal tract for optimum assimilation of nutrients into the bloodstream.

You can eat some raw nuts along with the broth as a snack. The protein and fat from the nuts will enhance sustained energy release, while the salted broth will generate an immediate energy boost.

Recipe 1

CALORIES: 467; Fat: 17 g; Protein: 61.4 g; Carbohydrates: 14 g

- ½ bone-in chicken or two whole legs, skin and fat removed
- 1 medium-sized onion, chopped
- 2–3 celery stalks, cut in 3-inch segments
- 1 medium-sized carrot, chopped

Recipe 2

CALORIES: 451; Fat: 16.9 g; Protein: 61.3 g; Carbohydrates: 10.2 g

- ½ bone-in chicken or two whole legs, skin and fat removed
- 1 medium-sized beet root, peeled and chopped
- 2 celery stalks

Recipe 3

CALORIES: 488; Fat: 16.7 g; Protein: 62.4 g; Carbohydrates: 19.8 g

- ½ bone-in chicken or 2 whole legs, skin and fat removed
- 1 6 to 10 inch lotus root, peeled and chopped

DIRECTIONS FOR ALL RECIPES

1. In a saucepan, add enough water to cover the chicken and vegetables, plus 3 more inches. Bring to a boil.
2. Reduce the heat to medium, and cook for 30 minutes. Then reduce heat to medium low, and cook for another 90 minutes. Add salt to taste.
3. Remove the chicken meat for other uses.
4. Strain vegetables from broth and use elsewhere.

NOTES:

1. Make sure you remove the skin and fat from the chicken before making the broth, and if there is still some oil left after boiling, skim the oil off with a spoon or shredded paper towel. Save the chicken meat for other uses, but be sure to use all bones for the broth.
2. Rotate the use of these three recipes for the greatest health benefits. The chicken broth should be made fresh daily in the morning, a different recipe each day.
3. Drink the broth as warm to hot as you can tolerate it, one cup each time. Do not reheat it in the microwave but rather on the stovetop.
4. Each recipe makes 3–5 cups. The longer you boil it, the less liquid will remain.
5. You can eat 2–6 ounces of the chicken meat before bedtime along with some nuts to combat sleep-onset insomnia or sleep-maintenance insomnia.

Dr. Lam's Beef Broth

SERVES: 1 | LEVEL: Easy

CALORIES: 174; Fat: 7.8 g; Protein: 23.7 g; Carbohydrates: 0.8 g

This broth invigorates the body and is nourishing for the blood.

¼ pound organic, extra-lean ground beef
2 cups water
2 slices ginger
Salt to taste

1. In a medium-sized pot, soak the ground beef and ginger in the water for 30 minutes. Stir to make sure the ground beef is loosened in the water. Bring the mixture to a boil. Reduce heat and simmer for 1 minute. Add salt to taste.
2. Strain the soup, and consume only the broth. Save the beef for casseroles or sauces.

> **NOTE:** If you have a weak constitution and issues with digestion, do not eat the beef.

Festive Butternut Squash Soup

CALORIES: 158; Fat: 6.6 g; Protein: 3.7 g; Carbohydrates: 23 g

SERVES: 8 | LEVEL: Medium

PARTIALLY RAW VERSION

- 1 red onion, cubed
- 1 large carrot, cubed
- 2 medium celery stalks, cubed
- 1 red or yellow bell pepper, cubed
- 3 medium-sized red potatoes, cubed
- 1 12-oz. bag of butternut squash, cubed
- ½ tsp. allspice
- ½ tsp. cinnamon
- ½ cup presoaked nuts
- 2 tbsp. olive oil or grape seed oil
- Mushroom extract to taste
- 8 tsp. cream

1. In a pot, boil water, then add the onion, carrot, celery, bell pepper, and potatoes. Simmer for 30 minutes on medium-low heat. Turn off heat and let sit 15 minutes.
2. Pour the contents of the pot into a blender. Add the butternut squash, allspice, cinnamon, nuts, oil, and mushroom extract. Blend until smooth, pour into soup bowls, and swirl 1 tsp. of cream in each bowl as decoration.

COOKED VERSION

1. Put in a pot the onion, carrot, celery, bell pepper, potatoes, butternut squash, allspice, and cinnamon with enough water to cover the vegetables plus 2 inches. Bring to a boil, then turn heat to low, simmer for 30 minutes. Immediately turn off the heat. Let stand 15 minutes.
2. Pour the contents of the pot into a blender. Add the nuts, oil, and mushroom extract. Blend on a low speed (does not need to be smooth). Pour into soup bowls and swirl 1 tsp. cream in each bowl as decoration.

NOTES:

1. You can use more cinnamon to improve your blood sugar balance.
2. For allergies, substitute sea salt for the mushroom extract.

Butternut squash gets its bright orange hue from an abundance of carotenoids, which are vital to eye health and can help protect against macular degeneration. One cup of butternut squash contains enough carotenoid compounds to provide three to four times your daily requirement.

The nutritional punch of butternut squash does not stop there. A cup of butternut squash contains about half the vitamin C you need each day, a powerful immune-boosting antioxidant. Butternut squash is also high in B-complex vitamins and a variety of minerals, including iron, zinc, copper, calcium, potassium, and phosphorus.

When buying fresh butternut squash, look for one heavy for its size with thick, blemish-free skin. It does not need to be refrigerated.

Gluten-free Macaroni and Cheese

SERVES: 8 | LEVEL: Medium

CALORIES: 329; Fat: 17 g; Protein: 12.5 g; Carbohydrates: 33.2 g

Macaroni and cheese, even when it is gluten free, is not generally considered a health food. However, it can be when you add a leafy green veggie such as **Napa cabbage.**

Napa cabbage is especially good for your skin. It contains high levels of vitamin C, which prevents blemishes and protects skin from damage resulting from sun exposure. Vitamin C also helps the body develop resistance against infectious agents and free radicals. Its juice extract can improve skin allergies.

Napa cabbage is also high in vitamin E, which combined with the vitamin C stimulates hair growth and saves the skin cells from potential damage. Its high iron content protects your hair against excessive shedding. Napa cabbage has adequate levels of vitamin K to promote osteotrophic activity in bone cells.

3 cups gluten-free macaroni
½ head Napa cabbage, coarsely chopped
1 cup bok choy or other greens, coarsely chopped
3 tbsp. coconut oil or butter
Salt and pepper to taste
½ tsp. garlic powder
4 oz. sharp cheddar cheese, cut into thin slices or small cubes
1 oz. mozzarella cheese, cut into small cubes
1 cup almond milk (see Chapter 2)

1. Follow the package instructions to cook the macaroni.
2. Heat a large frying pan or wok, and add the coconut oil or butter, cabbage, and other vegetables. Stir-fry them until tender. Stir in the salt, pepper, and garlic powder. Add ½–1 cup water, cover, and cook for 5–10 minutes. Add more water as needed.
3. Add almond milk, macaroni, and cheese. Stir until well mixed. Add water if you want it to be more runny; the mixture will thicken as it sits.

NOTE: For estrogen dominance and hypothyroid, use leeks, onions, summer squash, peas, or green beans instead of the Napa cabbage.

CHAPTER 7: **Catabolic State** 183

Grilled Apple

CALORIES: 35.7; Fat: 2.1 g; Protein: 0.1 g; Carbohydrates: 4.8 g

SERVES: 2 | LEVEL: Easy

1 Gala or Granny Smith apple, cut in half and cored
1 tsp. butter

1. Melt butter in a frying pan over medium heat.
2. Put apple halves face down in frying pan. Cover and cook over low to medium heat until soft.

When Ben Franklin said an apple a day keeps the doctor away, he was more accurate than he knew. **Apples** are a good source of quercetin, a flavonol known to boost the immune system. In a study of more than 100 different foods, two apple varieties, Granny Smith and Red Delicious, ranked in the top 20 for antioxidants.

Apples are high in pectin, a soluble fiber with a variety of health benefits. One medium-sized apple contains nearly four and a half grams of fiber to help relieve constipation, diarrhea, and irritable bowel syndrome (IBS). Apples also contain phlorizidin, a phytochemical that stimulates bile production. This, along with the fiber and vitamins found in apples, is an especially effective detoxifier.

NOTES:
1. For weight loss, this is a great dessert for those watching calories. It is delicious, and if you use a Gala apple, it is sweet and fragrant. If you use a Granny Smith apple, it will be more tart.
2. For blood sugar balancing, add more butter along with some chopped nuts and cinnamon.

Kelp Mung-Bean Porridge

SERVES: 1 | LEVEL: Easy

CALORIES: 234; Fat: 3.8 g; Protein: 15 g; Carbohydrates: 38 g

There are 30 different types of **kelp.** Kelp is a large seaweed in the brown algae family. Kelp is especially high in iodine, a trace element vital to healthy thyroid function. Iodine deficiency can lead to developmental delays in children and mental deficiency in adults. Iodine is added to table salt to help people get enough, but kelp is a better source. Iodine can help raise your energy levels while calming the body and reducing nervous energy. Studies have shown a link between energy levels and iodine intake.

Kelp is especially good for bone health. Research conducted in the 1950s found that hens given kelp supplements laid harder eggs. This led to research on humans that showed bone fractures healed significantly more quickly in patients given seaweed supplements. Kelp is also a natural diuretic that helps the body to flush water and toxins.

1 oz. shredded dried kelp, soaked until soft, cut into thin strips
¼ cup mung beans, soaked overnight
5 almonds, soaked overnight and roughly chopped
5 dried rose petals in a teabag or muslin bag
Brown sugar or honey to taste

1. In a small pot, put the kelp, mung beans, and almonds. Add 2 cups water and boil for 5 minutes. Turn down the heat and simmer another 30 minutes, making sure there is enough water.

2. Add the rose petal bag for the last 10 minutes of cooking. When ready to serve, remove the rose petal bag and add sweetener as desired.

CHAPTER 7: **Catabolic State**   185

Millet Jujube Porridge

CALORIES: 283; Fat: 2.5 g; Protein: 11 g; Carbohydrates: 54.4 g   SERVES: 2 | LEVEL: Easy

¼ cup black beans, soaked overnight
½ cup millet, soaked overnight
1 oz. dried jujubes, pits removed
Brown sugar, honey, or agave nectar to taste

1. In medium-sized pot, put 6 cups of cold water, black beans, and millet. Bring to a boil over high heat. Turn down the heat and simmer for 10 minutes.
2. Add jujubes, and continue to simmer for another 30 minutes. Make sure there is enough water every 15 minutes. Turn off the heat, and add sweetener to taste.

The **jujube** is a small fruit that resembles a date and tastes a bit like an apple. Jujubes are not especially high in many nutrients but are a good source of magnesium, copper, potassium, calcium, manganese, phosphorous, and niacin. Jujubes also contain a great deal of vitamin C, with 20 times more than any other citrus fruit. This makes them a great choice to strengthen the immune system and help you fight off infection.

Jujubes also contain a complex combination of phytonutrients, some of which have sedative properties. Ancient Chinese medical practitioners recognized this and used the fruit to help relieve anxiety and insomnia.

Jujubes are an especially good source of antioxidants that can support the liver. Studies have shown that consuming jujubes can even protect against liver injury. Eat a few dry jujubes to stimulate digestion and relieve constipation.

Potato Pea Soup

SERVES: 6 | LEVEL: Medium

CALORIES: 212, Fat: 5 g; Protein: 6.7 g; Carbohydrates: 36 g
Nutritional information is based on 6 servings.

Peas are a starchy vegetable and as such, not typically thought of as especially nutritious. Although peas do contain quite a bit of starch, they also pack a nutritional punch. Peas are a rich source of fiber and protein, both of which help to slow the breakdown of sugar, keeping blood sugar levels steady, which can help prevent sugar crashes. A cup of peas gives you more than 10 percent of your daily requirement of iron. An iron deficiency can lead to fatigue, especially at the end of the day.

Peas are a surprising source of omega-6 fatty acids as well as omega-3 fatty acids, a nutrient most commonly found in fish and vital to brain health. Peas are packed with antioxidants as a rich source of zinc and vitamins C and E.

PART A
2 tbsp. olive oil
1 medium-sized white or yellow onion, finely chopped

PART B
2 lbs. potatoes, peeled and cut into small chunks
5 cups vegetable stock

PART C
3 cups frozen peas

PART D
½ cup mint leaves, chopped
Salt and pepper to taste

GARNISH
6 whole mint leaves

1. **PART A:** In a large soup pot, sauté the onion in the olive oil over medium heat for 3–4 minutes, until softened.
2. **PART B:** Add the potatoes and vegetable stock, cover, and simmer for 10–12 minutes or until tender.
3. **PART C:** Add the frozen peas and cook 2 more minutes. Use a slotted spoon to remove ¼ of the vegetables, and set them aside.
4. **PART D:** Pour the rest of the contents of the pot into a blender and blend until smooth. Stir in the remaining vegetables, the chopped mint leaves, salt, and pepper. Garnish with the whole mint leaves.

Pumpkin Oatmeal

CALORIES: 245; Fat: 2.2 g; Protein: 6 g; Carbohydrates: 50 g

SERVES: 2 | LEVEL: Easy

- ½ cup brown rice, soaked overnight
- 2 cups pumpkin, cut into ½-inch cubes
- ⅓ cup oatmeal
- 1 stalk green onion, chopped
- Salt to taste

1. In a medium-sized pot, add brown rice and 2 cups of water and bring to a boil. Reduce heat and simmer for 20 minutes.
2. Add pumpkin and cook over low heat for 10 minutes.
3. Add oatmeal and cook over low heat for 10 minutes. Turn off heat and add green onion and salt.

Pumpkin and oatmeal are both low on the glycemic index, so this is an ideal food for breakfast to jumpstart the day. You can always add some nuts if you like.

Roasted Garlic

LEVEL: Easy

Packed with antioxidants, **garlic** is a powerful immune booster and especially helpful in the winter to ward off colds and flu. If you do feel a cold starting to take hold, chop a clove of fresh garlic and steep it in hot water, add some honey or ginger for flavor, and drink it to knock out the illness in no time flat.

In one study conducted over three months, subjects who took garlic every day had 63 percent fewer colds than subjects who took a placebo, and colds lasted less than two days in those who took garlic compared with five days for those taking the placebo. If you seem to catch every little virus that goes around, try finding ways to incorporate more garlic into your diet every day.

Garlic cloves
Olive oil

1. Preheat oven to 350°F.
2. Cut the tops off a few garlic cloves. Place the garlic on a baking sheet. Drizzle the garlic with olive oil. Bake for 30 minutes or until soft.

> **NOTE:** This recipe has many uses: squeeze out the garlic flesh and pop it in your mouth; crush and spread on bread; spread on any meat before cooking; mix in salad dressings; mix in cooked vegetables.

Spinach with Eggs

CALORIES: 206; Fat: 12.6 g; Protein: 13.6 g; Carbohydrates: 14 g

SERVES: 4 | LEVEL: Medium

PART A
2 tomatoes

PART B
2 tbsp. olive oil, coconut oil, or butter
1 medium-sized onion, finely chopped
1 garlic clove, finely chopped
1 fresh chili (optional), seeded and finely chopped

PART C
2¼ lbs. leaf spinach
⅓ cup water

PART D
4 eggs, whisked with salt and pepper to taste

1. **PART A:** Bring a medium-sized pot of water to boil. Fill another bowl with ice and water, and set it next to the stove. Remove the stems from the tomatoes and slice a shallow "X" at the bottom of each. Drop the tomatoes into the boiling water. The skins of the tomatoes should start to wrinkle and split at around 45–60 seconds. Scoop up the tomatoes, transfer them to the ice-water bath, and leave them in it for 5–10 minutes. Peel off the skin, and seed and dice the tomatoes.

2. **PART B:** In a large frying pan, stir-fry the onion, garlic, and chili over medium-high heat until lightly brown.

3. **PART C:** Add in the tomatoes, spinach, and water. Cook for about 15 minutes, stirring continuously, until the liquid has evaporated.

4. **PART D:** Stir in the eggs. Remove from the heat and adjust the seasoning to taste.

A nutritional powerhouse, **spinach** contains calcium, iron, potassium, manganese, zinc, selenium, carotene, folate, vitamins A and C, and fiber. Look for dark green spinach leaves that look crisp and vibrant. Not only are they more visually attractive but also they will have a higher concentration of nutrients than lighter green ones. Smaller leaves will be more tender than bigger leaves, and leaves kept in the light will have higher concentrations of nutrients than leaves stored in the dark.

Spinach is also high in oxalic acid, which can hamper the body's ability to absorb calcium and certain other minerals from the vegetable. Counter this by pairing spinach with ingredients high in vitamin C, or reduce the oxalic acid content by boiling the spinach for 2 minutes.

Egg yolks contain large amounts of both lutein and zeaxanthin, which help to prevent macular degeneration. In a controlled trial, it was shown that lutein in the blood is increased by 28–50 percent and zeaxanthin by 114–142 percent after eating 1.3 egg yolks per day for four to five weeks. Studies have shown that sufficient intake of eggs, spinach, and broccoli is associated with up to a 20 percent decrease in cataracts and up to a 40 percent decrease in age-related lens and retinal degeneration.

Spinach Fennel Soup

SERVES: 8 | LEVEL: Medium

CALORIES: 145; Fat: 5.4 g; Protein: 4.6 g; Carbohydrates: 21 g

Fennel contains the antioxidants quercetin and kaempferol. These substances are vital to recovering from the catabolic weakened state so devastating to individuals in advanced stages of AFS.

Fennel contains sulphur as well as certain amino acids and essential oils that can help strengthen hair and prevent it from falling out. Fennel functions as an emmenagogue, meaning that it can stimulate and regulate menstruation. It has been used in traditional herbal medicine to alleviate symptoms of PMS.

Fennel has antioxidants and amino acids that work to reduce inflammation throughout the body, but particularly in the eyes. This can help protect the eyes from macular degeneration and other detrimental effects of aging. There is even some evidence that the juice of fennel leaves can reduce eye fatigue when applied externally.

1 red onion, cubed
1 large carrot, cubed
2 medium celery stalks, cubed
1 red or yellow bell pepper, cubed
3 medium-sized red potatoes, cubed
1 lb. spinach
½ cup presoaked sunflower seeds
¼ cup fennel, chopped
1 clove garlic
2 tbsp. olive oil or grape seed oil
Mushroom extract
8 tsp. cream

PARTIALLY RAW VERSION

1. To a soup pot of boiling water, add the onion, carrot, celery, bell pepper, and potatoes. Simmer 30 minutes on medium-low heat. Remove from heat and let stand for 15 minutes.
2. Pour the contents of the pot into a blender. Add spinach, sunflower seeds, fennel, garlic, oil, and mushroom extract. Blend until smooth. Pour into soup bowls. Swirl 1 tsp. of cream into each bowl and garnish with a spinach leaf as decoration.

COOKED VERSION

1. Put in a soup pot of water the onion, carrot, celery, bell pepper, potatoes, spinach, sunflower seeds, fennel, and garlic. Bring to a boil. Lower the heat, and simmer for 15 minutes.
2. Pour the contents of the pot into a blender. Add oil and mushroom extract. Blend until smooth. Pour into soup bowls. Swirl 1 tsp. of cream into each bowl and garnish with a spinach leaf as decoration.

NOTES:

1. People who have allergies or cancer can substitute sea salt for the mushroom extract. You might also want to use more garlic and fennel and use flaxseed oil instead of olive oil.
2. For weight loss, do not be afraid of the oil. The oil helps maintain satiety and prevents you from getting hungry until the next meal.

Vanilla and Pears

SERVES: 4 | LEVEL: Easy

CALORIES: 148; Fat: 0.2 g; Protein: 0.6 g; Carbohydrates: 39 g

Pears are high in both fructose and glucose, making them a good source of energy without the caffeine jitters. Despite this, pears are low on the glycemic index, making them a good fruit to help regulate blood sugar levels. Caffeine increases cortisol levels, which leads to feeling stressed out. Excess cortisol also interferes with normal sleep patterns, which leads to a need for more caffeine, triggering a vicious cycle. Eating pears can provide a gentler energy boost without increasing cortisol or interfering with sleep.

Pears are not high in many of the more well-known antioxidants, but they are rich in a variety of flavonols and phytonutrients such as quercetin, kaempferol, catechin, epicatechin, and many more, all of which have strong antioxidant and anti-inflammatory properties.

4 small pears of any kind, peeled
4 cups water
¼ cup honey or maple syrup
1 tsp. stevia powdered extract
1 slice ginger
1 small piece lemon rind
1 tsp. vanilla

1. In a saucepan, put the pears, water, sweeteners, ginger, lemon, and vanilla. Cover the pan with a lid.
2. Cook the mixture over low heat for 30 minutes, or until pears are soft. Turn over the pears two times.

> **NOTE:** For diabetes and metabolic syndrome, omit the honey or maple syrup. Use stevia to taste. You can also sprinkle on some cinnamon to help balance blood sugar.

Vegetable Pesto Pasta

CALORIES: 415; Fat: 22.9 g; Protein: 15.8 g; Carbohydrates: 41.6 g

SERVES: 8 | LEVEL: Medium

2 small zucchini, cut into strips
1 small bunch asparagus, cut into small pieces
1 bunch of green beans, cut into pieces
1 package gluten-free penne pasta

SAUCE

1 cup fresh Italian parsley leaves
$1/3$ cup fresh tarragon leaves
1 cup fresh basil leaves
1 garlic clove
1 tsp. lemon zest
$1/3$ cup roasted pine nuts
1¼ cup Parmesan or Romano cheese
1 tsp. sea salt
½ tsp. ground pepper
½ cup extra-virgin olive oil

1. Follow the package instructions to cook the gluten-free pasta. When it is about ¾ done, add the zucchini, asparagus, and green beans and cook for another 3–5 minutes for crunchy veggies or 5–7 minutes for well-done veggies. Set aside 2 cups of the liquid.
2. Put the parsley, tarragon, basil, garlic, lemon zest, pine nuts, cheese, salt, and pepper in a food processor, and turn it on to a low speed. As it processes the ingredients, add ½ cup extra-virgin olive oil slowly until the ingredients stick to the sides.
3. When ready to serve, add the reserved liquid to the pesto sauce in a dish. Add the pasta and veggies and mix well. Salt to taste and garnish with more Parmesan or Romano cheese.

NOTE: For diabetes and metabolic syndrome, double the amount of veggies and cut down the pasta to half.

If you have heard about gluten-free food and thought it was just a fad or too difficult to be worth considering, we invite you to reconsider. The Center for Celiac Research at the University of Maryland estimates that 6 percent of the population has some degree of gluten sensitivity. For those with celiac disease, following a completely gluten-free diet is vital to avoiding malnutrition. In a person with celiac disease, gluten causes inflammation in the intestines and flattening of the intestinal villi, small fingerlike structures that absorb nutrients. When they become flattened, they are unable to absorb nutrients, leading to deficiencies and malnutrition as well as symptoms similar to those of irritable bowel syndrome (IBS).

For those with less severe sensitivity, it is not necessary to completely eliminate gluten, but reducing it may decrease symptoms of a number of conditions, from asthma to depression. If you suffer from digestive issues, headaches, foggy thinking, ADHD-like symptoms, depression, joint pain, muscle cramping, numb legs, or low energy, or if you think gluten sensitivity could be aggravating any symptoms you are experiencing, consider eliminating gluten from your diet for a couple of weeks.

CHAPTER 8

Snacks

What Are the Best Snacks?

Many people with Adrenal Fatigue Syndrome (AFS) find themselves hungry every two to four hours. This might be a result of their blood sugar needs as described in Chapter 1. So we thought of providing some wholesome recipes that can be used for snacks between meals to help with balancing the glucose when you encounter stress. Also, for people in advanced stages of AFS and therefore weak, these snacks can all be prepared ahead of time by their loved ones. The savory recipes can be eaten cold or warmed easily.

What Are the Best Snacks? 195

recipes
Apple Nachos 197
Apple Sandwiches 198
Cauliflower Strips 199
Garbanzo Snacks......................... 200
Kale Chips................................. 201
Rice Paper Wraps 202
Spinach Wraps 204
Sweet Potato Rolls 206

Apple Nachos

CALORIES: 310; Fat: 22.4 g; Protein: 5.3 g; Carbohydrates: 26.4 g

SERVES: 4 | LEVEL: Medium

1 large Granny Smith apple, cut in half and cored
1 large Fuji apple, cut in half and cored
3 tbsp. sunflower butter
1 tbsp. grape seed oil
2 tbsp. agave nectar, honey, or maple syrup
¼ cup almonds, coarsely chopped
¼ cup pecans, coarsely chopped
¼ cup dark chocolate bits
¼ cup unsweetened coconut flakes (optional)

1. Slice both apples thinly.
2. Put the sunflower butter, oil, and sweetener in a saucepan. Heat over a low temperature until melted, and mix.
3. On a plate, arrange one layer of apples, intermingling Granny Smith and Fuji. Use a spoon to drizzle the melted butter mixture evenly over the apples. Top with almonds, pecans, and dark chocolate bits. Repeat until all ingredients are layered.

Most love **chocolate,** and studies show that it is as good for you as it is delicious. The secret behind both the health benefits and the taste is cacao. Cacao is packed with chemical compounds that fight disease, but by itself, it is bitter and chalky. This is why the chocolate bar you pick up at the checkout stand is also packed with milk, sugar, and butter. For maximum health benefits, stick with chocolate that's at least 70 percent cocoa, and exercise moderation.

Chocolate boosts blood flow to the brain and to the heart, increasing cognitive function and mood. Chocolate contains the same chemical your brain makes when you fall in love, phenyl ethylamine (PEA), and PEA encourages the brain to release endorphins, which make you feel happy. Chocolate also contains small amounts of caffeine for a gentle energy boost.

The flavonoids in chocolate improve cell function and lower insulin resistance. Chocolate does not cause blood sugar to spike, though the kinds with lower concentrations of cacao will.

According to the U.S. Department of Agriculture, pecans are in the top 15 foods known for their antioxidant activity. Combine dark chocolate with **pecans** for a powerful dose of healthy minerals. A serving of pecans is packed with more than double the heart-healthy manganese you need in a day. They contain significant amounts of copper, vital to energy production in the cells; magnesium, vital to the immune system and regulation of nerve impulses; and zinc, vital to immune function, cell division, and protein synthesis.

> **NOTE:** For blood sugar balance, use less sweetener, more sunflower butter, or stevia for sweetener.

Apple Sandwiches

SERVES: 3 | LEVEL: Medium

CALORIES: 133; Fat: 4.8 g; Protein: 3 g; Carbohydrates: 22.3 g

1 large apple
½ tsp. salt dissolved in 1 cup water
5 tsp. sunflower butter
5 tsp. raisins
5 tsp. granola (optional)

1. Slice the apple horizontally into pieces 1–2-inch thick, so you have several slices with the core in the center. Cut out the centers with a core remover or small, round cookie cutter.
2. Dip the apple slices in the cup of saltwater or squirt them with lemon juice to prevent browning.
3. Spread sunflower butter on all the apple slices. Sprinkle raisins and granola on half the apple slices. Make sandwiches by placing the rest of the apple slices, spread side down, onto the ones with raisins and granola.

NOTE: You can also make these open-faced sandwiches.

Raisins are packed with insoluble fiber, which makes you feel full and stimulates the digestive process by reducing constipation. They can also help to stop loose stools by absorbing the liquid. They are high in fructose and glucose, natural sugars that provide a healthy energy boost.

Raisins are rich in potassium and magnesium, both of which have a high pH and are good for alkalizing the body. Also, magnesium helps soothe the nerves. Raisins are also high in calcium, which along with the potassium and magnesium is vital to bone strength.

Increase the nutrient power of this snack with sunflower seeds. Like raisins, sunflower seeds are high in magnesium, which keeps our nerves relaxed by preventing calcium from rushing into the nerve cells and activating them. Sunflower seeds are also high in selenium, an essential mineral that boosts the antioxidant power of vitamin E and can help support thyroid function.

CHAPTER 8: **Snacks** 199

Cauliflower Strips

CALORIES: 51; Fat: 2.8 g; Protein: 4 g; Carbohydrates: 3.4 g

SERVES: 6 | LEVEL: Medium

- ½ head of cauliflower, grated in the food processor
- 2 small eggs
- ¼ cup mozzarella cheese, shredded
- 1 cup Italian parsley, chopped
- 1 tsp. dried basil
- ⅛ tsp. ground oregano
- Salt and pepper to taste
- Olive oil

1. Preheat oven to 350°F.
2. Thoroughly mix the cauliflower, eggs, cheese, parsley, basil, oregano, salt, and pepper in a large bowl.
3. Line a baking sheet with foil, then line with parchment paper on top of the foil. Brush the parchment paper with the olive oil. Pour the cauliflower mixture onto the parchment paper. Spread evenly until it is about 1-inch thick. Square off the edges. Brush the top of the whole rectangle with olive oil. Bake for 40 minutes until brown and firm to the touch.
4. Remove from the oven, pick up one side of the parchment paper, and flip it over on the baking sheet. Peel off the parchment paper. Cut to approximately 1-inch-wide by 4-inch-long strips. Broil for 3 minutes. Take the baking sheet out of the oven and let the strips cool down.

NOTE: You can eat the cauliflower strips plain or with dipping sauce. For estrogen dominance or thyroid issues, do not use this recipe more than once a week, provided you have not used any other cruciferous vegetables during that week.

The modern diet is sorely lacking in nutritional value. **Cauliflower** can help you get more of several vital nutrients you might otherwise miss. A single serving contains significant amounts of vitamins C and K along with several B vitamins, protein, magnesium, manganese, phosphorus, potassium, and a variety of antioxidant phytonutrients, including quercetin, kaempferol, cinnamic acid, and rutin. The vitamin B12 in cauliflower can give you an energy boost between meals and help keep blood sugar levels stable throughout the day.

Cauliflower is especially beneficial to the brain. Containing choline and phosphorus, cauliflower can help repair cell membranes, a function vital to efficient brain function and the transmission of nerve signals. Potassium and vitamin B6 are vital to the synthesis of a variety of neurotransmitters such as dopamine and norepinephrine.

Cauliflower provides more than nine grams of fiber per 100 calories. Researchers found that the sulforaphane generated by a glucosinolate in cauliflower can help protect the lining of the stomach and prevent bacterial overgrowth of *Helicobacter pylori*.

Garbanzo Snacks

SERVES: 4 | LEVEL: Easy

CALORIES: 150; Fat: 4.7 g; Protein: 9 g; Carbohydrates: 20 g

Also known as **chickpeas, garbanzo beans** are not only healthy for you but also can help reduce the amount of unhealthy processed food you eat, according to research. Garbanzo beans are packed with fiber, and fiber provides satiety. One cup contains half of the fiber you need for the entire day. About 65–75 percent of the fiber is insoluble, which means it reaches the colon undigested. At that point, it is used as fuel by the bacteria found in that part of the digestive tract.

Garbanzo beans are also an excellent source of protein. Combining garbanzo beans with a whole grain such as millet or quinoa provides high-quality protein comparable with that of meat or dairy, with fewer calories and unhealthy fats. They are also a great source of manganese and iron, both of which are vital for energy production.

1 tbsp. expeller-pressed coconut oil
1 15-oz. can garbanzo beans, rinsed and drained

SEASONING MIX
2½ tbsp. nutritional yeast
¼ tsp. garlic powder
½ tsp. salt
¼ tsp. ground black pepper
⅛ tsp. paprika
⅛ tsp. crushed red pepper

1. In a medium-sized skillet over a medium temperature, heat the oil.
2. Rinse and drain the garbanzo beans well. Stir-fry them for 2 minutes, then stir in the seasoning mix.
3. Stir frequently, making sure the garbanzo beans do not burn. They should be golden and lightly charred in some places.

NOTE: For estrogen dominance, limit intake because garbanzo beans are high in phytoestrogen.

Kale Chips

CALORIES: 149; Fat: 8 g; Protein: 5.1 g; Carbohydrates: 18.8 g

SERVES: 6 | LEVEL: Medium

2 bunches of kale, washed and dried well; leaves separated from the stem

SAUCE

3 tbsp. olive oil (if dehydrating) or grape seed oil (if baking)
1 medium-to-large-sized lime, juiced
1 tsp. garlic powder
1 tbsp. honey
1 tsp. seasoned sea salt

1. Tear kale leaves into bite-sized pieces.
2. In a large bowl, sprinkle half of the sauce over the kale.
3. Use your hands to toss the kale and massage the sauce evenly on the pieces.
4. Repeat steps 2 and 3 with remaining kale.

BAKING METHOD

1. Preheat oven to 325°F.
2. Line 2 baking sheets with parchment paper. Spread the kale on baking sheets, and bake 10–15 minutes until crisp. Do not let the pieces turn brown. Remove from the oven, and sprinkle with salt.

DEHYDRATOR METHOD

1. Set dehydrator to 115°F.
2. Place the seasoned kale pieces on the dehydrator shelves. Drying time could take 4–14 hours. (It varies with type of dehydrator.)

Kale is a member of the cabbage family and is related to cauliflower, broccoli, and Brussels sprouts. Researchers have identified no less than 45 separate flavonoids in kale, all of which have anti-inflammatory and antioxidant properties, including quercetin and kaempferol.

Indeed, kale might well be one of the most nutrient-dense foods you can eat.

Kale is an excellent source of minerals of which many people do not get enough. Kale is rich in calcium, vital not only for bone health but also a variety of cellular functions. It is a good source of magnesium, which regulates nerve impulses and might be able to protect against heart disease and diabetes. It also contains potassium, which regulates electrical impulses in the cells. Although many leafy green vegetables contain these minerals, kale has an advantage in that it is low in oxalates, substances found in many plants that block the absorption of certain minerals.

Kale is high in fiber and rich in eye-protecting nutrients. It also contains vitamin K, which aids in blood clotting. The glucosinolates in kale produce isothiocyanates (ITCs), which help detox activities in the cells. Kale also contains compounds that might be able to protect against the bacteria that cause ulcers.

However, there is a compound in kale that interferes with your thyroid function. There must be a chain of reactions for the thyroid-interfering compounds—thiocyanates—to be released. Cooking kale stops that chain of reactions from happening, but eating raw kale in a salad or chewing it allows thiocyanates to form. A few ounces of raw kale should not affect your thyroid.

Rice Paper Wraps

SERVES: 4 Wraps
LEVEL: Medium

CALORIES: 130; Fat: 2.7 g; Protein: 8.6 g; Carbohydrates: 12.4 g

2 cups mixed spring salad
6 shiitake mushrooms, chopped
2 pieces five spice tofu
2 stalks spring onions, slivered
4 large rice-paper wraps

SAUCE
¼ cup fish sauce
¼ cup water
¼ cup rice vinegar
⅛ cup sugar
1 garlic clove, minced

Love them or hate them, **mushrooms** have long been used for both food and medicine. Much medical research has been done on shiitake mushrooms, but few studies have been done on their use in the human diet. The few studies do show that shiitake mushrooms provide health benefits to the immune system and have strong antioxidant properties.

Shiitake mushrooms are high in potassium, selenium, riboflavin, niacin, and iron. They also contain lentinan, a beta-glucan that might be able to stimulate the immune system, fight infection, and discourage the growth of tumors. Recent studies have also shown that shiitake mushrooms might also protect against cardiovascular disease.

With only 26 calories, a serving of four shiitake mushrooms contains less than a gram of fat, 2 grams of fiber, and almost 2 grams of protein. Snacking on shiitake mushrooms can help you feel full and energized.

1. Mix the mushrooms, tofu, and onions.
2. In a separate bowl, mix the fish sauce, water, vinegar, sugar, and garlic.
3. Dip the rice paper in warm water, take the rice paper out of the water, and lay it on a plate. The rice paper will soften in a few seconds.
4. Put a quarter of the spring salad and the mushroom-tofu mixture in the bottom ⅓ of the wrap. Fold the bottom wrap up, and roll it up to ¾ of its length. Fold in the two corners, and roll it to the end.
5. When ready to serve, dip the rice paper wraps into sauce.

NOTE: People with estrogen dominance and hypothyroid might want to substitute tempeh (fermented tofu) for the tofu. You can also use beef or chicken instead of tofu.

Spinach Wraps

SERVES: 8 wraps
LEVEL: Medium

CALORIES: 65; Fat: 3.2 g; Protein: 4.7 g; Carbohydrates: 5.3 g

- 1 box (10 oz.) frozen spinach, defrosted, or 1½ lb. fresh baby spinach, chopped
- 1 box firm tofu, cubed (season with salt and pepper)
- 1 medium-sized white onion, finely chopped
- ¼ cup sun-dried tomato, chopped
- 1 tbsp. olive oil or grape seed oil
- 8 large rice paper wraps

RAW VERSION

1. Mix the spinach, tofu, onion, sun-dried tomato, and olive oil.
2. Dip the rice paper in warm water, take the rice paper out of the water, and lay it on a plate. The rice paper will soften in a few seconds.
3. Put the spinach mixture in the bottom ⅓ of the wrap, fold the bottom of the wrap up, and roll it up to ¾ of its length. Fold in the two corners and roll to the end.

COOKED VERSION

1. In a frying pan, sauté the onion in the olive or grape seed oil. Add the spinach, tofu, sun-dried tomato and gently stir. Add salt and pepper to taste.
2. Dip the rice paper in warm water, take the rice paper out of the water, and lay it on a plate. The rice paper will soften in a few seconds.
3. Put the spinach mixture in the bottom ⅓ of the wrap, fold the bottom of the wrap up, and roll it up to ¾ of its length. Fold in the two corners and roll it to the end.

NOTE: For estrogen dominance and hypothyroid, you might want to substitute tempeh (fermented tofu) for the tofu. You can also use organic ground beef, organic ground chicken, or organic ground turkey instead of tofu.

The process of making **tofu** is similar to that of making cheese. Soy milk is curdled and the curds pressed into a block and cooled. Tofu has little flavor of its own but will take on the flavor of whatever is cooked with it, and the texture is influenced by the method of cooking.

Tofu is an excellent plant-based protein source and contains all eight essential amino acids, making it a valuable part of a vegetarian diet. It is also a great source of iron, calcium, manganese, selenium, phosphorus, magnesium, zinc, copper, and vitamin B1. The calcium in tofu might be able to reduce the risk of osteoporosis. Research has shown that fermentation of tofu might increase the antioxidant and free-radical-fighting health benefits.

Tofu and other soy-derived foods are thought to lower bad cholesterol. Tofu contains phytoestrogens similar enough to human estrogen that they mimic the action of estrogen produced in the female body. Estrogen levels drop during menopause, so for some women, consuming soy foods might act as a sort of natural hormone replacement. People with estrogen dominance and some thyroid conditions should be careful to consume soy foods in moderation.

Sweet Potato Rolls

SERVES: 6 | LEVEL: Medium

CALORIES: 221; Fat: 15.7 g; Protein: 2.6 g; Carbohydrates: 19.6 g

Nori is the seaweed used to wrap sushi, and it is an incredibly healthy snack. It has been considered a perfect food in China for more than 2,000 years. Nori is low in calories and contains a surprising amount of fiber. Nearly a full third of its dry weight consists of dietary fiber, so it can help you stave off between-meal cravings.

Another third of the dry weight of nori consists of protein. A serving of nori provides more protein than nearly any other plant-based protein, making it an excellent choice for vegetarians in particular. Nori is high in a variety of nutrients. A single sheet provides as many heart-healthy, anti-inflammatory, omega-3 fatty acids as two avocadoes. Two sheets give you as much blood-building iron as an egg or glass of milk.

In addition, nori provides significant amounts of vitamin A, thiamine, riboflavin, niacin, folate, phosphorus, potassium, zinc, and iodine. Vitamins C, E and K are found in nori as well. It may seem strange to snack on seaweed, but you cannot go wrong with nori. The organic iodine in nori aids in maintaining healthy thyroid function. The polysaccharides in nori help to stabilize blood sugar, increase the feel-good chemicals in the brain, and improve liver function.

- 3–4 sweet potatoes
- 2 carrots
- 1/3 cup olive oil
- 1/3 cup fresh dill, minced
- 1/3 cup fresh basil, minced
- 1 tbsp. sea salt
- Dash of cayenne pepper
- 8 nori sheets
- 12 red-leaf lettuce leaves
- 1 Japanese cucumber, cut into sticks
- 1 avocado, cut into thin wedges
- 1 cup bean sprouts

1. Preheat oven to 400°F.
2. Clean the sweet potatoes and carrots. Put them on a baking sheet and bake for 50 minutes. Remove from oven and let cool.
3. Remove the pulp from the skin of the sweet potato. Chop up the skin. Mash together the carrots with the potato pulp and skin. Mix in the olive oil, dill, basil, sea salt, and cayenne.
4. Lay out one sheet of nori on a plate. Place lettuce over the nori. Spread 2 tbsp. of the sweet potato mixture on the lettuce. Add cucumber sticks, avocado wedges, and sprouts. Roll tightly and serve immediately with wasabi and soy sauce.

About the Authors

Dorine Lam, MS, MPH, RDN

is a registered dietitian and holistic clinical nutritionist specializing in Adrenal Fatigue Syndrome (AFS) and natural hormonal balancing. She received her Bachelor of Science degree in dietetics, Master's degree in public health in nutrition, and Master of Science degree in nutrition from Loma Linda University, California. She is also an anti-aging health practitioner, board certified by the American Academy of Anti-Aging Medicine. She coauthored the books *Adrenal Fatigue Syndrome: Reclaim Your Energy and Vitality with Clinically Proven Natural Programs, Estrogen Dominance,* and numerous articles on AFS. Her personal research and writing focuses on the dietary aspect of hormonal imbalance and adrenal fatigue. She is wife of Dr. Lam and is an integral part of the nutritional coaching team helping people overcome AFS.

Dr. Michael Lam, MD, MPH, ABAAM,

is a Western-trained physician specializing in nutritional and anti-aging medicine. Dr. Lam received his Bachelor of Science degree from Oregon State University and his Doctorate of Medicine degree from the Loma Linda University School of Medicine in California. He also holds a Master's degree in public health. He is board certified by the American Board of Anti-Aging Medicine, where he has also served as a board examiner. Dr. Lam was first to coin the term ovarian-adrenal-thyroid (OAT) hormone axis and to describe its imbalances. He has written six books: *Adrenal Fatigue Syndrome: Reclaim Your Energy and Vitality with Clinically Proven Natural Programs, Advanced Symptoms of Adrenal Fatigue Syndrome: A Metabolic Perspective, Central Nervous System Disruptions and Adrenal Fatigue Syndrome, The 5 Proven Secrets to Longevity, Beating Cancer with Natural Medicine, How to Stay Young and Live Longer,* and *Estrogen Dominance.* In 2001, Dr. Lam established *DrLam.com* as a free, educational website on evidence-based alternative medicine for the public and for health professionals. His personal, telephone-based nutritional coaching services have enabled many around the world to regain control of their health using natural therapies.

Dr. Justin Lam, ABAAHP, FMNM

is a metabolic nutritionist specializing in Adrenal Fatigue. He earned his Bachelor of Science degree in Biology from Pacific Union College, California and his Doctor of Medicine degree from Ross University School of Medicine, a fully U.S. accredited medical school in Dominica. He is a diplomate in Anti-Aging Medicine and board certified by the American Board of Anti-Aging Health Practitioners. He has completed a fellowship in Metabolic and Nutritional Medicine from the American Academy of Anti-Aging Medicine in educational partnership with George Washington University. He is a lifestyle health coach certified by the Metabolic Medical Institute. He is the son of Michael Lam, MD, recognized pioneer in Adrenal Fatigue, and is an integral part of Dr. Lam's worldwide telephone-based nutritional coaching team. His research focuses on the neuroendometabolic ramifications of exertion intolerance.

Dr. Carrie Lam, MD,

graduated with a Bachelor of Science from Pacific Union College, California, and earned her Doctor of Medicine degree from Loma Linda University, California. Her career focus is on functional medicine and integrative primary care, with an emphasis on anti-aging, lifestyle, and nutrition. She is the daughter of Dr. Michael Lam.

Dr. Lam's Adrenal Recovery Series

Dr. Lam has created a miniseries of books as well as single chapter ebooks for your use to aid in your recovery. *Adrenal Fatigue Syndrome* is the comprehensive guidebook; the miniseries and single chapter ebooks allow you to have "select" sections that support and enhance your education and recovery. They are easier to carry with you for reference, allowing you to bookmark specific sections during your recovery program.

THE MINI SERIES OF PAPERBACK AND EBOOKS INCLUDE:

Psychology of Adrenal Fatigue Syndrome: How the Mind-Body Connection Affects Your Recovery

Central Nervous System Disruption and Adrenal Fatigue Syndrome

Anatomy of Adrenal Fatigue Syndrome: Clinical Stages 1–4

Natural Therapeutics to Adrenal Fatigue Syndrome: Proper Use of Vitamins, Glandulars, Herbs, and Hormones

Advanced Symptoms of Adrenal Fatigue Syndrome: A Metabolic Perspective

Dietary and Lifestyle Therapeutics to Adrenal Fatigue Syndrome: Your Personal Recovery Toolbox

Metabolic Complications of Adrenal Fatigue Syndrome

Estrogen Dominance: Hormonal Imbalance of the 21st Century (Expanded Version)

THE SINGLES SERIES OF EBOOKS INCLUDE:

Neuroendocrine Basis of Adrenal Fatigue Syndrome: The Physiology of Fatigue

Adrenal Crashes: How to Prevent and Recover Quickly

Diagnostic Testing for Adrenal Fatigue Syndrome: Everything You Need to Know

Adrenal Fatigue Syndrome Progression and Case Study: What is Coming Ahead

Your Constitution and Adrenal Fatigue Syndrome: How Your Genetic Makeup Can Affect Your Recovery

Travel Tips and Adrenal Fatigue Syndrome: How to Avoid Adrenal Crashes

Ovarian-Adrenal-Thyroid Axis Imbalance: Why Your Thyroid Medications May Not Be Working

7 Adrenal Recovery Mistakes: What Successful Recovery Avoid

Anti-aging and Adrenal Fatigue Syndrome:

Incorporating an Anti-aging Program Into Your Recovery

Myths of Adrenal Fatigue Syndrome: Separating the Facts from the Fiction

Individual copies can be ordered from www.DrLam.com as well as through online retailers.

Glycemic Appendix

Glycemic Index is a measure of how much blood sugar stress a food creates. Controlling blood sugar is one of the key pillars in a successful anti-aging diet. High blood sugar is a direct reflection of high sugar intake. Knowing what food to take that is low in sugar is important.

Below is a table of common foods and their glycemic index. These numbers use Glucose as a baseline, which is given a GI of 100. All the other values are relative to glucose.

To reduce blood sugar handling stress, concentrate on foods with an **index at or below 75.** This will help create a more even flow of glucose into the blood. If you are taking high glycemic index food like white bread, always try to mix it up low glycemic index food. If foods are mixed, the resulting index will be between the high and low values.

Recommended: GI < 60 | **Avoid:** GI > 60
Diabetes or hypoglycemia: avoid GI > 50

Legumes

Baked Beans, canned	68
Black Beans	30
Black Eyed Peas	42
Butter Beans	31
Chick Peas	33
Chick Peas, canned	42
Fava Beans	80
Kidney Beans	30
Kidney Beans, canned	52
Lentils, green	30
Lentils, red	25
Lima, baby, frozen	32
Pinto Beans	39
Soy Beans	18
Split Peas	32

Dairy Products

Ice Cream, regular	61
Ice Cream, low-fat	50
Milk, regular	27
Milk, skim	32
Yogurt, sugar	33
Yogurt, aspartame	14

Grains

Barley, pearled	25
Buckwheat (kasha)	54
Bulgar	47
Couscous	65
Cornmeal	68
Millet	71
Rice, brown	56
Rice, instant	85-91
Rice, white	70

Crackers

Graham Crackers	74
Rice Cakes	77
Rye Crispbread	67
Stoned Wheat Thins	68
Water Crackers	72

Cereals

All Bran	43
Bran Chex	59
Cheerios	75
Corn Bran	75
Corn Chex	83
Cornflakes	84
Cream of Wheat	71
Grapenuts	68
Life	66
Mueslix	60
Nutri Grain	66
Oat Bran	55
Oatmeal, regular	53
Oatmeal, quick	66
Puffed Wheat	74
Puffed Rice	90
Rice Chex	89
Rice Krispies	82
Shredded Wheat	69
Special K	54
Total	76

Pastas

Angel Hair	45
Bean Threads	26
Gnocchi	67
Pastas, brown rice	92
Pastas, refined	65
Pastas, whole grain	45
Star Pastina	38
Vermicelli	35

Snacks, misc.

Corn Chips	70
Fried Pork Rinds	OK
Olives	OK
Peanuts	10
Peanut M&M's	32
Popcorn	56
Potato Chips	55
Pretzels	82
Rice Cakes	77
Rich Tea Cookies	56
Vanilla Wafers	77

Vegetables

All green vegetables	0-30
Bean Sprouts	<50
Beets	64
Carrots	71-92
Cauliflower	<50
Corn	58
Eggplant	<50
All onions	<50
Parsnips	97
Peppers	<50
Potato, russet (baked)	90
Potato, instant mashed	83
Potato, fresh mashed	73
Potato, new, boiled	57
Potato, french fries	75
Radishes	<50
Sauerkraut	<50
Sweet Potato	54
Tomato	38
Water Chestnuts	<50
Yams	51
Yellow Squash	<50

Bread Products

Bagel	72
French Bread	96
Kaiser Roll	73
Melba Toast	71
Pita Bread	58
Pumpernickel Bread	49
Rye Bread	64
Rye Bread, whole	50
Stuffing	75
Tortilla, corn	70
Waffles	76
White Bread	95
Whole Wheat Bread	75

Fruits

Apple	39
Apple Juice	41
Apricots, dried	35
Bananas, ripe	60
Cantaloupe	65
Cherries	23
Grapefruit	25
Grapefruit Juice	49
Grapes	46
Kiwi	52
Mango	56
Orange	42
Orange Juice	51
Papaya	58
Peach	35
Pear	35
Pineapple	66
Pineapple Juice	43
Plum	29
Raisins	64
Strawberries	32
Watermelon	74

Adapted from D.J.A. Jenkins et. al., *American Journal of Clinical Nutrition*, Volume 34, 1981

Histamine Diet Appendix

1. Prepare and eat everything fresh from the allowed list

2. AVOID ready meals

3. AVOID food that has preservatives and artificial colorings

	AVOID	ALLOWED
Meat	Bacon Hot dogs ALL processed meats (salami, pepperoni, hot dogs) ALL left over cooked meets	Fresh meat (cooled, frozen immediately or fresh) Most fresh meats are low in histamine, with the exception of raw or cooked ground/chopped beef products.
Eggs	Raw egg white*	Egg yolk
Fish*	Anchovies Mackerel Mahi-mahi Sardines Smoked fish Tuna	Freshly caught fish Fresh fish are low in histamines, but improper fish handling can cause "scombroid poisoning" which tend to be very high in histamine.
Breads & Cereals	Wheat germ* Commercial products Products made with yeast and not allowed ingredients	Home made products with allowed ingredients and NO YEASTS
Legumes*	Garbanzo / Chickpeas Kidney beans Peanuts Soy (include miso, tofu)	All others

*****Histamine Trigger foods** - the food itself may not have histamine, but within some people, it can trigger histamine release.

 # Diamine Oxidase (DAO) blocker - DAO is the primary enzyme which metabolizes dietary histamine

	AVOID	**ALLOWED**
Nuts n Seeds*	Cashews Sunflower seeds Walnuts	All others
Dairy	Aged Cheese Buttermilk Cottage Cheese Goat cheese Kefir Milk Sour cream Sour milk Yogurt	Plain milk Ricotta Cheese Mascarpone Cheese Quark Butter Cream Cheese Cream Ice cream (w allowed ingredients) Milk substitutes (coconut milk, rice milk)
Fruits	Apricots Avocado Banana Citrus Fruits* Cranberry Date Figs Kiwi* Nectarine Papaya Peach Pineapple* Plums* Raisins, currants & sultanas Raspberries Strawberries	All others
Vegetables	Eggplant Pumpkin Sauerkraut Spinach Tomatoes*	All others

*Histamine Trigger foods - the food itself may not have histamine, but within some people, it can trigger histamine release.
Diamine Oxidase (DAO) blocker - DAO is the primary enzyme which metabolizes dietary histamine

	AVOID	ALLOWED
Condiments	Artificial dyes* Additives / Artificial preservatives* Chocolate / Cocoa Olives Pickles Soy sauce Vinegar or anything pickled in vinegar Commercial prepared syrups, fillings, frostings, sweets, candies Yeast	Most leafy herbs
Beverage	Beer# Champagne# Kombucha Wine# ALL tea# Energy drinks# Non-alcoholic beer and wines ALL flavored or carbonated drinks. All citric fruit juices	Plain milk Pure juices from allowed fruits and veggies Plain mineral water Plain carbonated water Coffee Hard Liquor: vodka, gin, white rum
Fats	Hydrogenized fats All fats with preservatives Margarine All packaged salad dressings and gravies	All others
Spices	Anise Cinnamon Cloves Curry powder Paprika Nutmey	All others
Herbs	Licorice*	

*Histamine Trigger foods - the food itself may not have histamine, but within some people, it can trigger histamine release.
Diamine Oxidase (DAO) blocker - DAO is the primary enzyme which metabolizes dietary histamine

Category Index

A

aches and pains, 89–90
acid
  alpha-linoleic, 101
  alpha-lipoic, 176
  omega-3 fatty, (see omega-3 fatty acid)
  carnosic, 82
  gallic, 111
  lactic, 20
  oxalic, 110, 189
  pantothenic, 176
  phytic, 121
adrenal breathing exercise, 39, 178
adrenal fatigue recovery, 208
Adrenal Fatigue Syndrome, (see AFS)
adrenaline, 34, 41
adrenals, 42, 57–58, 163
AFS (Adrenal Fatigue Syndrome), 3–5, 7–9, 33–34, 36, 42, 45, 57–58, 93–94, 97–98, 105, 135–36, 138–39, 163–64, 195, 207–9
  advanced, 34, 57–58, 136, 138, 139, 163, 177, 190, 195
  symptoms of, 3–5, 7, 42, 57, 90, 97–98, 136, 174, 209
aging, 78, 82, 110, 190
ailments, liver-related, 144
alcohol, 41, 58, 104
  excessive consumption, 144, 160
aldosterone, 58
  dysregulation, 138, 178
Aldosterone and Low Blood Pressure, 56, 58
Allergies, 19, 57, 79, 89, 93, 129, 132, 145, 151–52, 181, 190
  symptoms, 74, 90
allicin, 24, 146
almond, bitter, 119
alpha-linoleic acid, 101
alpha-lipoic acid, 176
alpha-tocopherol, 75
aluminum, toxicity of, 152
Alzheimer's disease, 20, 122, 159
anti-aging 146, 167, 210
amino acids, 27, 70, 158–59, 171–72, 176, 190, 204
  taurine, 42
  tyramine, 42
  tryptophan, 29, 36–37, 39–41, 75, 128
anthocyanins, 18, 20, 64, 111, 155
Anti-aging Program, 167, 209
antibacterial properties, 23, 24, 54, 65, 76
antifungal properties, 23, 24, 54, 65, 76
antiviral properties 18, 23, 24, 54, 127
anti-inflammatory properties, 9, 65, 122–23, 153, 154, 192, 201, 206
antinutrients, 121

antioxidants, 6, 9, 11, 14, 15, 16, 18, 20, 22, 27, 30, 51, 54, 64–66, 68, 72, 74, 75, 79, 80, 103, 111, 112, 123, 125, 128, 132, 146, 153–55, 160, 172, 176, 181, 183, 186, 188, 190, 192, 197, 198, 199, 202, 204
anxiety, 3, 8, 41, 42, 45, 57, 67, 68, 78, 90, 112, 152, 185
arthritis, 22, 57
  rheumatoid, 90
asparagine, 172

B

bacteria, 76, 98, 104, 106, 122,128, 139, 152, 199, 201
  "friendly", 19, 28, 103, 111,
  beneficial, 108–9, 129,
basal metabolic rate, 97
batatins, 65
B-complex vitamins, 106, 110, 150, 174, 178, 181
beta-carotene, 15, 66, 101, 123
beta-glucan, 130, 202
beta-lain, 144
bile, 30
birth defects, 24, 78
bloating, 49, 90, 97–98, 100, 105–6, 114, 121–22, 163
blood-brain barrier, 9
blood pressure, 7, 19, 42, 57–61, 82, 138, 178
blood sugar, 3–4, 6, 27, 34, 36, 37, 39, 40, 41, 45, 46, 54, 72, 97, 116, 122, 130, 132, 174, 176, 186,192 195, 197, 199, 210
  low, 4, 8, 42, 45, 97
  stabilize, 9, 34, 54,132, 206
bone marrow, 138, 178
bones, 13, 46, 62, 83, 167–68, 179
bowel movements, normal, 158
brain, 18, 20, 34, 37, 39, 41, 67, 78, 82, 111, 155, 159, 171, 176, 197, 199, 206
brain fog, 3, 42, 89, 97
brain functions, 51, 199
brain health, 72, 81, 186
breakfast, 32, 36, 39, 187
breathing exercises, adrenal, 39, 178
bromelain, 120

C

caffeine, 40, 42, 139, 192, 197
  free, 40
  jitters, 192
cage-free birds, 128
calcium, 6–7, 16, 37, 39, 46, 62, 70, 72, 76 83, 110, 118, 174–75, 178, 181, 185, 189, 198, 201, 204

calories, 14, 80, 163, 171, 178, 183, 199–200, 202, 206
cancer, 20, 30, 70, 79, 100, 122, 129, 132, 145, 151–52, 167, 190
   tumor, 16, 18, 159, 202
candida, 23, 97
carbohydrates
   complex, 8, 28, 76, 121, 176
   high-impact, 6
   low-glycemic-index, 41
carcinogenic toxins, 80
carcinogens, 172
carnosic acid, 82
carotenes, 128, 189
   beta-, 30, 123
carotenoids, 64, 112, 123, 154, 171, 176, 181
catabolic state diet, 164
catechins, 123, 192
cells, 15–16, 18, 46, 58, 76, 80, 106, 109, 153, 164, 172, 174, 177, 197, 201
charcoal, activated, 141
chelation, 152, 159
chemotherapy, 127
cholesterol, 8, 16, 18, 29, 46, 70, 101, 113, 118, 128, 178, 204
choline, 132, 144, 199
circulation, 46, 168, 176
civilization, early, 178
cleanses, 132, 135–36
   juice/soup, 138
cognitive function, 7, 29, 197
cognitive performance, 82
colds, 76, 168, 188
collagen, 15, 83, 146, 163, 164
colon, 76, 98, 120, 132, 200
coma, 40, 60
compounds, 11, 15, 23, 49, 70, 74, 80, 84, 109, 111, 117, 201
constipation, 62, 90, 97, 105–7, 113–14, 129, 139, 158, 163
contamination, 29, 151
cortisol, 3, 58, 148, 192
crops, genetically modified, 64, 81, 102, 128, 175
cyanogenic glycosides, 119

D

damage
   DNA, 149
   eyes, 123
   free radical, 18
   organ, 57
   repair, 120
   repair oxidative, 154
decaffeinated
   drinks, 42
   green teas, 40
degeneration, macular, 15, 181, 189–90
dehydration, 58, 60
   fluid depletion, 138, 178

delta-tocopherol, 75
dementia, 78, 155
dental hygiene, poor, 98
deodorant, natural, 152
depression, 42, 57, 67, 78, 193
dermatological disorders, 90
detox, 80, 134–36, 138-39, 160, 201
detoxifier, 28, 132, 152, 183
detoxify, 104, 140
detoxification, 70, 72, 149, 163, 172
detoxing properties, 168
DHA, 10, 81
diabetes, 6, 22, 66, 114–15, 145, 151, 155, 192–93, 201
diarrhea, 90, 105–6, 129, 139, 158, 183
diet,
   GAPS, 12, 104, 105
   gluten-free, 193
   histamine, 36
   rotational diet 93, 104
digest, 28, 40, 48, 70, 90, 97, 105, 108, 121, 138, 140, 167, 169, 173
digestion, 84, 97, 103, 109–11, 113, 115, 120, 131, 156, 158, 168, 180, 185
digestive imbalance, 96–97
digestive system, 90, 139, 150, 159, 164
   breakdown, 162, 164
digestive tract, 8, 28, 65, 81, 105–6, 108, 115, 120, 129, 132, 158, 167, 200
   healthy, 111
diseases, 4, 74, 101
   cardiovascular, 202
   celiac, 193
   chronic, 30, 164
   gum, 122
   heart disease, 30, 98, 100, 155, 201
   mad cow, 102
   progressive eye, 15
   respiratory, 98
dysbiosis, 97, 105

E

ECM, extracellular matrix, 164, 168
edema, 138, 178
energy, 4, 8, 13, 29, 33–34, 40, 42, 129, 136, 144, 150, 174–76, 178, 192, 207–8
   energy levels, 150, 184
   energy production, 46, 62, 174, 197, 200
environment, 83, 135
enzymes, 80, 103, 120–21, 134, 138–40, 146, 167, 176, 207
   digestive, 97, 105, 120, 139
   proteolytic, 120
epinephrine, 84, 126
ergothioneine, 16
estrogen dominance, 175, 204
expectorant, 76, 209

F

fat, 2–5, 8, 22, 27, 30, 34, 36, 40, 70, 101, 105, 112, 125, 178–79, 202
   healthy, 5, 22, 29, 40, 42, 118, 167
   monounsaturated, 22, 29
   polyunsaturated, 101
   saturated fat, 29, 46, 101–2
fatty acids, 102
   omega-3, 10, 37, 48, 66–67, 80–81, 101, 126, 132, 154, 168, 186, 206
   omega-6, 81, 118, 186
   short-chain, 106
fermentation, 103, 108, 204
fermented cuisine, unique, 103
fiber, 8, 14, 15, 18, 27, 30, 84, 109, 110, 111, 115, 118, 120, 132, 171, 186, 189, 199, 200, 201, 202, 206
   dietary, 14, 112, 114, 129, 130, 176, 206
   indigestible, 108
   insoluble, 158, 198
   soluble, 22, 76, 115, 130, 183
flavonoids, 24, 72, 123, 154–55, 176, 197, 201
flavonols, 183, 192
fluid depletion, 138, 178
folate, 14, 24, 27, 78, 132, 189, 206
folic acid, 16
foods, 5, 6, 22, 36, 37, 41, 61, 89, 90, 92-4, 97-8, 100-1, 105, 114, 123, 125, 130, 138, 151, 154, 158, 164, 167, 169, 171, 174, 183, 197
   alkaline, 168
   allergenic, 36
   altered, 101
   breakfast, 37
   comfort, 28
   complex, 97
   complex-carbohydrate-rich, 34
   decontaminate, 151
   digested, 164
   digest raw, 169
   effective, 160
   fermented, 103-4, 139
   fried, 125
   gluten-containing, 92
   high-glycemic, 36, 40, 210
   high-protein, 171
   histamine, 212-4
   Immune-Boosting, 162, 168
   low glycemic, 34, 210
   microbial-rich, 104
   miracle, 54
   non-nutritious, 125
   nourishing, 167
   nutrient-dense, 201
   organic, 101
   processed, 92, 97
   plant-based, 175, 206
   processed, 92, 97
   raw, 169
   salty, 60
   sensitivities, 36, 89–90, 93, 98, 105, 120, 193
   soy-derived, 204
   spicy, 42
   sugary, 8
   sugar-laden junk, 5
   super, 23, 28
   unhealthy processed, 200
free radicals, 15, 62, 65, 82, 120, 135, 144, 172, 182
frequency of meals, 2, 5
fructans, 76
fructo-oligosaccharides, 139
fructose, 7, 15, 98, 192, 198
fruits, 5, 9, 32, 34, 39–40, 46, 64, 89, 94, 97–8, 100, 118, 139, 141, 153
   fresh organic, 136

G

gallic acid, 111
GAPS, 104-5
gastrointestinal, 90, 130,
gastrointestinal tract, 97, 103–4, 122, 138, 163, 164,167, 169, 177–78
genetic makeup, 209
genetically modified, GMO, 64, 81, 102, 128, 138, 175
glandulars, herbs, and hormones, 209
glucose, 3, 84, 176, 192, 195, 198
glutathione, 144, 172
gluten, 46, 92, 109, 130, 182, 193
   allergies, 78, 155
   protein structures, 92
   sensitivity, 116, 130, 193
gluten-free, 46, 193
   alternatives, 92, 113,
   diet, 193
glycemic
   high, 36, 40
glycemic Index, 130, 174, 187, 192, 210-2
   high, 210
   low, 9, 41, 65, 210
grains, 27, 40, 92, 94, 121, 200
   easily digested, 109
   gluten-free, 130
   hearty, 37
green teas, 40
greens, 182
   beet, 142, 144–45
   leafy, 168
   mixed, 116
   mustard, 39
   rhubarb, 141
growth hormone, 3
   natural, 173
gut, 28, 76, 98, 100, 103–4, 106, 109, 117, 138
gut flora, 108, 158
   restoring healthy, 106
gut lining, 90

H

Harman alkaloids, 40
hair pigment melanin, 62
heal, 7, 93, 103–5, 144
heal or harm, 7, 93, 103–5, 144
healing, 7, 57, 104–5, 164, 207
Healing Diet, 96, 104
health, 6–7, 54, 61, 74, 76, 101, 105, 164, 169, 207
   benefits, 6, 18, 20, 22, 24, 28, 54, 75, 102, 125, 183, 197, 202
heartburn, 42
heart palpitations, 41, 57, 136
heart rate, 68, 89
heavy metals, 6, 65, 152, 159
   remove, 146, 152, 159
Helicobacter pylori, 199
hemoglobin production, 113
hemorrhoids, 158
hens, 92, 128, 184
herbal teas, 40
HFCS (high fructose corn syrup), 5–7, 64, 125
high fructose corn syrup. See HFCS
Himalayan pink salt, 61
histamines, 36, 74, 90, 168, 212-4
hormones, 3, 36–37, 39–40, 54, 58, 84, 101, 128, 138, 168
HPA (hypothalamus-pituitary-adrenal), 33
hypertension, 40
hypoglycemia
   reactive, 3–4, 34
   symptoms of, 3
hypoglycemia and dietary guidance, 3-7
hyponatremia, 60
hypothalamus-pituitary-adrenal (HPA), 33
hypothyroid, 9, 20, 22, 70, 78, 80, 114, 116, 120, 142, 152, 173, 182, 203–4
hybrid pea, 14

I

IBS (Irritable Bowel Syndrome), 96, 98, 105, 127, 183, 193
immune system, 7, 11, 15–16, 75–76, 78, 80, 90, 93, 111, 113, 146, 150, 183, 185, 202
Immune-Boosting Foods, 162, 168
inflammation, 76, 80–81, 93, 98, 122, 149, 168, 178, 193
insomnia, 31–33, 35, 41–42, 45, 47, 49, 51, 53–54, 57, 68, 74, 136, 185
insomnia and dietary guidance, 33-42
insulin, 3, 39, 81, 130, 132, 173
   balance, 4
   output, 9
   resistant, 6, 22, 197
   regulation, 34
intestines, 108, 110–11, 114, 120, 132, 193
iodine, 184, 206
   deficiency, 184
   intake, 184

iron, 6–7, 16, 27, 62, 68, 70, 122, 153, 175, 181, 186, 189, 200, 202, 204
Irritable Bowel Syndrome. See IBS

J

juice fasts, 136
juice/soup cleanses, 138
juicer, 153
   regular centrifuge, 141
   juicing machine, best, 141
juicing, 140–42
Juicing, Vegetable, Preparation Tips for, 141
juicing cleanse, 136

K

kaempferol, 24, 27, 123, 190, 192, 199, 201

L

lactic acid, 20
lactose, 28, 106
lactucarium, 68, 78
lifestyle, 4, 80, 135, 163
   healthy, 80
low blood pressure, 56–58, 60, 65, 67, 73, 75, 77, 79, 81, 83
Low Blood Pressure and Dietary Guidelines, 56, 58
low heat cooking, 74, 103
L-tryptophan, 171
lutein, 123, 153, 189
lycopene, 79, 125
lysine, 27, 173

M

macronutrients, science of, 138
magnesium, 7, 18, 24, 27, 36–37, 39, 41, 46, 54, 62, 70, 174–75, 178, 197–99, 204
manganese, 27, 68, 154, 176, 185, 189, 199–200, 204
meal plans, 5, 89, 93
   permanent, 36
melatonin, 9, 29, 36–37, 39–40, 67, 84, 171
menopause, 175, 204
mercury, 10–11, 81, 126, 152, 159
   levels, high, 126
   poisoning, 152
   risk, 10–11
metabolic syndrome, 115, 192–93
metabolic system imbalances, 34
metabolically neutral state, 163–64
micronutrients, 34
Mind-Body Connection, 209
minerals, 13–14, 37, 39, 41, 61, 68, 70, 103, 106, 109, 113, 118, 138, 140, 201
mitochondria, 109, 144, 174
molecules, 90, 92, 102, 109, 144
   small bioactive protein, 81
MRSA (methicillin-resistant Staphylococcus aureus), 23
muscles, 9, 13, 40–41, 163

N

nasunin, 18
nausea, 3, 5, 106, 127, 136
nerves, 40–41, 72, 90, 152, 174, 198
nervous system, 40, 62, 126, 172
    autonomic, 34, 57
    functions, 84
    parasympathetic, 178
neurodegeneration, 82
Neuroendocrine, Basis of Adrenal Fatigue Syndrome, 209
neuroendocrine
    ramifications, 208
    response mechanism, 163
neurological conditions, 68
neurotransmitter releases, excessive, 34
neurotransmitters, 29, 199
niacin, 16, 29, 118, 176, 185, 202, 206
    levels, 29
non-GMO products, 102
Non-GMO Project Verified seal, 175
norepinephrine, 34, 84, 199
nutrients, 7, 14, 16, 24, 27, 52, 64, 68, 70, 74, 100–101, 108, 109, 110, 112, 120, 121, 125, 126, 138–39, 148, 153, 155, 160, 168, 174, 176, 177, 178, 185, 186, 189
    absorption of, 70, 103, 106, 115, 158, 167, 193
    fat-soluble, 22
    sulfur-containing, 80
    vital, 72, 138, 148, 167, 177, 199

O

OAT (ovarian-adrenal-thyroid), 207, 209
oil, 102-3
    rancid, 100
oxalic acid, 110, 189
osteoporosis, 175, 204
osteotrophic activity, 182
ovarian-adrenal-thyroid (OAT), 207, 209

P

pantothenic acid, 176
parchment paper, 54, 80, 199, 201
Parkinson's disease, 122
pasteurizing, 128
pathogens, foodborne, airborne, 122, 151
pectin, 117, 132, 183
peptides, 11, 81
pesticides, 81, 101, 128, 135–36, 153
phosphorus, 16, 27, 37, 39, 70, 109, 176, 181, 199, 204, 206
phytic acid, 121
phytoestrogens, 204
phytonutrients, 72, 106, 149, 154, 185, 192
phytosterols, 70
polyphenols, 24, 74
pork, 94, 167, 211
potassium, 16, 18, 36, 39, 54, 58, 60, 68, 70, 72, 113, 181, 185, 198–99, 201–2

poultry, 5, 101
prebiotic, 109, 111, 129–30
premenstrual symptoms (PMS), 112, 175, 190
probiotics, 103–4, 106, 134, 138–39
probiotic use, excessive, 139
processed, 103, 156,
    desserts, 6, 42
    flour, 118
    food, 92, 97, 200
    fruit, 34
    meats, 41, 212
protein, texturized vegetable (TVP), 93
protein, 2–5, 8, 16, 27, 28, 29, 34, 36–37, 40–42, 46, 118, 120–21, 126, 129, 167–68, 176, 178, 206
    acidic meat, 168
    allergy-triggering, 19
    complete source, 27, 173
    dense vegetable, 121
    excellent source of, 39, 200
    fragment, 11
    high protein snack, 39
    high-quality, 29, 200
    plant-based, 206
    texturized vegetable, 93

Q

quercetin, 74, 123, 183, 190, 192, 199, 201

R

radicals, free, 15, 62, 65, 82, 120, 135, 144, 172, 182
relax, 29, 39, 41, 46, 171
Restless Leg Syndrome (RLS), 41, 54
rice paper, 203–4
rotational diet plan, 93, 104

S

salt, 58-61, 138, 172, 178, 184
    cravings, 19, 138, 178
    trace minerals in sea salt, 61
salting, 58
seasonal affective disorder, 65
seaweed, 60, 184, 206
selenium, 7, 11, 76, 146, 189, 198, 202, 204
serotonin, 29, 36–37, 40–41, 84, 171
silicon, 37, 39, 83
sleep
    daytime sleepiness, 54
    sleep-maintenance insomnia. See SMI
    sleep-onset insomnia. See SOI
SMI (sleep-maintenance insomnia), 32–34, 39, 77
sodium, 19, 58, 60, 164, 178
SOI (sleep-onset insomnia), 32–33, 37, 39, 179
soluble fiber, 22, 76, 115, 130, 158, 183
soups, 8, 92, 105, 107, 114, 134, 138–39, 149, 156, 159, 162, 167–68, 180
    benefit, 138
    cooked, 114
    drinking, 167
    hot, 167

soups *(continued)*
   mutton, 168
   nutrient-dense, 136
   pureed, 167
   reheat, 149
   thick, 8
steaming, 93
stimulants, 40–42
   adrenal, 36
stir-frying, 93, 103, 154
stomach acid, 49
stools, 114–15, 198
stress, 7, 12, 67, 174, 195
   adrenal, 6
   oxidative, 111
   stressed out, 192
   stressful, 7, 33
sugary
   foods, 8, 42
   drinks 33, 164
sulfur, 80, 160
superoxide dismutase, 144
Supplementing with Probiotics and Enzymes, 139
supplements, 75, 97
   adrenal, 138
   antioxidant, 154

T

taste buds, 60
taurine, 42
teas, 136
   detox, 139
   herbal, 140
texturized vegetable protein (TVP), 93
thiocyanates, 201
thyroid, 97, 109, 201
   function, maintaining healthy, 184, 206
   medications, 33, 209
toxins elimination, 28, 30, 68, 80, 101, 132, 135–36, 139, 144, 149, 160, 164, 172, 184
traditional Chinese medicine, 110, 167
tryptophan, 29, 36–37, 39–41, 75, 128
turmeric, 159, 168, 171
TVP (texturized vegetable protein), 93
tyramine, 42

U

ulcers, 201
   gastric, 117
   ulcers, peptic, 20
ulcerative colitis, 130
ultraviolet radiation, 146

V

velocity of blood sugar drop, 3
vitamin A, 15, 20, 24, 30, 68, 101, 102, 122, 123, 171, 206
vitamin B (B-complex), 11, 24, 29, 70, 110, 118, 132, 150, 174, 178, 181, 199
vitamin B1 (thiamin), 16, 132, 204, 206
vitamin B2 (riboflavin), 16, 132, 206
vitamin B3 (niacin), 132, 206
vitamin B6, 36–37, 84, 112, 113, 132, 176, 199
vitamin B12, 199
vitamin C, 14, 15,16, 20, 37, 66, 111, 112, 113, 120, 122, 146, 148, 150, 153, 154, 171, 172, 176, 181, 182, 185, 186, 189, 199, 206
vitamin D, 16, 54, 65, 82, 83, 101
vitamin D3, 159
vitamin E, 20, 27, 70, 75, 101, 102, 110, 112, 118, 139, 172, 174, 182, 186, 198, 206
vitamin K, 24, 72, 102, 108, 182, 201, 206
vitamins, 14, 54, 103, 106, 113, 121, 138, 140, 150, 177, 183, 199
   antioxidant, 20, 75
   synthesize, 123, 171

W

water
   drinking, 28, 60, 150
   ice, 72, 83, 172
   room temp. spring, ideal for drinking, 164
water consumption and healing, 164
weight loss, 9, 13, 22, 24, 78–79, 106, 120, 132, 135, 145, 151, 155, 183, 190
wrinkles, 15, 146, 189

Y

yoga exercises, 32, 39

Z

zeaxanthin, 123, 153, 189
zinc, 7, 16, 27, 34, 37, 75, 146, 154, 178, 181, 186, 189, 197, 204, 206

Food Index

A

acorn squash, 56, 66, 114
Acorn Squash, 56, 66
Acorn Squash Kale Soup, 96, 114
agave nectar, 6–7, 14, 17, 19, 50, 82, 153, 172, 185, 197
aged cheeses, 42
algae, 60, 184
allspice, 181
almond butter, 34, 40–41
Almond Meal Pizza, 96, 118
Almond Milk, 44
almond milk, 32, 40–41, 44–45, 51, 53, 92, 113, 156, 182
    unsweetened, 148
almonds, 27, 34, 37, 41, 46–47, 52, 74, 89, 93, 103, 108, 118–19, 168, 184, 197
    drying, 119
    meal, 118, 126
    raw, 46, 108
    substituting, 74
    toasted, 153
amaranth, 94
amino Soyu, 116
anise, star, 48
Apple Carrot Oatmeal, 32, 45
Apple Nachos, 196–97
apples, 2, 5, 20, 23, 32, 34, 39–40, 45–46, 51, 64, 67, 114, 183, 185, 197–98
    Fuji, 197
    Granny Smith and Red Delicious, 183, 197
    Juice, 67
    medium-sized, 10, 159, 183
    medium-sized green, 67
    medium-sized red, 67
    slices, 198
    strips, 45
    tart, 159
Apple Sandwiches, 196, 198
Apple Walnut Spring Green Salad, 56, 67
apricots, dried, 46
asparagus, 64, 96, 127, 129–30, 158, 162, 172, 193
Asparagus, Sauteed, 96, 129
Asparagus with Ginger-Miso Butter, 96, 127
Asparagus with Lemon-Basil-Yogurt Sauce, 172
avocados, 2, 5, 22, 98, 206

B

Baked Chicken with Honey-Mustard Sauce, 56, 82
Baked Lemon-Almond Cod, 96, 126
Baked Stuffed Pumpkin Bowl, 162, 171
Baked Sweet-Potato Rounds, 56, 65
baking soda, 118
bananas, 36, 40, 148

barley, 92, 94, 130, 158
    pearl, 19
    sprouted, 130
Barley, Date Asparagus Salad, 134, 158
basil, 62, 113, 132, 172, 193, 199, 206
    leaves, 113
    pesto, 122
    slivers, 132
Basil Cream Sauce, 56, 62
bay leaf, 24, 79, 117, 136, 138
bean sprouts, 121, 206, 211
beans, 5, 8, 10, 83, 94, 100, 121
    black, 185
    frozen edamame, 175
    garbanzo, 122, 200
    green, 56, 83, 96, 123, 155–56, 182, 193
    kidney, 94
    lima, 94
    mung, 94, 184
    navy, 94
    red, 110
    white, 10
beef, 101–2, 105, 116, 167, 180, 203
    ground beef
        lean, 68, 180
        marinated, 109
        organic, 204
beet, 72, 94, 144
    greens, 94, 144–45
    root, 142, 144–45, 179
bell peppers, 27, 74, 79, 112, 132, 144–45, 151, 156, 181, 190
    green, 112
    orange, 112
    red, 24, 27, 112, 142, 159
    yellow, 27, 79, 112, 132, 144–45, 151, 181, 190
berries, 111
beverages, 5, 58, 164
    kefir, 104
black-eyed pea, 8, 94, 210
Black-eyed Pea and Kale Soup, 2, 8
Blended Tomato Soup, 56, 79
blueberries, 23, 111
bok choy, 9, 120, 154
Bok Choy, Stir-fried, Baby, 134, 154
Bok Choy Cherry Salad, 2, 9
Bok Choy Pineapple Salad, 96, 120
bone marrow, 178
Braised Red Cabbage and Apple, 2, 20
Brazil nuts, 93
Bread
    Buckwheat, 9
    Ezekiel, 92

breakfast, 32, 36, 39, 187
    nutrient-dense recipes, 36
broccoli, 70, 149, 154, 160, 189, 201
Broccoli Leek Soup, 134, 149
broths, 105, 112, 138, 162, 167–68, 178–80
Brown Rice with Edamame, 173
brown sugar, 20, 66–67, 110, 115, 174, 184–85
Brown-Sugar Garlic Chicken, 162, 174
Brussels sprouts, 80, 201
buckwheat, 46, 94, 130
Buckwheat, Apple Granola Bar, 32, 46
butter, 8, 12–13, 15–16, 20, 50, 66, 68, 74, 83–84, 102–3, 117, 126, 127, 130, 149, 156, 159, 175, 182, 183, 189, 197, 213
    almond butter, 34, 40–41
    ginger-miso, 96, 127
    sunflower, 197–98
butternut squash, 159, 175, 181
Butternut Squash Edamame Casserole, 162, 175

C

cabbage, 20, 78, 116, 152, 154–55, 182
    green, 20
    Napa, 182
    red, 20, 56, 78, 142, 152, 155
cacao, 197
carrot, 19, 24, 30, 45, 74, 79, 114, 116, 132, 141, 142, 144–45, 151, 179, 181, 190, 206
Carrot Thyme Soup, 134, 151
cashew, 41, 62, 89, 93, 108, 171
    cream, 144–45
    raw, 62, 144–45
    soaked, 168
    sticks, 106
cauliflower, 56, 70, 100, 160, 199
Cauliflower Strips, 196, 199
cayenne pepper, 50, 112, 147, 206
celery, 8, 10, 13, 22, 27, 79, 117, 132, 144–45, 151, 181, 190
    stalks, 112, 117, 122, 132, 142, 144–45, 151, 179
Celery and Almond Salad, 2, 27
Celery Soup, 96, 117
cheese, 113, 128, 162, 175, 182, 193, 199
    aged, 42
    Asiago, 42
    cottage cheese, 13, 36, 128
    cream, 12–13
    hard, 42
    making, 204
    mozzarella, 118, 182
    organic, 168
    Parmesan, 28, 42, 117, 130, 193
    raw, 113
    Romano, 42, 193
    sharp cheddar, 182
    shredded, 175
cherries
    dried sweet, 9

regular, 37
sour Montmorency, 37
tart, 9, 37, 46, 54
Chia Coconut Milk Pudding, 32, 41, 48
chia seeds, 48
    golden, 48
Chicken, Brown Sugar Garlic, 162, 174
chicken, 23, 34, 56, 62, 76, 82, 94, 101, 105, 116, 138, 167, 174, 176, 179
    bone-in, 179
    breasts, 23, 82
    broth, 13, 105, 138, 168, 177–79
    free-range, 13, 68, 76
    free-range/pastured, 138
    meat, 179
        cooked, 122
    pieces, 174
    stock, 13, 138
    thighs, 19, 62, 76, 82, 174
Chicken, Teriyaki, 2, 19
Chicken Hash-Brown Casserole, 162, 176
Chicken in Basil Cream Sauce, 56, 62
chickpeas, 37, 94, 122, 200
chili, 159, 189
chilies, 68, 160, 175–76
    crushed red, 17, 65, 159, 160, 175, 176
    minced fresh, 68
chili sauce, 77
chipotle powder, 64
chives, 149
chocolate, 5, 41, 197
cilantro, 68, 75, 152, 160
cinnamon, 46, 107, 114, 181, 183, 192, 214
    sticks, 48
coconut, 48, 54, 103
    dried, 54
    flakes, unsweetened, 197
    flour, 76
    milk, 48, 54
    oil, 44, 49, 51, 54, 62, 64, 68, 76, 81, 102, 123, 128, 171, 174, 182
    sugar, 48
cod
    Alaskan, 126
    fillet, 115
coffee, 6, 58
cookies, 54
    soaked granola, 5, 32, 54
coriander, 159
corn, 64, 81, 130, 156
    chips, 39
cornstarch, 12–13, 19, 113
corn syrup, 64
    high fructose, 5–6, 64, 125
cottage cheese, 36, 128
    low-fat, 13
couscous, 56, 75
Couscous with Vegetables, 56

crab, 93, 126
crackers, 10, 106
cranberries, 54
cranraisins, 47–48, 64, 158
cream, 2, 8, 12–13, 42, 56, 62, 144–45, 151, 168, 181, 190
    cashew, 144–45
    cheese, 12–13
    sour, 8
Cream Cheese Chicken Casserole, 2, 12
Cucumber Lime Cod Salad, 96, 115
Cucumber Mint Yogurt, 96, 106
Cucumber-Pineapple Salsa, 2, 17
cucumbers, 2, 115, 142, 150
    English, 106, 115
    Japanese, 206
    shredded, 116
    sticks, 206
Cucumber Tomato Red Onion Salad, 134, 150
cumin, 50, 159
    seed, 8
Curried Butternut Squash and Apple Soup, 134, 159
curry powder, 159, 160

D

dairy products, 36, 98, 105, 167
date, 46, 94
    Madjool, 158
    sugar, 7
dessert, 111, 183
Detoxifying Beet Soup, 134, 144, 165
dill, 49, 206
Dilled Salmon Patties, 32, 49
dough, 47, 54, 118–19
dressing, 14, 67, 93, 120, 153, 158
    readymade, 9
drinks
    caffeinated, 33, 42
    carbonated, 214
    decaffeinated, 42
    energy, 42
    sugary, 33, 164, 214
duck, 94

E

edamame, 93, 113, 162, 173, 175
eggplant, 18, 75, 94, 211, 213
    Japanese, 118
eggs, 29, 34, 36, 49, 72, 76, 84, 92, 94, 101, 128, 175, 184, 189, 199
    large, 29, 76
    medium-sized, 29, 118
    organic, 128
    pasteurized, 128
    raw, 44, 128, 199
    vegetarian, 128
extra-virgin olive oil, 10, 14, 18, 28, 67, 70, 74, 78, 83, 103, 150, 160, 167, 175, 193
Ezekiel bread, 94

F

fennel, 50, 190
Festive Butternut Squash Soup, 162, 181
fillets
    cod, 115, 126
    mahi mahi, 17
    salmon, 81
fish, 5, 10, 17, 81, 93, 105, 115, 126, 152, 168, 186
    broth, 168
    fillets, 126
    freshwater, 94
    oily, 66
    saltwater, 10, 94
    sashimi (raw), 115
fish sauce, 68, 115, 121, 154, 203
    Vietnamese fermented, 103
flaxseeds, 37, 48, 50, 107, 148
Flaxseed Soup, 37, 96, 105, 107

G

Garbanzo and Zucchini Salad, 96, 122
Garbanzo Snacks, 37, 196, 200
garlic, 2, 8, 23–24, 27, 30, 74, 76, 79, 83–84, 132, 144–46, 149, 154, 168, 188–90
    clove, 24, 49, 68, 76, 79, 123, 132, 144–45, 190
    cloves, 19, 83, 146–47, 149, 154, 171, 188–89, 193, 202
    minced, 18, 160, 174
    powder, 65, 118, 128, 182, 200–201
    salt, 112, 120
Garlic, Ginger Lemon Drink, 134, 147
Garlic, Roasted, 56, 83, 162, 188
Garlic Tea, 134, 137, 146
garnish, 70, 73, 83, 112–15, 117, 120–21, 126, 132, 149, 152–53, 155, 160, 186, 190, 193
gelatin, 13
ginger, 9, 48, 81, 120–21, 125, 127, 144–45, 154, 168, 180, 188, 192
    grated fresh, 19, 125
    root, 147
Gluten-free Macaroni and Cheese, 162, 182
gluten-free
    macaroni, 162
    penne pasta, 193
    spaghetti, 28
granola, 54, 111, 198
    bars, 46, 47
grape juice, 5
Grated Zucchini Basil Soup, 96, 104, 132
Greek yogurt, 103, 172
Green Bean Potato Pine Nut Salad, 134, 155
Green Beans with Cherry Tomatoes, 96, 123
green onions, 8, 17, 76, 113, 116, 187
green peas, 14–15, 84, 173
greens, 182
    beet, 142, 144, 145
    mixed, 116
    rhubarb, 141
    salad, 10

Grilled Apple, 162, 183
Grilled Eggplant Fans, 2, 18

H

Harissa paste, 75
hash brown flakes, dehydrated, 49
hash browns, dehydrated, 175, 176
herbs, 33, 49, 93, 139, 151, 168, 207, 209
HFCS (high fructose corn syrup), 5–7, 64, 125
high fructose corn syrup (see HFCS)
hoisin sauce, 9, 78, 120, 155
honey, 6, 37, 51, 54, 81–82, 100, 107, 120, 125, 172–73, 184–85, 188, 192, 197, 201
   raw, 6, 37, 46, 51
Honey-Mustard Sauce, 56, 82
Honey Teriyaki Salmon, 56, 81

I

Italian parsley, 76, 122, 199
   fresh, 193

J

Japanese cucumber, 206
Japanese eggplants, 75
Japanese miso, 103
Japanese raw fish (sashimi), 115
Japanese rice sprinkles, 116
jicama, 94
   shredded, 115
juice, 9, 23–24, 37, 80–81, 136, 139, 172, 190
   apple, 67
   citrus, 173
   fresh apple, 67
   fresh lemon, 23, 28, 64, 70, 108, 122, 172
   fresh pineapple, 17
   lemon, 28
   vegetable, 34
juicer, 153
   regular centrifuge, 141
   juicing machine, best, 141
juicing, 140–42
Juicing, Vegetable, Preparation Tips for, 141
jujube, 166, 185

K

kale, 8, 22, 39, 72, 76, 114, 201
   bunch, 22
   raw, 201
Kale Chips, 39, 196, 201
Kale Salad with Avocado, 2, 22
Kale Sweet-Potato Chicken Patties, 56, 76
kamut, 94
kecup manis, 116
kefir, 104
kelp, 168, 184
Kelp Mung-Bean Porridge, 162, 184
ketchup, 125
Ketchup-Ginger Glaze, 96, 125
kiwis, 94

Korean Cold Noodles, 96, 116
Korean kimchi, 103

L

lamb, 101, 168
   soup, 168
lamb loin chops
   conventional, 101
   organic, 101
Lam's Beef Broth, 162, 180
Lam's Chicken Broth, 162, 177
leafy vegetables, dark green, 168
leeks, 2, 13, 24, 74, 113, 130, 171, 182
Leeks with Lemon and Garlic, 2
legumes, 8, 34, 121, 173
lemon
   juice, 10, 22–24, 28, 64, 67, 73, 108, 121, 126, 146–47, 158, 173, 198
   mixture, 24
   peel, 126
   rind, 172, 192
   wedges, 24, 126
   zest, 23, 24, 158, 172, 193
Lemon Basil Pasta, 2, 28
Lemon-Basil-Yogurt Sauce, 162, 172
Lemon Chicken Breasts, 2, 23
lemons, 2, 23–24, 28, 60, 72, 126, 146–47, 192
Lemon-Tahini Broccoli and Cauliflower, 56, 70
lentils, 94, 210
lettuce, 9–10, 68, 70, 78, 116, 120, 145, 151, 152
   butter, 68
   red-leaf, 206
   romaine, 20, 68, 78, 152
   mixed green, 22
Lettuce Chicken Cups, 56, 59, 68
lima beans, 94
lime, 27, 68, 78, 142, 160, 173, 201
   juice, 17, 27, 68, 160

M

macaroni, gluten-free, 182
mackerel, 126
mahi mahi, 2, 17, 126
Mahi Mahi with Cucumber-Pineapple Salsa, 2, 17
Maple Chipotle Corn and Asparagus Salad, 56, 64
maple syrup, 6, 9, 19, 64, 67, 70, 82, 108, 120, 172, 192, 197
marinade, 81
marinara sauce, 119
marinate, 17, 30, 62, 68, 176
Marinated Carrots with Mint and Garlic, 2, 30
meat, 5, 61, 68, 82, 115, 126, 167–68, 188, 200
milk, 39, 62, 92, 102, 106, 148, 197, 206
   almond, 32, 40–41, 44–45, 51, 53, 92, 113, 156, 182
   coconut, 48, 54
   camel's, 92
   chocolate, 41
   cow's, 92

grass-fed, 106
oat, 148
rice, 45, 148,
millet, 109, 130, 185, 200
Millet Jujube Porridge, 162, 166, 185
mint, 2, 15, 30, 60, 72, 106, 114, 130, 158, 186
    chopped, 186
    dried, 72
    fresh, 15, 19, 130
Mint Dressing, 134, 158
mirin (Japanese sweet rice wine), 81
miso, 42, 108, 127
Miso Dressing, 96, 108
monosodium glutamate / MSG, 138, 177
molasses, bootstrap, 54
mushroom extract, 8, 79, 112, 114, 129, 132, 144–45, 151–52, 181, 190
Mushroom Millet Porridge, 96, 109
mushrooms, 13, 16, 100, 109, 116, 168, 202–3
    button, 78
        can/jar/fresh, 12
        needle, 116
    oyster, 16
        king oyster, 16
    shiitake, 202
        fresh, 109
mustard, 64, 76, 82
    Dijon, 64, 67, 82
    greens, 39

N

Napa and Red Cabbage Salad, 134, 152
Noodle, Korean glass, 96, 116
nori, 206
Nut and Seed Mix, 32, 50
nutmeg, 114
nutritional yeast, 64, 114, 128, 200
nuts, 5, 34, 36, 41, 45–46, 50–52, 67, 70, 94, 98, 132, 144–45, 151, 178–79, 181
    macadamia, 94
    pine, 54, 62, 72–73, 78, 144–45, 152, 155, 159, 193
    roasted, 193
    pistachio, 37, 64, 93, 106
    presoaking, 52

O

oatmeal, 32, 35, 37–39, 45, 49, 51, 62, 128, 187
    gluten-free, 128
Oatmeal with Walnut and Apple, 35, 38, 51
oats, 39, 47, 51, 54, 130
    rolled, 46–47, 51, 54
oil
    canola, 102–3
    coconut, 44, 49, 51, 54, 62, 64, 68, 76, 81, 102, 123, 128, 171, 174, 182
    extra-virgin olive oil, 10, 14, 18, 28, 67, 70, 74, 78, 83, 103, 150, 160, 167, 175, 193
    flaxseed, 79, 129, 151–52, 167, 190
    grape seed, 12–13, 79, 83, 102–3, 132, 144–45, 149–51, 153, 159, 181, 190, 197, 201, 204
        reusing, 100
    sesame, 9, 14, 78, 103, 116, 120–21, 127, 152, 154–55
olives, 22, 29, 68, 98, 103, 171, 204
    black, 22, 28
onions, 13, 15, 24, 27, 72, 74, 112, 114, 132, 144–45, 150–51, 159, 181–82, 189–90, 203–4
    green/scallions/spring, 8, 17, 76, 113, 116, 187
    red, 15, 49, 7
    white, 62, 204
    yellow, 72, 84, 156, 186
Orange and Mint Peas, 2, 15
orange, 23, 36, 94, 211
    juice, 15, 125, 153
    peel, 15
oregano, 23, 74, 168, 199
oyster sauce, vegetarian, 9, 14, 78, 116, 120, 125, 155

P

paprika, 17, 70, 76, 80, 126, 153, 171, 176, 200
parsley, 10, 72, 74, 78, 117, 123, 126, 193, 199
    flat-leafed, 12, 123, 126
    Italian, 76, 122
pasta, 28, 42, 92, 105, 113, 193
    penne pasta, 193
    gluten-free, 193
patties, 77, 128
peanuts, 52, 93, 103
Pearl-Barley Risotto, 96, 130
pears, 89, 94, 162, 192
peas, 15, 94, 100, 121, 130, 182, 186
    black-eyed, 8, 210
    green, 84, 170
    hybrid pea, 14
    snow, 121
    sugar snap, 2, 14, 96, 100, 121
pecans, 56, 65, 67, 93, 197
pectin, 117, 132, 183
pepper
    bell, 27, 74, 79, 112, 132, 144–45, 151, 156, 181, 190
        green, 112
        orange, 112
        red, 24, 27, 112, 142, 159
        yellow, 27, 79, 112, 132, 144–45, 151, 181, 190
    black, 12, 23, 50, 64, 66, 74, 83, 121, 172, 200
    cayenne, 50, 112, 206
    chili, 8
    crushed, 8
    crushed red, 27, 128, 200
peppermint leaf, 139
pesto, 96, 122
Pesto, Garbanzo and Zucchini Salad, 96, 122
pickles, traditional American, 103
pimiento pieces, 112
pineapple, 120
    frozen, 17

Pineapple Salsa, 2, 17
poppy seeds, 74, 153
pork, 94, 167, 211
porridge, 109, 110, 162, 166, 184, 185
potatoes, 84, 105, 151, 156, 176, 181, 186, 190
    cubed, 155
    mashed, 109
    purple, 155
    red, 79, 112, 132, 144–45, 151, 181, 190
    sliced, 84
    sweet, 65, 149, 206
    white, 155
Potato Onion Frittata, 56, 84
Potato Pea Soup, 162, 186
pre-bedtime snacks, 36–37
presoaked nuts, 32, 51–52, 67, 79, 114, 132, 144–45, 151, 181
pumpkin, 39, 94, 171, 187, 213
    seeds, 34, 50, 75
Pumpkin Oatmeal, 162, 187
Pumpkin Seeds with Almond Milk, 32, 53

Q

quinoa, 2, 12–13, 27, 94, 130, 200
Quinoa, Celery and Almond Salad, 2, 27

R

radish, white, 115
raisins, 198
Red Bean and Black Sesame Seed Porridge, 96, 110
Red Cabbage, Romaine, Mushroom Salad, 56, 78
red onion, 18, 20, 68, 79, 132, 144–45, 150–51, 181, 190
rice, 72, 94, 105, 109, 117, 130, 171, 173
    bread, 92
    brown, 12, 19, 109–10, 162, 173, 187
    cooked, 72
    cooked long-grain, 171
    long-grain, 173
    milk, 45, 92, 148
    short-grain, 117
    wild, 12
Rice and Celery Soup, 96, 117
Rice Paper Wraps, 196, 202
rice paper wraps, 196, 202-3, 204
Roasted Bell Pepper Soup, 96, 112
Roasted Brussels Sprouts, 56, 80
Roasted Cauliflower, 134, 160
Roasted Garlic, 56, 83, 162, 188
Roasted Onions with Walnut Crumbs, 56, 74
Romaine and Mushroom Salad, 56, 78
romaine lettuce, 20, 68, 78, 152
root vegetables, 168
rosemary, 82
rose petals, dried, 184

S

salad, 9, 22, 67–68, 78, 99, 103, 120–21, 150–51, 155, 158, 201
    dressings, 70, 92, 103, 188
    greens, 10
    ingredients, 115
    spring mix, 67, 122, 142, 158, 202
salmon, 10, 81, 96, 125–26
    cans wild Alaskan, 49
    wild caught, 81
Salmon with Ketchup-Ginger Glaze, 96, 125
salsa, 17, 22
salt
    bamboo, 61
    Himalayan pink, 61
    table, 61, 184
Salty Snacks, 60
sauerkraut, German, 103
sauté, 15, 27, 83, 174, 186, 204
Sautéed Asparagus with Thyme, 96, 129
Sautéed King Oyster Mushrooms, 2, 16
sautéing, 102–3
scallions, 10, 27, 29, 76
sea bass, 126
seafood, pluses and minuses, 118, 126
sea salt, 28, 61, 76, 106, 114, 193, 206
    pinch, 54
    seasoned, 201
    substitute, 129, 132, 145, 151, 152, 181, 190
seasoning
    Italian, 118–19
    Spike, 16
seeds, 34, 37, 66, 98, 112–13, 115, 121, 132, 171
    chia, 41, 48
    flax, 37, 48, 50, 107, 148
    pumpkin, 34, 50, 75
    sesame, 70, 74, 121, 153, 155
    sunflower, 41, 46, 47, 50, 54, 75, 94, 103, 120, 155, 190, 198, 213
        butter, 197
sesame
    oil, 9, 14, 78, 103, 116, 120–21, 127, 152, 154–55
    seeds, 70, 74, 121, 153, 155
shrimp, 10, 93, 126
smoothies, 98, 162, 167
snacks
    bedtime, 36, 41
    best Snacks, 195–96
    convenient, 37
    good, 74
    great, 60
    light, 36
    overlook, 34
    packaged, 6
    portable, 5
    small, 4, 36
Soaked Granola Cookies, 32, 64
soups, 8, 104, 107, 112, 114, 117, 132, 144, 149, 151, 156, 159, 165, 167–68, 177, 180, 181, 186, 190

sourdough, English, 103
soy, 19, 36, 42, 81, 93, 108, 175
    fermenting, 108
    foods, 175, 204
    GMO, 175
    milk, 93, 204
    modified, 175
    products, 81
        fermented, 42
soybeans, 19, 103
    young, 175
soy sauce, 9, 14, 19, 42, 68, 81, 108, 121, 153, 176, 206
    gluten-free, 78, 116, 120
    sweetened, 116
    wheat-free, 19
Spaghetti Squash Edamame Casserole, 96, 113
spices, 8, 23, 48, 93, 151, 159, 168
spinach, 8, 22, 39, 78, 94, 114, 116, 128, 148, 153, 154, 189, 190, 204, 213
Spinach Fennel Soup, 162, 190
Spinach Patties, 96, 128
Spinach Strawberry Salad, 134, 153
Spinach with Eggs, 162, 189
Spinach Wraps, 196, 204
sprouts, bean, 121, 206, 211
squash, 94
    acorn, 66, 114
    butternut, 159, 175, 181
    spaghetti, 113
    summer, 29, 132, 182
    winter, 75
    yellow, 118, 211
star anise, 48
steaming, 93
stevia, 6, 115, 139, 192, 197
Stews, 162, 167
Stir-fried Baby Bok Choy, 96, 134
Stir-fried Bean Sprouts and Sugar Snap Peas, 96, 121
stir-frying, 93, 103, 154
strawberries, 36, 111, 148, 153
Strawberry Green Smoothie, 134, 148
sugar, 2, 5–8, 37, 40, 45, 48, 102, 105–6, 111, 125, 132, 139, 152, 197, 203
    brown, 20, 66–67, 110, 115, 174, 184–85
    date, 7
sugar snap peas, 2, 14, 96, 100, 121
Sugar Snap Peas with Wasabi Dressing, 2, 14
sunflower seeds, 41, 46, 47, 50, 54, 75, 94, 103, 120, 155, 190, 198, 213
    butter, 197
sweet potatoes, 65, 149, 206
Sweet Potato Rolls, 196, 206
Swiss chard, 8, 72, 114, 154
Swiss Chard Rolls, 56, 72–73

T

tahini, 70
tarragon, 193
tart cherries, 46
tea, 6, 76, 127, 134, 138–39
    caffeinated, 58
    caffeine-free, 40
    chamomile, 40, 49
    detox, 139
    drinkers, 40
    green, 33
    herbal, 40, 139
    soothing, 49
tea-like beverage, 168
teff, 94
Teriyaki Chicken with Summer Squash, 2, 19
teriyaki sauce, 19, 42
thyme, 23, 27, 65, 84, 96, 114, 129, 151, 156, 168, 171, 176
tofu, 42, 93, 168, 175, 203, 204, 212
    fermented (tempeh), 203, 204
    five spice, 202
tomato, 22, 62, 79, 118
    skin, 22
    paste, 118–19
    pieces, 22
    sauces, 118–19, 125
    sun-dried, 204
tomato-based foods, 42
tomatoes, 29, 74, 79, 120, 123, 125, 150, 171, 189
    cherry, 75, 96, 123
    diced, 8
    fresh, 8, 29, 146
    processed, 79
    red, 79
    sliced, 29
tree nuts, 89, 93, 118
trout, 10, 126
truffles, 94
tuna, 10–11, 37
    ahi, 126
    albacore, canned, 10, 126
    canned light, 10
    fresh, 11
    wild ahi, 10
Tuna Salad Wraps, 2, 10, 37
turkey, 34, 40, 68
    breast, 40
    Thanksgiving, 171
turmeric, 159, 168, 171
TVP (texturized vegetable protein), 93

V

vanilla, 44, 148, 192
Vanilla and Pears, 162, 192
Vegetable Chowder, 134, 156
Vegetable Pesto Pasta, 162, 193
vegetables, 18, 75, 79, 118, 121, 132, 136, 139, 141, 144, 153–54, 156, 179, 181–82, 186
    cruciferous, 8–9, 70, 78, 105, 114, 120, 142, 152, 154, 160, 199
    dark green leafy, 168
    root, 168
vegetable stock, 24, 72–73, 117, 130, 156, 186

vegetarian oyster sauce, 9, 14, 78, 116, 120, 125, 155
vinegar, 54, 146, 150, 152–53, 203
    apple cider, 30, 67, 70, 150, 168
    balsamic, 20
    red wine, 18
    rice, 202
    seasoned rice, 153
    white wine, 150

W

Walnut Crumbs, 56, 74
walnuts, 9, 32, 35, 37, 39, 51–52, 54, 67, 74, 93, 98, 106, 158
wasabi, 14, 206
watermelon, 40, 125
wheat, 19, 27, 36, 46, 92, 94, 100
wheat berries, 152
wheat-flour products, 105
white flour, refined, 6
wine
    cooking, 13, 176
    dry white, 23
    Japanese sweet rice, 81
    mirin, 81

Y

yams, 65, 76
yeast, 68, 104, 212, 214
    nutritional, 64, 114, 128, 200
yogurt, 5, 13, 39, 96, 98, 103, 106, 111, 144–45, 162, 167, 169, 172
    Greek yogurt, 103, 172
    live-culture, 106
    nonfat, 13
    organic, 169
    plain, 106
    sugar-free strawberry, 111
    whole milk, 5, 111, 145, 146
Yogurt Parfait, 39, 96, 111

Z

zucchini, 19, 27, 83, 118, 122, 132, 193
    yellow, 83
Zucchini and Roasted Garlic, 56
Zucchini Salad, 96, 122